BRITISH AND IRISH AUTHORS

Introductory critical studies

ANDREW MARVELL

ANDREW MARVELL

ROBERT WILCHER

Department of English Language and Literature
University of Birmingham

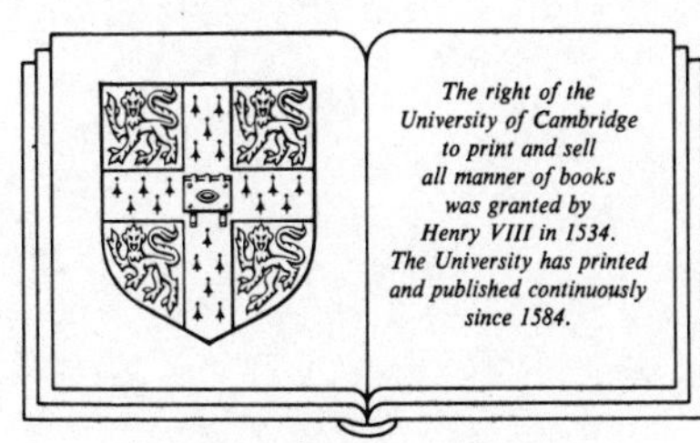

CAMBRIDGE UNIVERSITY PRESS

CAMBRIDGE

LONDON NEW YORK NEW ROCHELLE

MELBOURNE SYDNEY

Published by the Press Syndicate of the University of Cambridge
The Pitt Building, Trumpington Street, Cambridge CB2 1RP
32 East 57th Street, New York, NY 10022, USA
10 Stamford Road, Oakleigh, Melbourne 3206, Australia

First published 1985

Printed in Great Britain at
the University Press, Cambridge

Library of Congress catalogue card number: 84–21472

British Library cataloguing in publication data

Wilcher, Robert
Andrew Marvell.–(British and Irish authors)
1. Marvell, Andrew–Criticism and
interpretation
I. Title II. Series
821'.4 PR3546

ISBN 0 521 25819 7 Hardcovers
ISBN 0 521 27722 1 Paperback

GG

For Miriam, Jessica, Thomasin, Victoria

Contents

Preface

An author who undertakes the task of introducing the work of Andrew Marvell to new readers faces several problems. Not only do individual poems contain the usual complexities of metaphor and argument associated with the conceited style of the earlier seventeenth century, but their essentially allusive nature demands a wide range of information about both literary and historical contexts. It is the purpose of this book to supply such information not merely as background to the poetry and prose, but as a vital element in the detailed explication of each poem or group of poems – as part of the fabric of the texts themselves. To that end, the introductory chapter on Marvell's career and personality provides no more than a brief sketch of the times in which he lived, to be filled out in later chapters in relation to specific works. Since the volume is designed for the use of sixth-form students and undergraduates, attention has been concentrated on the lyric poetry and *Upon Appleton House*, but for the sake of completeness the final chapter includes a more selective account of Marvell's activities as political panegyrist and satirist in verse and prose.

Anyone writing about Marvell inevitably incurs innumerable debts to the body of distinguished scholarship and criticism that has been generated by his literary and political achievements. In the absence of footnotes, the Select bibliography must serve as a general acknowledgement of the many discoveries and insights that have been silently appropriated in the pages that follow. Among more personal debts of gratitude, I owe most of all to the supervisor of my apprentice-work on seventeenth-century poetry as a post-graduate student, Elsie Duncan-Jones, whose expert scrutiny of much of the typescript saved me from a number of errors and whose generosity made available to me unpublished material. I am also grateful to my colleagues Tony Davies and H. Neville Davies, who found time during a busy academic year to read the entire first draft and whose valuable suggestions have greatly improved the finished version. Thanks are also due to Valerie Edden and Sue Roberts for helpful comments on early portions of the text, and to Terence Moore and Pauline Leng of Cambridge University Press for their courtesy and care at later stages of its preparation for the press. Whatever shortcomings remain are, of course, no one's responsibility but my own. Finally, I take this opportunity to record my gratitude for the unquantifiable contribution that my wife and daughters made to the writing of this book simply by being there.

Birmingham,
August 1984

R.W.

Note on texts

Quotations from Marvell's poems are generally taken from Elizabeth Story Donno's Penguin edition of 1972. In the following instances, however, I have preferred the readings of H. M. Margoliouth's Oxford edition: 'Clorinda and Damon', line 2, omit the semi-colon after 'too late'; 'To His Coy Mistress', line 44, 'gates' rather than 'grates'; 'The Second Chorus from Seneca's Tragedy *Thyestes*', line 2, 'Tottering favour's pinnacle' rather than 'Giddy favour's slippery hill', and line 11, 'Country man' rather than 'countryman'. I have made the necessary modernization of 'born' to 'borne' in line 53 of 'An Horatian Ode', and have adopted Thomas Cooke's 1726 emendation of the 1681 Folio's 'plum' to 'plume' in line 34 of 'Upon the Hill and Grove at Bilbrough' in preference to the 'plump' found in most modern editions. With minor modifications to spelling, the 'Statue' poems, omitted from the Penguin edition, are quoted from Volume One and the Letters from Volume Two of Margoliouth's edition, *The Rehearsal Transpros'd* from D. I. B. Smith's Oxford edition, and Marvell's other prose works from Volume Four of Grosart's 'Fuller Worthies' Library' edition of 1875. Passages from Latin poets are quoted from the following Penguin Classics volumes: *Virgil: The Pastoral Poems*, translated by E. V. Rieu, *The Odes of Horace*, translated by James Michie, and *The Metamorphoses of Ovid*, translated by Mary M. Innes.

Footnotes have been avoided, and page references to editions of Marvell's prose and to secondary materials are included in the text. Details of all editions, books, and articles cited can be found in the Select bibliography.

1

Introduction

Andrew Marvell died on 16 August 1678. He was commemorated in some anonymous verses as 'this island's watchful sentinel' and 'the people's surest guide and prophet too' – a man whose unfailing 'truth, wit, and eloquence' had defended his country against 'the grim monster, arbitrary pow'r'. The epitaph composed by his nephew, William Popple, alludes to 'his inimitable writings', but pays more attention to his 'unalterable steadiness in the ways of virtue' and his twenty-year service as Member of Parliament for Kingston-upon-Hull. On the title-page of *Miscellaneous Poems*, the volume in which his poetry was printed (most of it for the first time) in 1681, he is described as 'Andrew Marvell, Esq; Late Member of the Honourable House of Commons'. Although he was remembered as 'an excellent poet in Latin or English' in John Aubrey's *Brief Lives* and honoured in another set of anonymous verses as a 'Prodigy of Wit', whose achievements with a pen placed him far above 'the scribbling crowd', it was his career as a politician and controversialist that shaped his reputation in his own day and for many years afterwards. But that career did not begin until he was appointed Latin secretary in the office of John Thurloe, Secretary to the Council of State, in 1657. During the thirty-six years of his life before that, he had had, in his own words, 'not the remotest relation to public matters'. It is true that his further assertion, in the same passage from *The Rehearsal Transpros'd: The Second Part* (1673), that he had had no 'correspondence with the persons then predominant, until the year 1657' (p. 203), does not quite square with his previous employment by both Lord Fairfax and Oliver Cromwell, but the broad contrast between his later activities as civil servant, M.P., and diplomat and his earlier life as a student and private tutor still holds good. And indeed, most commentators assume a similar chronological transition in his literary work from mainly lyrical poetry in the 1640s and early 1650s to political verse and controversial prose. The search for lines of continuity between the poet of gardens and meadows and the champion of liberty and toleration exercises biographer and critic alike, and it is evident that the conflicting demands of the self and the world, which in one guise or another inform many of his most celebrated poems, need to be seen not only in relation to his own enigmatic personality, but also in the context of what one historian has dubbed the Century of Revolution.

The facts of his life can be quickly rehearsed. He was born on 31 March 1621 at Winestead-in-Holderness, Yorkshire, where his father was rector. In 1624, the family moved to Hull, following the Reverend Andrew Marvell's election as Master of the Charterhouse (an almshouse) and as lecturer in Holy Trinity Church. Young Andrew probably attended Hull Grammar School, and from there proceeded to Trinity College, Cambridge, in 1633. Having graduated B.A. in 1639, he abandoned his M.A. studies soon after his father's accidental death by drowning in 1641. Two of his three older sisters had married into the families of well-to-do Hull merchants, and there is a local tradition that he entered the trading-house of one of his brothers-in-law to learn the business after leaving Cambridge. Recently discovered documents, however, indicate that he was not in Hull, but in London in February 1642. Two further documents reveal that he was present in person to complete the sale of some family land and other property in Meldreth, Cambridgeshire, in November and December 1647. It must, therefore, have been between these two dates that Marvell spent the 'four years abroad in Holland, France, Italy, and Spain' mentioned in a letter written in 1653 by John Milton. It is usually assumed that he travelled as tutor to some young man of rank and wealth, but this has not been proved, and it may be that he was able to finance his continental tour from the sale of family property after he came of age in 1642. At the end of the 1640s he was back in London, but by early 1651 he had taken up a post in Yorkshire as tutor to Mary Fairfax, the twelve-year-old daughter of the successful general who had resigned as commander of the parliamentary armies in June 1650 and retired to his northern estates.

Marvell had left Fairfax's service and returned to London by February 1653, when Milton wrote to John Bradshaw, Lord-President of the Council of State, recommending him for government employment and explaining that 'he comes now lately out of the house of the Lord Fairfax, who was General, where he was intrusted to give some instruction in the languages to the Lady, his daughter'. His application for a post in Whitehall was not successful, but he had apparently come to the attention of Oliver Cromwell, Fairfax's successor. In July 1653, Marvell was writing to Cromwell from the house of the Reverend John Oxenbridge, a fellow of Eton, where he had just been installed as private tutor to William Dutton, a young protégé of the great soldier. During 1656 Marvell and Dutton were in France at Saumur on the Loire, where there was a famous

Protestant academy. In September of the following year, however, a public appointment at last came his way as assistant to Cromwell's Secretary of State. He retained this office until late 1659 or early 1660, although by this time Cromwell was dead and preparations were being made for the restoration of the Stuart monarchy. He was first elected M.P. for Hull in January 1659 and again in April 1660 to serve in the Convention Parliament which recalled Charles II from exile; and he was returned for a third time in May 1661 to the Cavalier Parliament, in which he continued to represent his native town until his death. During his long career in the House of Commons, he sat on various committees and reported regularly to the Hull Corporation and Hull Trinity House on general parliamentary affairs and matters of particular interest to his constituency. He was absent from the House during the second half of 1662 on what seems to have been clandestine political business in Holland, and from July 1663 till January 1665 he was abroad again as secretary to the Earl of Carlisle on an extended diplomatic mission which took him to the court of the Czar in Moscow, to Stockholm, and to Copenhagen.

Once back in England, Marvell became associated with the Opposition forming itself around the Duke of Buckingham, husband of Mary Fairfax, and contributed both in speeches in the House of Commons and in satirical verses to the campaign which led to the overthrow of the king's chief minister, the Earl of Clarendon, in 1667. Five years later, he was again active politically, supporting Charles II's attempt to extend toleration towards religious dissenters in the work for which he was most renowned in his own lifetime, *The Rehearsal Transpros'd.* With the rise to power of Sir Thomas Osborne, the future Earl of Danby, however, Clarendon's policy of maintaining the supremacy of the Church of England was revived. Throughout the rest of his life, Marvell was a leading member of the opposition Country Party, and may even have been involved in a Dutch intelligence organization which aimed at breaking the Anglo-French alliance and ending the war against Holland in 1673–4. He spoke in the House of Commons in March 1677 against a bill which would have strengthened the intolerant Anglican establishment, and later in the same year wrote *An Account of the Growth of Popery, and Arbitrary Government in England*, setting out his fears for the future of constitutional government and his suspicions of a Roman Catholic, pro-French conspiracy.

Marvell died suddenly of a fever, after returning from a visit to Hull, in a house which he had leased in 1677 as a hide-out for two bankrupt friends. Eight months after his death, his former landlady,

Mary Palmer, in whose name he had taken the house in Great Russell Street, claimed that she was his widow. This seems to have been part of a stratagem to prevent a sum of five hundred pounds belonging to one of the bankrupts from falling into the hands of the creditors. It was, perhaps, to reinforce her claim to have been married to the poet that 'Mary Marvell' published the *Miscellaneous Poems* of 1681, prefaced by a declaration that 'all these Poems, as also the other things in this Book contained, are Printed according to the exact Copies of my late dear Husband, under his own Hand-Writing, being found since his Death among his other Papers'. Although she succeeded in obtaining administration of Marvell's estate, there is no indisputable evidence that this woman was his wife and most biographers believe that he remained a bachelor to the end of his days.

Before one can begin to guess at the personality that might animate this bare recital of facts, it is necessary to call to mind some of the main features of the world in which Marvell lived. Men of his generation grew to maturity in what one of his contemporaries at Trinity College – Abraham Cowley – was later to describe as 'a warlike, various, and a tragical age'. It was an age which saw radical changes in the institutions of church and state and the questioning of many fundamental beliefs about the nature of man and the society and universe he inhabits.

Neither the Church of England nor the monarchy, those twin pillars of the established order of things, survived the revolutionary decade of the 1640s. Already before the end of the sixteenth century, the more radical members of the national church were making known their antagonism towards the ruling hierarchy of bishops and their conviction that the process of reformation had not gone far enough. The ecclesiastical policy fostered by Charles I and ruthlessly implemented by William Laud alienated the Puritan faction within the church even further. First as Bishop of London, and then from 1633 as Archbishop of Canterbury, Laud used his authority to enforce strict conformity to the Prayer Book of the Church of England and to introduce religious practices which many regarded as steps on the path back to Roman Catholicism. The Long Parliament, which assembled for the first time on 3 November 1640, imprisoned Laud in the Tower and over the next few years undertook what Milton was to call 'the reforming of Reformation itself': the episcopacy was abolished, the Anglican Book of Common Prayer was replaced with the Directory of Public Worship, and a Presbyterian system of church government

– with elected elders rather than appointed priests and bishops – was adopted. Laud was eventually brought to trial and beheaded in January 1645.

The struggle for political power between king and House of Commons, which had dominated the earlier years of Charles I's reign, entered a new phase in 1640. Since 1629, Charles had contrived to raise the money necessary for government without summoning a parliament. The grievances that had built up over those eleven years of personal rule now burst upon him, and, given the obstinacy of his character and the zeal of his opponents, it was inevitable that the constitutional debate should turn into armed conflict. The Civil War, which began with the indecisive Battle of Edgehill in October 1642, culminated in victory for Parliament and the New Model Army under Fairfax and Cromwell at the Battle of Naseby in June 1645. After the defeat of Royalist risings in 1648 – the Second Civil War – the king was tried and executed on 30 January 1649. Monarchy and the House of Lords were abolished in March, and in the new Commonwealth authority was vested in a Council of State made up of M.P.s and army officers. Cromwell was appointed commander of the army in July 1650 in place of Fairfax, who had resigned rather than lead a campaign against Charles II and the Scots. Having beaten a Scottish army at Dunbar, Cromwell followed Charles and his remaining forces down through England and finally defeated them at the Battle of Worcester on 3 September 1651. The rest of the 1650s were dominated by a policy of mercantile expansion abroad and a series of abortive attempts to find a constitutional settlement at home. Cromwell was made Protector at the end of 1653, but when he died in September 1658 he had not succeeded in establishing a form of government that could survive his departure from the political scene. After a period of confusion caused by the abdication of the new Protector, his son Richard Cromwell, order was restored in the person of Charles II, who landed at Dover in May 1660.

Under Oliver Cromwell, there had been a large measure of religious freedom. Like many of his colonels, he was an Independent, and must have shared John Milton's disillusioned judgement of 1646 on 'the New Forcers of Conscience under the Long Parliament' – '*New Presbyter* is but *Old Priest* writ large'. But the restoration of the monarchy also saw a return to the policy of conformity to the restored Church of England. In a series of acts of Parliament known as the Clarendon Code various restrictions were imposed upon the activities of both Catholic recusants and Nonconformists or Dissenters, as the Presbyterians and members of the Puritan sects that had proliferated during the previous twenty years were called. Foreign affairs were dominated by relations with the France of Louis XIV, with whom Charles II entered into the secret Treaty of Dover in 1670, and with Holland, England's great trading rival, against whom two wars were fought in 1664–7 and 1672–4. At home the question of religious toleration was complicated by the avowed Roman Catholicism of Charles II's brother and heir, James, Duke of York, and by the king's own Catholic sympathies. Marvell died on the eve of Titus Oates's spurious revelation of a Popish Plot to murder Charles and set James on the throne.

The protracted battles for power between the supporters of uniformity and freedom of conscience in the church and between absolutism and constitutional parliamentary government in the state were naturally accompanied by an ideological war of words and ideas, in the course of which new philosophical positions were hammered out. Biblical texts and historical precedents were called upon to validate theories as diverse as the Divine Right of Kings and the egalitarianism of such groups as the Diggers and Levellers, which held that 'the poorest he that is in England hath a life to live, as the greatest he'. Thomas Hobbes's systematic analysis of the nature of man and the state – 'that great Leviathan' – swept aside older notions of natural or divinely ordained rights in favour of a rational theory of absolute sovereignty based on effective power; and James Harrington's *Oceana* (1656) argued along similarly secular and rationalistic lines for a republican constitution that would safeguard the liberties achieved in the Civil War, while avoiding the dangers of more radical democracy.

Advances in the physical sciences and the growing spirit of scepticism promoted even more fundamental changes in man's conception of the universe and his place in it. The medieval belief in a system of concentric spheres carrying the planets and stars round the earth had been gradually discredited by developments in astronomy associated with the names of Copernicus, Kepler, and Galileo, which were to culminate in the publication of Sir Isaac Newton's *Principia Mathematica* less than a decade after Marvell's death. It was still possible for a writer like Sir Thomas Browne to perceive the world around him as a hierarchical continuum – 'a Stair, or manifest Scale of creatures, rising not disorderly, or in confusion, but with a comely method and proportion' – or as a network of beautiful and significant relationships or 'correspondencies' (*Religio Medici* (1643)). But such a view, which could find meaningful parallels between the microcosm and the macrocosm and discover in the natural world emblems of moral and metaphysical truth, was giving ground during Marvell's lifetime in the face of Hobbes's materialistic conception of the human creature – 'For what is the *Heart*, but a *Spring*; and the *Nerves*, but so many *Strings*; and the *Joints*, but so many *Wheels*, giving motion to the whole Body, such as was intended by the Artificer?' (*Leviathan* (1651)) – and the Newtonian conception of the universe as a great machine, operating according to mathematical principles. And while the seventeenth-century inventions of telescope and microscope were extending the range of human perception, they were also underlining the deceptiveness of appearances and the elusiveness of truth. Both the life and the writings of Andrew Marvell can be interpreted as the responses of an intelligent and sceptical mind to the need to find new bearings amid the confusions and the challenges to inherited assumptions of a period of revolutionary change.

The earliest influences on the young Marvell must have been the moderate Puritanism of his father, who had been educated at Emmanuel, the most Puritan of the Cambridge colleges, and who was later to be described by the poet as 'a Conformist to the established Rites of the Church of *England,* though I confess none of the most over-running or eager in them' (*The Rehearsal Transpros'd: The Second Part*). As lecturer at Holy Trinity, the Reverend Andrew Marvell did not hold a church living, but was hired by the congregation in the capacity of a preacher. His attitude to the Anglican establishment is indicated by the reprimand he received from the Archbishop's court at York in 1639 for not making sufficient use of the Book of Common Prayer with his weekly sermons. The Cambridge of the 1630s, when Marvell was a student at Trinity, was less compliant with Laudian policy than Oxford, where Laud himself was Chancellor. There was, however, some infiltration by Jesuits, particularly at Peterhouse. Richard Crashaw, who was to become a convert to Roman Catholicism, was elected a Fellow there in 1635 and may well have been acquainted with Marvell, since they published poems in the same collection of Cambridge verse in 1637 and Marvell's later poetry shows a close familiarity with the work of the older man. However that may be, there is some evidence to support a family tradition that Marvell temporarily embraced the Roman religion and ran away to London in 1639, where he was found by his father and sent back to college. By the early 1650s, his religious views must have been such as to make him acceptable to John Milton, the chief propagandist for the Puritan cause, who considered him 'a man whom both by report and the converse I have had with him of singular desert for the State to make use of', and to Oliver Cromwell, who entrusted him with the education of William Dutton. In a letter written on taking up his post as tutor in July 1653, Marvell expresses gratitude to Cromwell 'for having placed us in so godly a family as that of Mr Oxenbridge whose Doctrine and Example are like a Book and a Map'. Although he had a consistent record of opposition to the penal measures taken against Nonconformists after the Restoration, he does not seem himself to have belonged to a dissenting congregation. A letter of 1675, however, contains a passing jibe at the Book of Common Prayer in an account of a Privy Counsellor who died suddenly, 'notwithstanding his Church's Litany, *From sudden Death, good Lord,* &c', and the description of him written soon after his death in the journal of a contemporary physician as 'a man not well affected to the Church or Government of England' is near enough to the mark.

His disaffection towards the 'Government of England' under Charles II is readily substantiated not only from his actions as an M.P. and his public writings, but also from his private letters, in which we find him in 1670 condemning one piece of legislation as 'the Quintessence of arbitrary Malice' and another as 'a Piece of absolute universal Tyranny'. That Cromwell earned his respect, and indeed his admiration, is clear from poems written to celebrate the first anniversary of his rule as Protector in 1654 and to lament his death in 1658. Much more problematic is the question of his earlier political allegiance. His four years of travel in the 1640s saw him out of England during much of the Civil War, and the debate over his commitment to the royalist cause at the time of the king's execution continues to this day. As we shall see in Chapter 6, the evidence of the poetry, which is all there is to go on in this period of his life, points to a crisis of adjustment to the new political realities of the Commonwealth in 1650.

His famous comment on the turmoil of the 1640s, as he looked back from the vantage point of 1672, characteristically refuses to simplify the tangle of human experience and introduces a note of paradox into the moral evaluation: 'Whether it were a War of Religion, or of Liberty, is not worth the labour to enquire. Which-soever was at the top, the other was at the bottom; but upon considering all, I think the Cause was too good to have been fought for' (*The Rehearsal Transpros'd*, p. 135). The same wary distaste for partisan fervour, which created the stance of detached amusement in so many of the poems, but which also led him eventually to commit himself to the struggle against ecclesiastical intolerance and political oppression, is evident in a remark in *A Short Historical Essay* (1677): 'Whereas truth for the most part lies in the middle, but men ordinarily look for it in the extremities' (p. 155). The cumulative impression made by the poetry, the prose works, and the letters is of a man who preferred to stay in the background and to keep his own counsel – partly because of his own temperament, partly because he lived in dangerous times, but perhaps above all because he was acutely conscious of the human capacity for misunderstanding, distortion, and over-simplification. His letters to the Hull Corporation, for instance, confine themselves to a scrupulously objective record of the proceedings in the House and other matters of public interest in the capital. On one of the rare occasions when he allows a more personal note to intrude, it is to urge caution with regard to what he has written:

> These things I have been thus careful to give you a plain account of, not thinking a perfunctory relation worthy your prudence but must in exchange desire you will not admit many inspectors into my letters. For I reckon your bench to be all but as one person: whereas others might chance either not to understand or to put an ill construction upon this openness of my writing & simplicity of my expression. (Letter dated 8 November 1670)

In the more informal letters to his favourite nephew, William Popple, Marvell does permit himself to convey the alarm and disgust he feels at the turn of political events, and now and then reveals a glimpse of that tendency to hold aloof from an intransigent situation which may have kept him abroad during the Civil War:

> It is also my Opinion that the King was never since his coming in, nay, all Things considered, no King since the Conquest, so absolutely powerful at Home, as he is at present. Nor any Parliament, or Places, so certainly and constantly supplied with Men of the same Temper. In such a Conjuncture, dear *Will,* what Probability is there of my doing any Thing to the Purpose? (Letter dated 21 March 1670)

Most of Marvell's prose works were printed anonymously, although he was stung into putting his name defiantly on the title-page of the Second Part of *The Rehearsal Transpros'd.* Anonymity was a natural precaution in books critical of the establishment, but his practice of covering his tracks in his private correspondence by referring to himself in the third person and omitting a signature also seems to have something in common with his habit of concealing himself behind a persona in the poetry. Writing to Sir Edward Harley on 1 July 1676, he places his tongue firmly in his cheek to comment on the reception of *Mr Smirke: Or, The Divine in Mode,* a pamphlet attacking the Anglican hierarchy:

> The book said to be Marvell's makes what shift it can in the world but the Author walks negligently up & down as unconcerned. The Divines of our Church say it is not in the merry part so good as the Rehearsal Transpros'd, that it runs dregs: the Essay they confess is writ well enough to the purpose he intended it but that was a very ill purpose. The Bishop of London's Chaplain said it had not answered expectation.

The bulk of his poetry remained in manuscript until after his death, and although the political satires of his later years were widely circulated, the lyrical poems on which his reputation now chiefly rests might well have been lost but for Mary Palmer's publication of *Miscellaneous Poems.* The few poems printed during his lifetime – such as the commendatory verses on Richard Lovelace's *Lucasta* (1649) and Milton's *Paradise Lost* (1674), the elegy on Lord Hastings (1649), and the panegyric on Cromwell's Protectorship (1655) – can be dated, as can other occasional pieces that relate to specific public events. The majority of the lyrics, however, can only be assigned to a particular period by biographical inference. *Upon Appleton House,* 'The Garden', and the Mower poems, for example, probably belong to the years when he was in Yorkshire as tutor to Mary Fairfax, and the Puritan tone of 'Bermudas' and 'The Coronet' may derive from the time of his residence with the 'godly' Oxenbridges. Some of the poems associated with Marvell's name – notably post-Restoration satires, but also the elegy on Lord Francis Villiers and the very early pastoral, 'A Dialogue between Thyrsis and Dorinda' – are even of doubtful attribution.

Given the many gaps in our knowledge, the discussion of Marvell's work in the chapters that follow will concentrate on the detailed analysis of individual poems, arranged according to theme and literary method rather than along some hypothetical line of development. Further historical information – and in particular that relating to the literary traditions that lie behind Marvell's writing – will be introduced as it becomes relevant to the consideration of specific texts. The overall intention is to put together a coherent picture of the poet's characteristic manner of turning his experience of his seventeenth-century world into literary form.

2

Silent judgements

Reading a poem by Andrew Marvell can be a disquieting and sometimes frustrating experience for those who expect from poetry the straightforward communication of meaning, personality, or point of view. Since the revival of widespread interest in Marvell in the 1920s, there have been numerous, often quite contradictory, assessments of the religious, political, and philosophical allegiances embodied not only in his work as a whole, but even in individual lyrics. The words most frequently called upon to describe the distinctive qualities of the mind and temperament that lie behind the poetry are 'wit', 'control', 'balance', 'poise', 'irony', and even 'elusiveness'. The term 'wit' relates Marvell to the tradition of poetry associated with the name of John Donne and with his imitators in the 1630s and 1640s – notably Cowley, Crashaw, and Cleveland – and it is as one of the 'Metaphysical Poets' that he is often first introduced to new readers.

'Metaphysical' wit manifests itself most obviously in the kind of hyperbole which led Donne to find a parallel to the high temperature of his mistress in scholastic eschatology:

> Oh wrangling schools, that search what fire
>   Shall burn this world, had none the wit
> Unto this knowledge to aspire,
>   That this her fever might be it?
>
> ('A Fever')

Or in the kind of conceit which ingeniously discovers similar properties in pure gold and souls united and refined by love:

> Our two souls therefore, which are one,
>   Though I must go, endure not yet
> A breach, but an expansion,
>   Like gold to aery thinness beat.
>
> ('A Valediction: Forbidding Mourning')

Or in the kind of self-mocking fantasy woven about the idea of testing the genuineness of a lover's grief:

> Hither with crystal vials, lovers come,
>   And take my tears, which are love's wine,

And try your mistress' tears at home,
For all are false, that taste not just like mine.
('Twicknam Garden')

Marvell's poetry furnishes many examples of this brand of intellectual ingenuity, from the conceit of the lover captivated by the voice of his lady in 'The Fair Singer':

But how should I avoid to be her slave,
Whose subtle art invisibly can wreathe
My fetters of the very air I breathe?

to the more extended flight of hyperbolical fancy in 'The Match', reminiscent of 'A Fever', which combines the chemistry of gunpowder with a mythological narrative about Cupid's provisions against old age:

Love wisely had of long foreseen
That he must once grow old;
And therefore stored a magazine,
To save him from the cold.

He kept the several cells replete
With nitre thrice refined;
The naphtha's and the sulphur's heat,
And all that burns the mind.

He fortified the double gate,
And rarely thither came;
For, with one spark of these, he straight
All Nature could inflame.

Till, by vicinity so long,
A nearer way they sought;
And, grown magnetically strong,
Into each other wrought.

Thus all his fuel did unite
To make one fire high:
None ever burned so hot, so bright:
And, Celia, that am I.

The comparison with Donne, however, should not be taken too far. Ingenious conceits and outrageous hyperboles are merely ingredients in a poetic art which acknowledges no single master and owes as much to the classical elegance and urbanity of Ben Jonson – and indeed to the Roman poets Horace and Catullus and Virgil – as to the flamboyant wit of the 'metaphysical' style. The 'balance', 'irony', and 'elusiveness' that characterize Marvell's poetic temperament are to be sought not in isolated images or turns of wit, but in the carefully controlled articulation of whole poems and often in the subtle and mischievous undermining of the conventional attitudes implicit in the models he is imitating. For he is, indeed, a poet thoroughly dependent on literary tradition. He takes up devices, images, even phrases, from English and European writers, both contemporary and ancient, and mobilizes the resources of many of the dominant genres of the earlier seventeenth century. But this does not mean that he is an unoriginal poet, content to retread the paths marked out by his predecessors. On the contrary, his acutely critical and alert mind is well aware that a poetic genre is not merely a collection of formal conventions and stereotyped images, but constitutes a way of enshrining a particular perspective on mankind's encounter with the world. Every attempt to pin down some aspect of human experience in words will inevitably oversimplify the endless complexities of man's predicament – whether the focus is on the physical, the emotional, the moral, or the spiritual dimension of his relationship with another person, or the state, or nature, or nature's God. This perception is central to Marvell's technique as a poet, and it accounts for that air of detachment – that refusal to endorse the assumptions of a particular rhetorical mode or to adjudicate between competing points of view – which can irritate some readers as a lack of firm commitment. Others, who regard what T. S. Eliot called the 'constant inspection and criticism of experience' (p. 303) as one of the most valuable qualities of the poet's art, will find much to admire in the wit and skill with which Marvell contrives to preserve that very openness to the possibility of alternative emphases or attitudes which the conventional formulations of experience in language tend to preclude.

A preliminary discussion of two poems that draw upon a well-established literary tradition will serve to demonstrate Marvell's versatility in assimilating and refashioning familiar materials and to open up some of the peculiar features of his own artistic vision and methods. 'Eyes and Tears' and 'Mourning' both exploit the topic of weeping, which was widespread in European literature and which was equally suitable for erotic and religious purposes. In English, Donne had built a witty argument out of it in 'A Valediction: Of Weeping', beginning with a double conceit of tears as coins and wombs bearing the image of the woman who causes them to flow:

Let me pour forth
My tears before thy face, whilst I stay here,
For thy face coins them, and thy stamp they bear,
And by this mintage they are something worth,
For thus they be
Pregnant of thee.

Richard Crashaw had strung together a series of conceits – including, appropriately enough, the idea that each tear is a bead of a rosary – on the theme of Mary Magdalene's penitent tears in 'The Weeper'. One of them may look back to the lines just quoted from Donne and almost certainly provoked a direct allusion by Marvell:

Say wat'ry Brothers
Ye simpering sons of those fair eyes,
Your fertile Mothers.
What hath our world that can entice
You to be born? what is't can borrow
You from her eyes' swoll'n wombs of sorrow?

Donne's poem, as is so often the case in his *Songs and Sonnets,* is spoken out of a fully imagined dramatic situation, in which the lover weeps at parting from his mistress and addresses her directly and intimately. The weeping Magdalene is more of an emblem than a living woman, and functions as the pictorial occasion for fanciful conceits on her eyes and tears as 'thawing crystal', stars sown like seed from the heavens, April showers, drops replacing sand in Time's hour-glass, and the jewels and the wombs of sorrow. She does, however, provide a specific external focus for Crashaw's exercise of wit and devotion.

Marvell's 'Eyes and Tears', by contrast, begins with generalizations:

1

How wisely Nature did decree,
With the same eyes to weep and see!
That, having viewed the object vain,
We might be ready to complain.

2

Thus since the self-deluding sight,
In a false angle takes each height,
These tears, which better measure all,
Like watery lines and plummets fall.

The first stanza states the proposition that the rest of the poem is going to support with an accumulation of observations, conceits, and witty examples: anything that belongs to the material world – 'the object vain' – which is revealed to us by the organs of sight can induce nothing but dismay, and therefore the wise economy of Nature has placed our chief means of expressing sorrow in the self-same organs. The opening couplet of the second stanza is a typical example of Marvell's habit of sliding one meaning over another, like two transparencies, so that we can choose to attend to one or the other, or both together. We can limit the reference to the fallibility of man's perceptive faculties, in which case the lines remind us that sight is frequently mistaken in its judgement of the height of physical objects. On the other hand, we can read the couplet metaphorically, and interpret 'the self-deluding sight' as referring to the deception of the self of the perceiving human agent, who misjudges the true value of things which are mistakenly accorded high status in this 'vain' world. Tears, the next couplet maintains, descend in undeceiving straight lines and 'better measure all' in a moral or spiritual sense – just as 'plummets' or plumb-lines give a surer and more direct indication of physical height than the dubious calculations made with a sextant.

Up to this point, neither context nor speaking source has been established for the words of the poem, although the allusion to '*These* tears' hints at something more specific than a generalized reverie on weeping. In the third stanza, we discover that the speaker is himself at the centre of his own contemplation:

3

Two tears, which Sorrow long did weigh
Within the scales of either eye,
And then paid out in equal poise,
Are the true price of all my joys.

What kind of impression do we form of this figure, who is neither giving vent to the healthy and familiar emotion of Donne's departing lover, whose tears are a sign of his commitment to another human being, nor meditating devotionally on a standard emblem of penitential sorrow, like Crashaw's rapt votary? That judicious weighing of the two tear-drops, before they are allowed to roll slowly down the cheeks, seems to imbue him with the same unruffled 'poise' that he attributes to the tears. His carefully contrived conceit of weighing them out two at a time to pay for his joys has a self-absorbed and self-satisfied air, which contrasts sharply – and to his disadvantage – with the uncontrolled passion of Donne's lover, who pours forth *his* tear-coins unstintingly and only considers them 'something worth' because they reflect the image of his beloved.

In the next three stanzas, the evaluating centre shifts from the generalized 'we', via the personal 'I', to the 'all-seeing sun' as the observer in the best position to make a universal judgement on the vain objects of this world:

4

What in the world most fair appears,
Yea, even laughter, turns to tears:
And all the jewels which we prize,
Melt in these pendants of the eyes.

5

I have through every garden been,
Amongst the red, the white, the green,
And yet, from all the flowers I saw,
No honey but these tears, could draw.

6

So the all-seeing sun each day
Distills the world with chemic ray,
But finds the essence only show'rs,
Which straight in pity back he pours.

The images of tears as 'pendants' and 'honey', which suggest that weeping is a decorative and sweetly pleasurable activity, reinforce the earlier note of self-centred indulgence; while the insistence on '*these* pendants' and '*these* tears' keeps the presence of the individual speaker before us, even when he is generalizing the evidence for his case under the plural 'we'. And the 'all-seeing' sun, who finds that tears are the quintessence – the purest distillation – of the whole world, appears at the climax of a movement that has run from the tears 'which better measure *all*' in stanza 2, through '*all* my joys' in stanza 3, '*all* the jewels which we prize' in stanza 4, and '*all* the flowers' in stanza 5. Whatever the eyes light upon in their function as organs of perception is unable to entice the speaker away from his absorption in the delights of weeping.

The next stanza begins with a paradox which increases the suspicion that the speaker so far has been rationalizing a maudlin enjoyment of the experience of shedding tears for its own sake:

7

Yet happy they whom grief doth bless,
That weep the more, and see the less:

And, to preserve their sight more true,
Bathe still their eyes in their own dew.

The 'Yet' marks a turn in the poem's development, and the traditional formula 'happy they who' usually implies some longed-for ideal beyond the reach of the speaker – as in the opening lines of Cowley's translation of one of Horace's epodes:

Happy the Man whom Bounteous Gods allow
With his own Hands Paternal Grounds to plough!
Like the first golden Mortals Happy he
From Business and the cares of Money free!

The tears celebrated in the first six stanzas have been tears of complaint (stanza 1) or sorrow (stanza 3) or pity (stanza 6) – all of which were induced by the passive contemplation of the vanity of the world. Grief, which implies a more active provocation on the part of the world, would be a blessing, because it would afford a stronger motive for allowing the tears to flow. As an example of one whose tears of grief were instrumental in preserving a 'sight more true' – a capacity for spiritual insight, perhaps, as opposed to mere visual perception – he cites the subject of Crashaw's poem:

8

So Magdalen, in tears more wise
Dissolved those captivating eyes,
Whose liquid chains could flowing meet
To fetter her Redeemer's feet.

Mary Magdalene is one of the supreme examples in Christian story and iconography of the repentant sinner, who turned from a life of depravity to devote herself to the service of Christ. The eyes which had been misused as a means of 'captivating' men – for seduction rather than perception – dissolved into 'tears more wise' as the nature of her sin came home to her. The second couplet derives from the concluding stanza of Crashaw's 'The Weeper', in which the tears of the Magdalene themselves speak:

We go not to seek
The darlings of *Aurora's* bed,
The Rose's modest cheek
Nor the Violet's humble head.
No such thing; we go to meet
A worthier object, *Our Lord's* feet.

These tears, too, turn from the flowers of this world, as Marvell's speaker did in stanza 5; but having 'viewed the object vain', they do not merely shrink from it in negative complaint. They positively seek out a 'worthier object' to pay their tribute of loving grief to. The phrase 'tears more wise' prompts the question, 'More wise than what?' An answer supplied by the immediate context would be, 'more wise than the seductive eyes that shed them'. In the larger context of the poem as it has developed up to this juncture, the answer may equally well be, 'tears more wise than the self-indulgent tears that have been celebrated in stanzas 1 to 6'. Read in this way, stanzas 7 and 8 stand as an indictment of the timid passivity of a speaker whose limited experience of the world – as an observer rather than a participant in life – has never exposed him to the passionate intensities of lust or penitence symbolized by the Magdalene. He has not earned the right to weep.

But he does not appear to have taken this lesson to heart. The next three stanzas offer a rapid accumulation of conceits which dwell on the aesthetic beauty or the soothing effect of tears:

9

Not full sails hasting loaden home,
Nor the chaste lady's pregnant womb,
Nor Cynthia teeming shows so fair,
As two eyes swoll'n with weeping are.

10

The sparkling glance that shoots desire,
Drenched in these waves does lose its fire.
Yea, oft the Thunderer pity takes
And here the hissing lightning slakes.

11

The incense was to heaven dear,
Not as a perfume, but a tear.
And stars show lovely in the night,
But as they seem the tears of light.

In stanza 9, Marvell has taken the conceit of eyes as the 'swoll'n wombs of sorrow' from Crashaw and separated it into its component parts. Now, the swollen eyes become a standard of beauty against which the ship swollen with cargo and the womb swollen with a child – both images which suggest active participation in the processes of life – and the aesthetic symbol of the full moon, also imagined as breeding, are judged to be inferior. These eyes, unlike those of Crashaw's poem, are no longer associated with the metaphor of procreation, but are deliberately opposed to it. The next stanza applauds the power of tears to quench the passions of lust and anger, symbolized by the fire shot from a lady's eye and the thunderbolts of Jove. The moral satisfaction of the speaker's tone may seem a poor compensation for the loss of the animal vitality in that 'sparkling glance'; and a vivid flash of lightning which fizzles out in mere 'hissing' may come as something of an anticlimax to those who thrill to the roll of thunder. Both stanzas, although offered by the speaker as enhancements of the value of weeping, subtly undermine his persuasive intent by the life-denying implications of their imagery. The two couplets of stanza 11 effect a rapid shift of perspective, rather like that in stanza 2, which measures height from below by taking an angle and then from above by letting down a plumb-line. Incense, viewed from heaven, and stars, viewed from earth, are both said to be valued only insofar as the imagination can transform them into tears. The crucial question for the reader – and this holds good for many of Marvell's most characteristic poems – is how far he feels that the evaluations embodied in these reductive conceits are the evaluations demanded by the whole poem, and how far he feels that Marvell's strategy has been to build into the text reservations about the reliability of the fictive speaker's judgement.

In the last three stanzas, this speaker finally abandons the restraint that has typified his approach throughout, and, with an air of passionate commitment, allows himself to be overwhelmed by the one experience he can morally endorse:

12

Ope then, mine eyes, your double sluice,
And practise so your noblest use;
For others too can see, or sleep,
But only human eyes can weep.

13

Now, like two clouds dissolving, drop,
And at each tear in distance stop:
Now, like two fountains, trickle down;
Now, like two floods o'erturn and drown.

14

Thus let your streams o'erflow your springs,
Till eyes and tears be the same things:
And each the other's difference bears;
These weeping eyes, those seeing tears.

The images of the 'double sluice' and the 'two floods' suggest a recklessness quite at odds with the careful weighing and 'equal poise' of stanza 3. There is a release of long pent-up energy in the emphatic repetitions of stanza 13; and the obliteration of separate identities in the final four lines, as eyes and tears merge and 'each the other's difference bears', has something of the triumphant ring of Donne's assertion in 'The Ecstasy' that love fuses the souls of lovers, 'And makes both one, each this and that'.

Looking back over the entire poem, we can see that it is cleverly structured with six stanzas on either side of the pivotal stanzas 7 and 8. Magdalene, blessed with a grief born of genuine experience, which validates both her tears and the devotional attention that a poet like Crashaw gives them, stands at the centre of the poem. Rather like Donne's more light-hearted challenge in 'Twicknam Garden' to other lovers to test the genuineness of their tears against his, Marvell tacitly invites us to measure the self-absorption, reductive arguments, smugly confident conceits, and final wild indulgence of the speaker of his poem against the true tears of the repentant sinner. There is no open questioning of the speaker's assertion of the absolute value of tears, and it is only by careful attention to his mode of expression that we become aware of an alternative point of view hovering behind the argument, which warns us that weeping, like any other human activity, is not as simple as it might seem, and that some tears are more worthy of celebration than others.

'Mourning', though it has its own kind of sophistication, employs a simpler strategy for setting diverse evaluations of the act of weeping against each other. The persona from which the voice emanates begins by acknowledging a difficulty in interpreting the particular instance that forms the subject of the poem:

1

You, that decipher out the fate
Of human offsprings from the skies,
What mean these infants which of late
Spring from the stars of Clora's eyes?

2

Her eyes confused, and doubled o'er,
With tears suspended ere they flow,
Seem bending upwards, to restore
To heaven, whence it came, their woe.

3

When, moulding of the watery spheres,
Slow drops untie themselves away,
As if she, with those precious tears,
Would strow the ground where Strephon lay.

Astrologers are called upon to 'decipher' the tears that Clora is shedding over the grave of Strephon. Her eyes 'seem' to be bending heaven-wards, in humble, but perhaps slightly reproachful, acceptance of the accident that has snatched her lover from her; her tears fall 'as if' in sorrowful tribute to her lost partner. But doubts raised by these words, and by the conditional 'would' at the end of stanza 3, are strengthened by the implications of tears 'suspended ere they flow', which slowly 'untie themselves away', as the moisture gathering behind her eyelids is moulded off in 'watery spheres'. 'Eyes and Tears' has made us suspicious of the sorrow that weighs its tears before paying them out, and one wonders whether Clora's are 'precious' because they have real value, or 'precious' because they are merely a fashionable affectation, carefully controlled by the weeper.

The speaker next reports two explanations of her weeping that are current among gossip-mongers:

4

Yet some affirm, pretending art,
Her eyes have so her bosom drowned,
Only to soften near her heart
A place to fix another wound.

5

And, while vain pomp does her restrain
Within her solitary bow'r,
She courts herself in am'rous rain;
Herself both Danaë and the show'r.

6

Nay, others, bolder, hence esteem
Joy now so much her master grown,
That whatsoever does but seem
Like grief, is from her windows thrown.

7

Nor that she pays, while she survives,
To her dead love this tribute due,
But casts abroad these donatives,
At the installing of a new.

The first rumour, in stanzas 4 and 5, is that only the 'vain pomp' of social convention is keeping her from replacing Strephon with a new lover at once. While her tears fall in order to prepare a place for Cupid's arrow to pierce her as soon as the proper period of mourning is over, she finds her own way of consoling herself for the absence of a male partner: 'she courts herself', as the poet puts it, in a scurrilous adaptation of the myth of Danaë's sexual conquest by Jupiter, who turned himself into a shower of golden rain and thus gained access to the brazen tower where she had been confined by her father to preserve her from the embraces of men. The second rumour is that she has already installed a successor to Strephon. Her tears can therefore be wittily interpreted as a discarding of the symbols of grief, like household slops thrown into the gutter; or as largesse – 'donatives' – distributed to celebrate the accession of a new lover. Each of these conceits is a cynical refurbishing of a traditional image: that of the eyes as the windows of the soul; and that of tears as coins, which may be of genuine value in a poem like 'A Valediction: Of Weeping'.

Marvell's narrator is quick to dissociate himself from the distasteful imaginations of the gossip-mongers, and interposes a disclaimer couched in the most richly resonant language of the poem:

8

How wide they dream! The Indian slaves
That dive for pearl through seas profound
Would find her tears yet deeper waves
And not of one the bottom sound.

Clora keeps her mystery, declares the poet, despite the dirty thoughts of a dirty world. Her salt tears are more unfathomable than the tropic seas in which pearls of true price are to be sought. The Indian divers themselves could not sound the depth of her grief. Such is the meaning that the wondering tone created by the exotic imagery and the slow rhythmic effects of the long open vowels urges us to adopt. But superimposed on that meaning is the suspicion that the bottom of not one of her tears is really sound – that the only thing profound about Clora is her inscrutable cunning.

Having planted his seed of doubt, in the very act of expressing his rejection of the scandalous rumours recorded earlier, the speaker withdraws enigmatically from the problem posed by Clora's tears:

9

I yet my silent judgement keep,
Disputing not what they believe:
But sure as oft as women weep,
It is to be supposed they grieve.

Keeping his opinion to himself, as Marvell so often does by refusing to resolve some dispute activated by his poetry, he offers a final neatly balanced assessment of the situation: either, 'whenever women weep, it is in order to give the impression that they are truly grief-stricken'; or, 'whenever women weep, it is tactful and generous to give them the benefit of the doubt and accept that their grief is genuine'. Marvell's debt to Jonson is evident in these lines, and elsewhere in the poem, as can readily be seen by placing them beside the opening of a lyric from *Epicoene*:

> Still to be neat, still to be dressed,
> As you were going to a feast;
> Still to be powdered, still perfumed:
> Lady, it is to be presumed,
> Though art's hid causes are not found,
> All is not sweet, all is not sound.

The suspicious male attitude towards the artifice of women; the rhythmic mastery of the octosyllabic line – a form largely ignored by Donne, but much favoured by Marvell; the emphasis borne by the word 'sound'; and most strikingly, the superb sarcasm of the impersonal passive construction, 'it is to be presumed': all these may well have been among the ingredients that went into the making of Marvell's poem. But, just as he wove features of Crashaw's 'The Weeper' into the much more intricately wrought fabric of 'Eyes and Tears', so in 'Mourning' he contrives a characteristic pressure of ambiguity upon his use of the word 'sound' and his impersonal passive, 'It is to be supposed'. Hiding behind the skill of an art that avoids all temptation to simplify the enigma of experience – even so trivial an enigma as that of Clora's tears – Marvell keeps his 'silent judgement'.

'Eyes and Tears' and 'Mourning', although neither could be counted among his finest achievements, represent two of Marvell's most frequent techniques for calling into question the adequacy of the interpretation of experience that a poem seems to be offering or for balancing one set of attitudes against another. Sometimes, as in the former, a single voice is permitted to dominate, but gradually the limitations of its vision are disclosed through the very conceits and rhetorical devices that constitute its medium of expression. Sometimes, as in the latter, a narrative voice will supervise our responses to the arguments being presented, but will evade the task of reaching a clear-cut verdict. A third ploy is to let two speakers have their say in dialogue form without adjudicating between them. Whichever method is operating, the reader is likely to become aware of an ironic intelligence holding itself aloof, observing, smiling, seeing more of the game than the participants. The next chapter will discuss four poems which illustrate Marvell's awareness of the complexities that are so often simplified by the conventions of love-poetry.

3

Loves and lovers

'The Gallery' is based on an extension of the commonplace conceit that, as Henry Constable puts it in the second of his *Diana* sonnets (1592), 'Love . . . within my heart thy heavenly shape doth paint.' Donne had already had fun with it in 'The Damp', where he suggests that if his friends carry out a postmortem examination and 'have me cut up' to ascertain the cause of death, 'they shall find your picture in my heart'. The wit of Marvell's poem is also a matter of taking the metaphorical to absurdly literal lengths: if the lover's heart can contain one likeness of his lady, why not a whole portrait-gallery? He invites her to accompany him on a guided tour:

1

Clora, come view my soul, and tell
Whether I have contrived it well.
Now all its several lodgings lie
Composed into one gallery;
And the great arras-hangings, made
Of various faces, by are laid;
That, for all furniture, you'll find
Only your picture in my mind.

The opening couplet warns us that the pictures Clora is about to see and the soul in which they are displayed are a contrivance. Like all human attempts to formulate experience, they are fashioned by art. In fact, the 'furniture' of this gallery is at two removes from reality, since it consists of verbal descriptions of paintings: outside the fictional frame of the speaker's bid for Clora's admiration at his ingenuity as an interior decorator is Marvell's bid for our applause at the imaginary situation he has invented in the poem we are about to read. Within the fiction, the 'various faces' that formerly had a place in the lover's mind have been cleared away like the old-fashioned 'arras-hangings', which the modern taste of Charles I's reign had replaced with painted canvases.

The next four stanzas present four portraits of Clora, arranged in contrasting pairs:

2

Here thou art painted in the dress
Of an inhuman murderess;
Examining upon our hearts
Thy fertile shop of cruel arts:
Engines more keen than ever yet
Adorned a tyrant's cabinet;
Of which the most tormenting are
Black eyes, red lips, and curlèd hair.

3

But, on the other side, th' art drawn
Like to Aurora in the dawn;
When in the East she slumbering lies,
And stretches out her milky thighs;
While all the morning choir does sing,
And manna falls, and roses spring;
And, at thy feet, the wooing doves
Sit perfecting their harmless loves.

4

Like an enchantress here thou show'st,
Vexing thy restless lover's ghost;
And, by a light obscure, dost rave
Over his entrails, in the cave;
Divining thence, with horrid care,
How long thou shalt continue fair;
And (when informed) them throw'st away,
To be the greedy vulture's prey.

5

But, against that, thou sit'st afloat
Like Venus in her pearly boat.
The halcyons, calming all that's nigh,
Betwixt the air and water fly;
Or, if some rolling wave appears,
A mass of ambergris it bears.
Nor blows more wild than what may well
Convoy the perfume to the smell.

That the contrasts are part of a schematic arrangement which Marvell wants us to notice is indicated by the phrase 'on the other side' in stanza 3 and 'against that' in stanza 5. Each pair sets an image of the cruel and destructive – Clora as 'murderess' and 'enchantress' – in apposition to an image of the seductive and sensuously appealing – Clora as Aurora and Venus. Stanzas 2 and 4 draw upon the implications of sadism, pitiless arrogance, and sorcery inherent in much of the conventional imagery of Elizabethan amatory verse. The 'lovely hue' of Spenser's lady is merely an 'allurement', 'That she the better may, in bloody bath / Of such poor thralls, her cruel hands imbrue' (*Amoretti*, sonnet 31); and the beauty of Drayton's is an 'evil spirit', that haunts and possesses him:

> And when by means to drive it out I try,
> With greater torments then it me doth take,
> And tortures me in most extremity. (*Idea*, Sonnet 20)

Torturer, murderess, and witch come together in Carew's song, 'Murd'ring Beauty':

> I'll gaze no more on her bewitching face;
> Since ruin harbours there in every place;
> For my enchanted soul alike she drowns
> With calms and tempests of her smiles and frowns.
> I'll love no more those cruel eyes of hers,
> Which, pleas'd or anger'd, still are murderers.

Little exaggeration in needed to produce the parodic portraits of Clora. In stanza 2 she is imagined gloating over the 'engines' of her craft, which turn out, in the finely managed bathos of the last line, to be the familiar attributes of the mistress of the sonneteers. In stanza 4, in a sinister chiaroscuro setting – 'by a light obscure' – she callously inspects the entrails of her dead admirer, like a pagan priestess, in quest of the one secret that interests her vanity: how long her beauty will last. Stanzas 3 and 5 exploit the mythic imagination which peoples an idyllic landscape or seascape with personifications of natural processes: the goddesses of dawn and sexual desire, surrounded by symbols of harmless pleasure and languid contentment.

What might Clora's reactions be to these paintings, one wonders, since each of them purports to be a likeness of her. Does she recognize herself in each of these roles, or does she smilingly interpret them as the erotic fantasies bred of an artistic tradition dominated by the masculine imagination? Her lover has, after all, introduced each of them as a 'picture in my mind'; and he seems to be deliberately sending up the poetic stereotype of the cruel mistress and inviting her to share his amusement.

There is an unexpected development in the next stanza, however, as the tour of the gallery is cut short:

6

These pictures and a thousand more
Of thee my gallery do store
In all the forms thou canst invent
Either to please me, or torment:
For thou alone to people me,
Art grown a numerous colony;
And a collection choicer far
Than or Whitehall's or Mantua's were.

The lover claims that the pictures derive not from *his* invention, but from *hers*, as she exercises her feminine ingenuity to please and torment him by turns in the manner already demonstrated in stanzas 2 to 5. Are they both sophisticated players in the game of love, who get aesthetic pleasure rather than passionate fulfilment from their relationship? That is certainly the implication of the final image of this stanza. The lover is a connoisseur, whose gallery contains 'choicer' exhibits of Clora's tantalizing performance than the most famous collections of paintings in recent history.

By another witty manipulation of the poem's structure, Clora's attention is finally brought to rest on a painting that was passed by in silence as we entered the gallery:

7

But, of these pictures and the rest,
That at the entrance likes me best:
Where the same posture, and the look
Remains, with which I first was took:
A tender shepherdess, whose hair
Hangs loosely playing in the air,
Transplanting flowers from the green hill,
To crown her head, and bosom fill.

This description of a 'tender shepherdess' brings with it from the tradition of pastoral an innocence and natural freshness, which provide an unspoken criticism of the melodramatic 'murderess' and 'enchantress', and of the languid sensuality and cloying perfume associated with Venus and the dawn goddess who 'stretches out her milky thighs'. It is this image from the very beginning of their relationship that the lover treasures most. The cynic might ask, however, whether it was merely another of the 'forms' that Clora is so adept at inventing. Was there ever a time when she was truly innocent? Was there ever a time when the lover's responses were spontaneous and untainted by an aesthetic taste for the refinements of the game of love? Marvell keeps his 'silent judgement', as he did over the question of Clora's (the same Clora's?) tears in 'Mourning'.

The withholding of the portrait of Clora as a shepherdess until the end of the poem is one of Marvell's most brilliant ploys for simultaneously releasing and exposing to sceptical scrutiny the expressive potentialities of a literary convention. What the fiction of the poem does is to leave us with an image of a worldly-wise man and woman gazing at an artistic impression of artlessness and experiencing who knows what yearnings for a lost, or perhaps merely imagined, golden world. And in so doing, it both dramatizes the impulse towards nostalgia and escapism that Laurence Lerner sees at the heart of the Renaissance pastoral, 'the wish to find in country life a relief from the problems of a sophisticated society' (p. 19), and demonstrates Patrick Cullen's further insight that 'while pastoral can portray an escape from reality, or a desire to escape reality', it also involves, 'implicitly or explicitly, a critical exploration and counterbalancing of attitudes, perspectives, and experiences' (p. 1). Since it is precisely the habit of counterbalancing one view or expressive mode against another that characterizes Marvell's practice as a poet, it comes as no surprise to find an important study of his work based squarely on the premise 'that all cf Marvell's good poetry responds in some degree to the demands of the pastoral vision, considered as one of the major ways of literary thinking that the European mind has found and followed' (Friedman, p. 4). Although it will be necessary more than once to come back to particular ramifications of the pastoral way of thinking as our discussion of Marvell's work proceeds, it will be useful at this early stage to have before us some idea of the general features and history of pastoral as a literary genre.

The term 'pastoral' derives from the Latin word *pastor*, a shepherd, and pastoral poetry as a distinct literary kind goes back to the Idyls of Theocritus, a Greek poet writing under court patronage in the great city of Alexandria in the third century B.C. Theocritus had been born in Syracuse, and in some of his Idyls recorded his early memories of the song-contests, rustic ceremonies, and simple way of life of the shepherds in Sicily and on the island of Cos. It is important to stress at the outset that pastoral poetry is not the folk art of actual countrymen, but the product of the highly developed culture of city or court. As W. W. Greg, one of the earliest historians of the genre, puts it, 'a constant element in the pastoral as known to literature is the recognition of a contrast, implicit or expressed, between pastoral life and some more complex type of civilization' (p. 4). Theocritus had his Greek imitators, but the next decisive step in the development of the genre was taken by the Latin poet, Virgil, whose ten Eclogues were published in 37 B.C., when Octavius Caesar ruled the Roman Empire. (The term 'eclogue' originally meant merely a 'selection', but in time it came to refer specifically to a poem in the pastoral manner.)

Virgil modelled his work directly on that of Theocritus, but took much further the process of idealization that was incipient in the Greek poet's affection for a less complex way of life. He relocated the pastoral world in Arcadia – in actuality a rugged region in Greece, but, because of its remoteness from centres of civilization, capable of being transformed into a distant and idyllic landscape of the mind; and he turned his shepherds both into vehicles for contemporary political allegory and elaborate compliments to powerful patrons and into embodiments of the unhappy lover and the aspiring poet. The result of these innovations was to bring the underlying contrasts between city and country, sophistication and artlessness, into thematic prominence and to discover significance in the paradoxical celebration of ideal simplicity in a poetic medium that was self-consciously artificial.

Virgil also opened the way for later developments by importing into pastoral the motif of a Golden Age, which had once existed on earth and which would return again in due course. The belief in a pristine time of innocence was widespread in ancient literature. Ovid gives a detailed account of it in the first book of his *Metamorphoses*:

In the beginning was the Golden Age, when men of their own accord, without threat of punishment, without laws, maintained good faith and did what was right . . . The peoples of the world, untroubled by any fears, enjoyed a leisurely and peaceful existence, and had no use for soldiers. The earth itself, without compulsion, untouched by the hoe, unfurrowed by any share, produced all things spontaneously, and men were content with foods that grew without cultivation . . . Then there flowed rivers of milk and rivers of nectar, and golden honey dripped from the green holm-oak.

In his Fourth Eclogue, Virgil celebrates the birth of a divine child who will rule over a new Golden Age, in which justice will return to the earth, peace will be established among men and beasts, and Nature will flourish without need of human labour. From quite early in the Christian era, this poem was interpreted as a prophecy of the birth of Christ, the during the Middle Ages the figure of the shepherd with his flock naturally became associated with the biblical imagery of Christ the Good Shepherd, who appointed St Peter and his successors to 'feed my sheep'.

In the late fifteenth century, the Italian Sannazaro rediscovered Arcadia as an idyllic realm in which love is the dominant concern and aristocratic values prevail. Tasso's *Aminta*, Guarini's *Il Pastor Fido*, and Montemayor's Spanish work, *Diana*, took their inspiration from Sannazaro's *Arcadia* and ensured that the new Arcadianism would leave an indelible stamp on the pastoral vision of Renaissance Europe. In England, a lively vernacular stream of pastoral lyrics flowed through into the sixteenth century, and Alexander Barclay produced the first eclogues in English early in the reign of Henry VIII, drawing upon both popular native sources and the classical inheritance. By the time Elizabeth I came to the throne, continental Arcadianism was also beginning to make an impact in England and the scene was set for an extraordinary flowering of pastoral. Sidney's prose romance, *Arcadia*, the twelve eclogues of Spenser's *The Shepheardes Calender* and the sixth book of his *Faerie Queene*, Shakespeare's *As You Like It* and *The Winter's Tale* are merely the greatest among a host of works large and small – from the briefest of songs to William Browne's Arcadian epic, *Britannia's Pastorals* – in which English poets and dramatists of the later sixteenth and early seventeenth centuries explored the artistic and philosophical possibilities offered by the many-sided genre of pastoral. For many, of course – and increasingly as the seventeenth century wore on – the idyllic landscape peopled by love-sick swains and coy or willing shepherdesses was no more than a literary convention cut off from the serious issues of life and providing a pretty setting for endless variations on the theme of love's joys and sorrows. But many more were fascinated by pastoral because it provoked, rather than evaded, important questions about the nature of man and his relation to both the natural and the civilized worlds. The poet who projects himself into the persona of a shepherd or recounts the activities of simple country folk may be impelled in the process to look more closely at the value of both their simplicity and his own sophistication. As we shall see, Andrew Marvell wrote in full consciousness of the rich and varied pastoral tradition that he was heir to, and was drawn time and time again to the complex relationships between innocence and experience, nature and art, contemplation and action, withdrawal and commitment which lie at the core of cultivated man's yearning for escape into a less demanding mode of existence.

The end of 'The Gallery' might be taken as a paradigm of the situation created by pastoral: a sophisticate pays homage to an artistic representation of an image of nature grace, which is itself recognized as being a symbol contrived by art. 'The Unfortunate Lover' also invokes pastoral as a point of reference, but confines it to the opening rather than the concluding stanza:

1

Alas, how pleasant are their days
With whom the infant Love yet plays!
Sorted by pairs, they still are seen
By fountains cool, and shadows green.
But soon these flames do lose their light,
Like meteors of a summer's night:
Nor can they to that region climb,
To make impression upon time.

The 'fountains cool, and shadows green', with their echoes of many an idyllic landscape going back to Virgil's 'mossy springs, and banks of grass softer than sleep', where 'green arbutuses' cast a network of shade in the Seventh Eclogue, are the setting for a vision of innocent, perhaps pre-sexual, love. But the very first word, 'Alas', establishes a perspective of superior wisdom upon the figures in this landscape, and the word 'Sorted' diminishes their dignity with its suggestion that they are unconscious victims of the playfulness of Cupid, 'the infant Love', in the same way that the pairs of young people in *A Midsummer Night's Dream* are made sport of by Puck. In the second half of the stanza, love conceived as an idyllic game – as pastoral lyric so often conceives it – is shown to be inconsequential and short-lived. The 'flames' (a conventional metaphor for lovers' passions) of this kind of immature love last no longer than a shooting-star. But the fact of transitoriness, implied throughout by the insidious accumulation of time-references – 'their days', 'yet plays', 'still are seen', 'a summer's night' – is less significant in itself than the failure to 'make impression upon time', to leave some more permanent memorial of their passing than the fast-fading track of a meteor in the night sky. The rest of the poem will draw upon an alternative poetic tradition for sharply contrasting images of a love which is far from 'pleasant', but which challenges oblivion by the sheer violence of its passion.

The version of Courtly Love embodied in Petrarch's sonnets to Laura had dominated English amatory verse of the sixteenth century ever since Sir Thomas Wyatt had set the fashion for translating and imitating Italian sonnets in the reign of Henry VIII. The torments of frustration willingly endured by the lover in his devotion to an unattainable or obdurately unyielding lady found their outlet in the sort of hyperbole and paradox illustrated by two lines from Samuel Daniel's sonnet sequence, *To Delia*:

No succour find I now when most I need;
Th' Ocean of my tears must drown me burning.
(Sonnet 29)

In Wyatt's rendering of one of Petrarch's sonnets, the lover's psychological situation is projected in the elaborate conceit of a ship tossing helplessly in a storm of passion:

My galley charged with forgetfulness
Thorough sharp seas in winter nights doth pass
'Tween rock and rock . . .

An endless wind doth tear the sail apace
Of forced sighs and trusty fearfulness.
A rain of tears, a cloud of dark disdain
Hath done the wearied cords great hindrance.

. . .

Drowned is reason that should me comfort
And I remain despairing of the port.

A century later, the same conceit was still very much alive in a poem by Thomas Carew, entitled 'Upon Some Alterations in my Mistress, After my Departure into France':

O gentle love, do not forsake the guide
Of my frail bark, on which the swelling tide
Of ruthless pride
Doth beat, and threaten wrack from every side.
Gulfs of disdain do gape to overwhelm
This boat, nigh sunk with grief, whilst at the helm
Despair commands;

. . .

My sighs have rais'd those winds, whose fury bears
My sails o'erboard, and in their place spreads fears;
And from my tears
This sea is sprung, where naught but death appears.

Marvell works witty variations on this tradition of metaphor in the stanzas which introduce his 'Unfortunate Lover':

2

'Twas in a shipwreck, when the seas
Ruled, and the winds did what they please,
That my poor lover floating lay,
And, ere brought forth, was cast away:
Till at the last the master-wave
Upon the rock his mother drave;
And there she split against the stone,
In a Caesarean section.

3

The sea him lent those bitter tears
Which at his eyes he always wears;
And from the winds the sighs he bore,
Which through his surging breast do roar.
No day he saw but that which breaks
Through frighted clouds in forkèd streaks,
While round the rattling thunder hurled.
As at the funeral of the world.

The curious reference to 'my poor lover', with its emphasis on the first person pronoun, serves two purposes: it indicates that the figure whose career is to be the subject of the poem is the fictional creation of the narrator and it asserts the contrast between this lover and those 'with whom the infant Love yet plays' in stanza 1. His story begins with the disaster of his birth, expressed in a conceit which maintains a complex relation between the images of a ship splitting against a rock and a mother's womb being cut open in a Caesarean delivery. From his earliest moments, he is surrounded by convulsions of the elements scarcely distinguishable in the poem's rhetoric from the convulsions of grief that roar 'through his surging breast'. If these stanzas seem designed to outdo in violence and ingenuity one set of traditional Petrarchan images, another set receives similar treatment in the account of what befalls the lover under the 'cruel care' of his cormorant guardians:

4

While Nature to his birth presents
This masque of quarrelling elements,
A numerous fleet of cormorants black,
That sailed insulting o'er the wrack,
Received into their cruel care
Th' unfortunate and abject heir:
Guardians most fit to entertain
The orphan of the hurricane.

5

They fed him up with hopes and air,
Which soon digested to despair,
And as one cormorant fed him, still
Another on his heart did bill,
Thus while they famish him, and feast,
He both consumèd, and increased:
And languishèd with doubtful breath,
The amphibium of life and death.

Samuel Daniel had presented himself as 'Th' Orphan of Fortune, born to be her scorn, / Whose clouded brow doth make my days so sad' (Sonnet 24); and had bewailed his 'Vulture-gnawn heart' and his 'hunger-starven thoughts so long retained, / Fed but with smoke, and cherish'd but with fire' (Sonnet 15). Marvell has ingeniously invented a situation in which the image of the 'orphan' has narrative as well as metaphorical point, since we must assume that the mother of his Unfortunate Lover died as a result of the 'Caesarean section'. Being an orphan, he passes into the custody of guardians, who simultaneously starve and feed him with the unfulfilled hopes that traditionally held the Petrarchan lover suspended between death and life. It is typical of Marvell's method in this poem that he should have replaced the conventional vultures with the startling 'fleet of cormorants black' and found the more extreme words 'famish' and 'feast' to express the familiar paradox.

By stanza 6, the protagonist seems to have grown into manhood and is forced into displays of gladiatorial valour against Fortune and Love:

6

And now, when angry heaven would
Behold a spectacle of blood,
Fortune and he are called to play
At sharp before it all the day:
And tyrant Love his breast does ply
With all his winged artillery,
Whilst he, betwixt the flames and waves,
Like Ajax, the mad tempest braves.

This 'play' is no harmless game, like that of 'the infant Love' of stanza 1. The weapons are unbated ('at sharp'), and the arrows ('winged artillery'), loosed by a Love who now bears the title 'tyrant', have the power to produce 'a spectacle of blood'. With a slight shock, we realize that the Unfortunate Lover is still on the rock where he was born, still being assaulted by lightning and tempest 'betwixt the flames and waves', like Ajax Oileus, who was destroyed in a storm for defying the gods. In the next stanza, we are called to witness his final heroic gesture, as he is overwhelmed by his adversaries:

7

See how he nak'd and fierce does stand,
Cuffing the thunder with one hand,
While with the other he does lock,
And grapple, with the stubborn rock:
From which he with each wave rebounds,
Torn into flames, and ragg'd with wounds,

> And all he says, a lover dressed
> In his own blood does relish best.

The final couplet contains a textual crux, which has divided the critics. Some take the last line and a half to be words – the only words, '*all* he says' – spoken by the Lover himself. They would contain the declaration that a lover covered in the blood pouring from his own wounds gives most pleasure – presumably to those who, like 'angry heaven', enjoy 'a spectacle of blood'. Others regard 'says' as an abbreviated form of the verb 'assays', meaning 'endeavours', and arrive at the following interpretation: 'A lover covered in his own blood is able to appreciate most fully everything that the Unfortunate Lover attempts to do.' A third possibility, and the one which seems to me preferable because it does least violence to the words as they stand in the text, is to accept 'says' as equivalent to 'speaks' and to read 'all he says' as the object of the verb 'relish'. The entire couplet would then be glossed: 'A lover covered in his own blood can best appreciate everything that this unfortunate lover says.' Whichever reading is adopted, there remains a witty play on the word 'dressed': its primary meaning of 'clothed' is supplemented by the secondary meaning 'garnished as a dish for the table' by association with 'relish' in the next line.

The Lover's career of misfortune, governed by 'the malignant stars', is now over, and the final stanza sums up his achievements and rewards:

> 8
>
> This is the only banneret
> That ever Love created yet:
> Who though, by the malignant stars,
> Forced to live in storms and wars,
> Yet dying leaves a perfume here,
> And music within every ear:
> And he in story only rules,
> In a field sable a lover gules.

A banneret is a knight dubbed on the field of battle for acts of bravery. King Charles had conferred this honour for the first time for many years at Edgehill in 1642 and Marvell almost certainly derived his use of the term here from a conceit in Richard Lovelace's 'Dialogue: Lucasta. Alexis':

> Soldiers suspected of their courage go,
> That ensigns and their breasts untorn show:

> Love near his standard when his host he sets,
> Creates alone fresh-bleeding bannerets.

The Unfortunate Lover has a breast far from 'untorn' and deserves to be uniquely honoured by Love. Dying, he leaves behind him ' a perfume', 'music', a memory of his exploits 'in story', and the striking device on his coat-of-arms of a blood-red lover on a black background ('gules' and 'sable' being heraldic terms for these colours).

This initial reading has left many questions unanswered. Why is there no mention of the object of the Unfortunate Lover's passion? What is the significance of his progress from calamitous birth to defiant death? What is the function of that opening evocation of the pastoral world? And, perhaps above all, what attitude does the poet expect us to take towards the figure he brings before us with such a proprietary air as 'my poor lover'? Many explanations have been offered. 'The Unfortunate Lover' has ben interpreted as an allegory of the suffering of the time-bound soul (Berthoff), or of Christ's Incarnation and Sacrifice (King), or of the fate of Charles I, the martyred king (Patterson). While not wishing to preclude the possibility that some such hidden meanings may lurk behind the images out of which the Unfortunate Lover is created, I prefer to follow Marvell's own hints that we should direct our attention towards the nature and status of those images themselves as constructs of the artistic imagination.

Within the poem's neatly schematic structure, which devotes two stanzas each to birth (2 and 3), upbringing (4 and 5), and fatal contest with Fortune and Love (6 and 7), between the framing stanzas 1 and 8, there are frequent reminders that the Lover belongs to the domain of art and has been invented for the entertainment of an audience. As well as the constant suspicion that the Petrarchan style is being burlesqued, there are the invitations to adopt the stance appropriate to readers of fiction in the narrative gambit, ''Twas in a shipwreck'; to regard the contents of stanza 3 as a 'masque of quarrelling elements', an example of the court shows put on in the Stuart period to celebrate a royal event; to join 'angry heaven' as spectators of the 'spectacle of blood' staged in stanza 6; and to admire the emblematic picture of the Lover defying the gods like a latter-day Prometheus in stanza 7. Indeed, it has been suggested that the entire poem is based on the series of emblems depicting the lover's torments in Otto van Veen's *Amorum Emblemata* (1608) and Crispin de Passe's *Thronus Cupidinis* (1618). But, in fact, the central section of 'The Unfortunate Lover' does not consist of a series of emblematic pictures; it tells a story. From the introductory ''Twas in a shipwreck' through to the end of stanza 5 finite verbs in the past tense recount the hero's history – what he did and what was done to him. By contrast, the pictorial images of Clora in 'The Gallery' are conveyed in present-tense verbs and present participles – what she is represented as doing in each portrait. And whereas the speaker's mental review of his relationship with Clora is arranged in spatial terms ('Here', 'on the other side', 'here', 'against that', 'at the entrance'), temporal conjunctions and adverbs articulate the narrator's conception of his 'poor lover' ('when', 'ere', 'Till at the last', 'While', 'While', 'soon', 'still', 'while'). In the last three stanzas of the poem, there is a gradual transition from the narrative to the pictorial, from the dynamic to the static. The 'And now' of stanza 6 signals the movement into the present tense, and the injunction 'See' at the start of stanza 7 freezes the action into a portrait of the Lover in his posture of defiance. Narrative has given way to emblem by way of 'spectacle', as participles and periphrastic verb-forms take over ('does stand', 'Cuffing', 'does lock, And grapple', 'torn', 'ragg'd).

The last four lines of the poem enact the process by which the Unfortunate Lover's significance for posterity is formulated. The perfume and the music that are his immediate legacy fade upon the air – 'Like meteors of a summer's night'; but 'in story', he continues to hold sway over the imagination, and his coat-of-arms survives as a more concrete memorial of his fate and his honour. Unlike the pastoral 'pairs' of stanza 1, this lover has managed to 'make impression upon time' and attain the immortality and permanence that art affords. But a price has to be paid for this achievement. Only the extraordinary leaves its mark, so the experiences of the Lover must set him apart from those unmemorable 'pairs' who pass their 'pleasant' days in a pastoral idyll. Like the lovers of Wyatt and Daniel and Carew, he is interesting to the consumers of art because of the intensity of his inner torments. The lady of the Petrarchan tradition functions merely as the occasion of the frustrated male passions which hold the centre of the stage. As such, she has no significant identity, and so Marvell omits all mention of her in the creation of his 'poor lover', who is conceived in direct contrast to those 'sorted' by Cupid into 'pairs'. Indeed, the Unfortunate Lover is, perhaps, best interpreted as a deliberate construct of the artistic imagination out of materials supplied by one particular poetic convention. But conventions become blunted with use, and a process of inflation sets in, as the poet strives to give new edge to his idiom with ever more extravagant variations on the inherited stock of hyperboles, paradoxes, and conceits. It is not a matter of parody, as those who seek for profound allegorical meanings in the poem are aware. There is genuine expressive power in the images of violence and suffering, which holds the suspicion of a simple burlesque intention at bay. Nevertheless, it is not possible to ignore the element of the ridiculous in the picture of the naked hero 'Cuffing' the thunder with one hand as he grapples the 'stubborn rock' with the other. This may be why the reader who can best savour 'all' that the lover-poet 'says' (in the many lengthy sonnet-sequences of the late Elizabethan age) is the 'lover dressed / In his own blood' – the man who is closest to the subjective realities that validate the extreme nature of the Petrarchan idiom. But those who can take a more objective view may well feel that there is something self-indulgent, and even masochistic, in the careful dressing of one's own pain as an artistic dish to be relished.

The choice and manipulation of words in the final couplet register a further reservation about the Petrarchan version of human experience. The Unfortunate Lover 'in story only rules': he alone has a tale worth telling, in contrast to those 'with whom the infant Love yet plays'; or he rules only in story, only in a fictional world which stands apart from the facts of real existence. This latter reading is reinforced by the specialized vocabulary of the last line: just as heraldic devices present a highly stylized image of the human form – simplified to a much greater degree than the emblematic portrait of stanza 7 – so the metaphors of Petrarchanism simplify, as all art must, the complexities of life in space and time.

Clora was invited to 'come view my soul' and to judge the good taste of her connoisseur admirer. The invitation extended to the unnamed lady in 'To His Coy Mistress' is for a more active participation in the game of courtship. The dramatic situation of the lover's attempt to persuade a reluctant virgin into sexual compliance has more immediacy than the fanciful conceit of the picture-gallery of the mind, and the movement of the poem has a correspondingly greater urgency. In place of the rather static arrangement of self-contained stanzas, which can be lingered over like the paintings they describe, there is the forward impulse of a three-part syllogistic argument. This speaker is just as ironically disposed towards the conventions of amatory verse as Clora's lover, but he makes much more vigorous use of them.

The conditional tense casts a mockingly regretful tone over the hyperboles of the first paragraph:

> Had we but world enough, and time,
> This coyness, Lady, were no crime.
> We would sit down, and think which way
> To walk, and pass our long love's day.

Thou by the Indian Ganges' side
Shouldst rubies find: I by the tide
Of Humber would complain. I would
Love you ten years before the flood:
And you should, if you please, refuse
Till the conversion of the Jews.
My vegetable love should grow
Vaster than empires, and more slow.
An hundred years should go to praise
Thine eyes, and on thy forehead gaze.
Two hundred to adore each breast:
But thirty thousand to the rest.
An age at least to every part,
And the last age should show your heart:
For, Lady, you deserve this state;
Nor would I love at lower rate.

The opening couplet strikes the keynote straight away: *if only* they were not subject to the inexorable laws of space and time, they could live out the fantasy of a love which slowly expanded over the face of the earth like an empire and which lasted right through human history, from Noah's flood to the Second Coming of Christ heralded by the 'conversion of the Jews'. Such fantasies are among the resources that human art has invented for coping imaginatively with the facts of time and mortality. An example from Abraham Cowley's *The Mistress* (1647) must have been in Marvell's mind as he composed this poem:

On 'a *sigh* of Pity I a year can live,
  One *Tear* will keep me twenty 'at least,
  Fifty a gentle *Look* will give:
An hundred years on one *kind word* I'll feast:
  A thousand more will added be,
If you an *Inclination* have for me;
And all beyond is vast *Eternity*.

But what in Cowley's 'The Diet' is an artificial and rather thin-blooded expression of the Petrarchan lover's abject devotion to his lady is transmuted into a powerful ploy in the seduction strategy of a more worldly-wise and witty wooer. If time did not make the project patently ridiculous, he would gladly play the conventional game of protracted courtship, and tune his sorrowful complaint – the technical name for the song of a love-sick swain – beside Marvell's own native stream, the Humber, while the lady gathered jewels from the more exotic banks of the Ganges. The very incongruity of linking the two rivers, with the difference in sophistication implied between the travelled lady and the provincial lover, begins a strain of gentle teasing which culminates in the suggestion that 'the last age' before the end of the world prophesied in the Revelation of St John would 'show' the secret of her heart. The Coy Mistress is no naîve country girl to be taken in by the poet's flattering combination of the traditional catalogue of female charms with Cowley's mathematical conceit in lines 13–16. Each turn of his wit is offered as a joke to be shared – sometimes at his own expense, sometimes at hers, and sometimes at the expense of the poetic conventions he mocks in the very act of exploiting them for his own purposes. But the jesting is not incompatible with a serious undertone of resentment and regret at time's defeat of human idealism:

For, Lady, you deserve this state;
Nor would I love at lower rate.

This elegant compliment prepares us for the next stage of the syllogism, introduced by the 'but' that has been looming ever since the conditional verb with which the poem began:

But, at my back I always hear
Time's winged chariot hurrying near:
And yonder all before us lie
Deserts of vast eternity.
Thy beauty shall no more be found;
Nor, in thy marble vault, shall sound
My echoing song: then worms shall try
That long-preserved virginity:
And your quaint honour turn to dust;
And into ashes all my lust.
The grave's a fine and private place,
But none, I think, do there embrace.

In place of the fantasy of a courtship stretching through millennia, the chilling prospect of a bleak and sterile eternity opens up, and the uncompromising future tense takes over from the dream-permitting conditional. That bodily perfection, which deserves the homage only hyperbole can express, will vanish from the face of the earth, and even the poet's record of his devotion will eventually be lost. The reference to his song exposes the futility of another of imagination's stays against the encroachments of time. Shakespeare, for example, had found consolation for the losses inflicted on human beauty in the thought that it would survive in *his* 'echoing song':

Time doth transfix the flourish set on youth
And delves the parallels in beauty's brow,
Feeds on the rarities of nature's truth,

And nothing stands but for his scythe to mow:
And yet to times in hope my verse shall stand,
Praising thy worth, despite his cruel hand.
(Sonnet 60)

Marvell's realism gives the lie to this illusion. Neither singer nor song will outlast even the 'marble vault' in which the lady's body moulders into dust, whatever poets may assert to the contrary:

Not marble, nor the gilded monuments
Of princes, shall outlive this powerful rhyme.
(Shakespeare, Sonnet 55)

The macabre humour of lines 27–32 allows no escape into the abstract or the general: the lady may keep herself intact during her life, but she will not evade the ultimate plundering of her virginity by the phallic worms of the grave. One way or another, the ravening hunger of Nature will overcome her coyness. With a final sardonic couplet, the lover leads into the third stage of his syllogistic argument.

To appreciate the achievement of the climactic paragraph – or indeed of the whole poem as a carefully articulated work of art – it is helpful to read it against other examples of the *carpe diem* lyric (literally 'seize the day', or 'enjoy life before it is too late'). Perhaps best known is the song Robert Herrick published in his *Hesperides* (1648):

Gather ye Rose-buds while ye may,
Old Time is still a flying:
And this same flower that smiles today,
Tomorrow will be dying.

The glorious Lamp of Heaven, the Sun,
The higher he's a getting;
The sooner will his Race be run,
And nearer he's to setting.

Closer in tone to Marvell's poem are some lines from the final stanza of 'Corinna's going a Maying', also from *Hesperides*:

Come, let us go, while we are in our prime;
And take the harmless folly of the time.
We shall grow old apace, and die
Before we know our liberty.
Our life is short; and our days run
As fast away as does the sun.
And as a vapour, or a drop of rain
Once lost, can ne'er be found again.

Ben Jonson's 'Song. To Celia', and the lines by the Roman poet Catullus on which it is based, seem to lie even nearer the heart of Marvell's inspiration:

Come my Celia, let us prove,
While we may, the sports of love;
Time will not be ours, for ever:
He, at length, our good will sever.
Spend not then his gifts in vain.
Suns, that set, may rise again:
But if once we lose this light,
'Tis, with us, perpetual night.

Phrases are echoed and the central idea is carried over in 'To His Coy Mistress', but there is a physical immediacy and a desperate recklessness which eschews the sentimental evasions of gathering 'Rose-buds' and enjoying 'harmless folly':

Now, therefore, while the youthful glue
Sits on thy skin like morning dew,
And while thy willing soul transpires
At every pore with instant fires,
Now let us sport us while we may;
And now, like amorous birds of prey,
Rather at once our time devour,
Than languish in his slow-chapped power.
Let us roll all our strength, and all
Our sweetness, up into one ball:
And tear our pleasures with rough strife,
Thorough the iron gates of life.
Thus, though we cannot make our sun
Stand still, yet we will make him run.

The urgently repeated 'Now', and the transition to present tense and imperative verb-forms, sweep the lady from the grim contemplation of her own decay towards the physical consummation that is the lover's goal. The dramatic sense of her sexual arousal – every pore of her glistening skin is alert and responsive, as if her 'willing soul' were burning its way through from the inside – excites the lover to images of brutal forthrightness. There is no mention of love or the gaze of adoration in this paragraph. Instead, there is the rapacious devouring of two 'amorous birds of prey' and the tearing of pleasures 'with rough strife'. Lines 41–6 have received many scholarly and ingenious interpretations. It may be that behind them lie the kind of hyperboles that Donne so often resorted to in order to embody his highest vision of reciprocal love. In 'The Good-Morrow' he tells his mistress, 'Let us possess one world, each hath one, and is one'; and says of their reflection in each other's eyes, 'Where can we find two better hemispheres?' In 'The Canonization' he imagines the male Eagle and the female Dove fused into the neutral Phoenix in the act of love-making. The rolling of strength and sweetness into a single ball may be a conflation of these two images, or others like them in poems that celebrate the perfect union of lovers. The final couplet may contain an allusion to the feat of the biblical hero, Joshua, who made the sun stand still while he took revenge on Israel's enemies. It may equally well contain echoes of Herrick and Jonson, and an ironic glance at Donne's claim, in 'The Anniversary', that though the sun, 'which makes times, as they pass', itself grows older, his love 'no tomorrow hath, nor yesterday, / Running it never runs from us away'; or at his fantastic command, in 'The Sun Rising', that the sun should stay its journey over him and his mistress:

> Shine here to us, and thou art everywhere;
> This bed thy centre is, these walls, thy sphere.

If Donne's poetry is meant to be brought to mind here, then it is a final instance of the speaker's wry undercutting of the ingenuity with which the human imagination avoids the stark facts of lust and time. A man and a woman rolled 'up into one ball' are too preoccupied with the 'rough strife' of exacting their physical 'pleasures' to trouble their minds with riddles about phoenixes. They would not presume, like Donne, to command *their* sun to stand still; but they can, during their desperate love-making, speed up the effects of time as the minutes rush by: that much control over time, at least, is in their hands, though they know that ultimately there is no escape from his 'slow-chapped power'.

Whatever the specific allusions behind these images and the equally contentious 'iron gates of life', there can be no disputing the unsentimental realism with which Marvell's lover concludes his appeal. The consummation he invites her to share with him takes on the air of a contest, in which he and the Coy Mistress pit themselves against a harsh world that will not yield its joys without a fierce struggle. He urges her not to *submit* to him, but to *join* him in overcoming, if only temporarily, the united forces of time and space that consign all poetry's most cherished dreams to the realm of illusion. How far Marvell endorsed the conclusion of his poem's argument and how far he expected his readers to condemn its reckless commitment to the merely physical satisfactions of sex, there is no way of knowing. Either interpretation is possible, although the title – 'To

His Coy Mistress' – may be taken as indicating the independent dramatic status of the speaker. Perhaps, like the other poetic approaches to the subject of love that he toys with and dismisses, his is one more oversimplification of the inexpressible complexity of man's life in time.

'The Definition of Love', as its title implies, affords a very different treatment of human experience from that in 'To His Coy Mistress'. In place of a lover's appeal to a lady whose dramatic presence is postulated by the mode of expression, we hear a voice speaking into the void and attempting definition rather than persuasion:

1

My love is of a birth as rare
As 'tis for object strange and high:
It was begotten by Despair
Upon Impossibility.

2

Magnanimous Despair alone
Could show me so divine a thing,
Where feeble Hope could ne'er have flown
But vainly flapped its tinsel wing.

It is a curious feature of this poem that the goal of the speaker's yearning is never once named or even accorded the minimal status as a human person that the pronouns 'she' or 'her' would impart. Having been introduced in these stanzas as an 'object strange and high' and 'so divine a thing', the beloved ceases to have any existence except in association with the lover in the plural pronouns 'us' and 'we'. This has led one critic to interpret the poem as an allegory of 'the love of the incarnate soul for its heavenly life' (Berthoff, p. 106). Others are adamant that there must be 'a girl of flesh and blood' in the case, whose social superiority or politically hostile family kept the lovers apart (Bateson, pp. 109–11). The fact that the poem seems deliberately to withhold the kind of information that would enable us to decide one way or the other should perhaps direct our attention away from the identity of the object and towards the nature of the love itself. The witty teasing of our expectations in the opening two lines certainly encourages this. The first, with its reference to birth, suggests that 'My love' is a human being of high social standing, presumably the conventional Petrarchan lady; the second forces us to revise this reading and interpret 'My love' as the emotion of the speaker. Riddle and paradox reign, as the origin of this strange passion is traced to the impossibility of its desires ever being fulfilled. The grand epithet

'Magnanimous' reinforces the tone of lofty self-satisfaction with which the speaker contemplates the superiority of his love to that of amatory poets whose more commonplace ambitions are sustained by the 'tinsel wing' of 'feeble Hope'.

The next two stanzas explain why consummation is unachievable:

3

And yet I quickly might arrive
Where my extended soul is fixed,
But fate does iron wedges drive,
And always crowds itself betwixt.

4

For Fate with jealous eye does see
Two perfect loves, nor lets them close:
Their union would her ruin be,
And her tyrannic power depose.

Physical images are used to express the forced separation of the lovers: iron wedges drive them apart, Fate 'crowds itself' between them like an ill-mannered jostler, and they are not permitted to 'close' in an embrace. Fate is given a degree of personality denied to the object of the speaker's devotion, as it – or she, in stanza 4 – jealously watches over them and exerts her 'tyrannic power' to prevent the impossible union. And yet, for all the particularity of the expression, the nature of the processes being described remains abstract and out of touch with familiar experience. The central idea seems to be that the 'union' of 'two perfect loves' would transgress the laws that govern the state of things as they are and so result in the 'ruin' of Fate, the embodiment and guardian of those laws. It is the very perfection of the loves that disables them from success in the material world associated with Fate's activities (and it is worth remarking that perfection is claimed not for the *lovers*, but for the 'loves' which they have for each other).

Having proclaimed the genesis of his love and identified the antagonist who stands in the way of its fulfilment, the poet goes on to amplify his present predicament:

5

And therefore her decrees of steel
Us as the distant Poles have placed,
(Though Love's whole world on us doth wheel)
Not by themselves to be embraced,

6

Unless the giddy heaven fall,
And earth some new convulsion tear;

And, us to join, the world should all
Be cramped into a planisphere.

These lines serve to display the speaker's wit rather than to advance the argument of the poem, in spite of the gestures towards logical structure in the linking words 'therefore' and 'unless'. Stanza 5 is a repetition of the idea more succinctly expressed in the phrase 'nor lets them close'; and stanza 6 is an even more fantastic elaboration of the claim that 'ruin' would attend the lovers' union. Together these stanzas amount to a virtuoso performance in the 'metaphysical' manner – ingenious variations on a conceit which goes back to Donne's 'Let us possess one world, each hath one, and is one' and 'This bed thy centre is, these walls, thy sphere.' The same conceit had been developed by the Cavalier poets to express the very subject of absence and separation that lies at the heart of 'The Definition of Love'. Among others, Richard Lovelace, for whose volume of poetry Marvell had written dedicatory verses, had used it in 'To Lucasta, Going beyond the Seas':

Though Seas and Land betwixt us both,
    Our Faith and Troth,
  Like separated souls,
    All time and place controls:
Above the highest sphere we meet
Unseen, unknown, and greet as Angels greet.

Marvell's speaker glances patronizingly at Donne's hyperbolical assertions of the self-contained fulfilment and universal significance of his love in a dismissive parenthesis: '(Though Love's whole world on us doth wheel)'. The love he is celebrating has an equal claim on hyperbole: it keeps the lovers as far apart as the human imagination can reach – to the poles of the universe. For them to embrace, therefore, the spheres of the Ptolemaic system would need to be compressed into a two-dimensional planisphere, so that the poles could come together. As in earlier stanzas, the strikingly physical connotations of the words – 'giddy', 'convulsion', 'tear', 'cramped' – are played off against the essentially immaterial nature of the love being defined.

The conceit and the challenge to Donne are continued in the next stanza:

7

As lines (so loves) oblique may well
Themselves in every angle greet:

But ours so truly parallel,
Though infinite, can never meet.

The lines of longitude on a chart graphically representing the spherical world meet at the poles, forming angles; the lines of latitude are parallel. Hovering behind this stanza is the famous conceit at the end of 'A Valediction: Forbidding Mourning' – another classic version of the 'separation' theme – in which Donne imagines himself on his journey as the moving foot of a pair of compasses which must 'obliquely run', while his lady, as the 'fixed foot', waits confidently at home and ensures his return by her 'firmness'. Marvell seems to be mischievously demonstrating that the same kind of imagery and ingenious exploitation of mathematical logic can be used to support opposite conclusions. Donne convinces himself that mere physical distance cannot part two souls that are truly united by love; Marvell's speaker assures us that 'parallel' souls – the 'Two perfect loves' of stanza 4 – 'can never meet'. As before, nothing but contempt is shown for the sort of love that seeks the satisfaction of 'greeting', whether platonically 'above the highest sphere' in Lovelace's poem or more carnally 'in every angle' (or dark corner) that offers convenient opportunity.

The poem concludes with a schematic setting forth of the definition towards which it has been working:

8

Therefore the love which us doth bind,
But Fate so enviously debars,
Is the conjunction of the mind,
And opposition of the stars.

Paradox is still the only available linguistic device for formulating the quality of a love that draws together and drives apart with equal force. The terms 'conjunction' and 'opposition' carry forward the earlier astronomical conceit into the related field of astrology, and put the final seal on a definition which insists on the role of Fate or the stars in maintaining the hopelessness from which this lover derives his smug sense of uniqueness. As in 'Eyes and Tears', which has much in common with this poem, no overt judgement is passed on the speaker or on the attitudes he expresses. Nevertheless, the lack of passion with which he contemplates his predicament, and indeed the lofty pleasure he takes in denigrating other kinds of love and analysing his own, are an inescapable part of the experience communicated by the controlled flow of the rhythm and the cool mastery of paradox, hyperbole, and conceit. If the seducer of 'To His Coy Mistress' finally commits himself to a vision of love that is disturbingly brutal and uncompromising in its stress on the physical, it is a vision which generations of readers have recognized as more profoundly and movingly human than the self-absorbed philosophizing of a mind more interested in defining love than in consummating it.

4

Pastoral and Puritan

The kind of compromise impossible for the 'Two perfect loves' of 'The Definition of Love' is easily accommodated by the participants in a slight, if witty, poem that can serve to introduce Marvell's varied use of the dialogue form. A frank acceptance of the imperfections of love in this world soon resolves the pastoral debate in 'Ametas and Thestylis Making Hay-ropes':

1
AMETAS
Think'st thou that this love can stand,
Whilst thou still dost say me nay?
Love unpaid does soon disband:
Love binds love as hay binds hay.

2
THESTYLIS
Think'st thou that this rope would twine
If we both should turn one way?
Where both parties so combine,
Neither love will twist nor hay.

3
AMETAS
Thus you vain excuses find,
Which yourselves and us delay:
And love ties a woman's mind
Looser than with ropes of hay.

4
THESTYLIS
What you cannot constant hope
Must be taken as you may.

5
AMETAS
Then let's both lay by our rope,
And go kiss within the hay.

Ametas warns his coy mistress that his ardour will soon cool if his desires are not granted; she points out that love thrives on contraries and opposition; he counters with charges of prevarication and inconstancy. The crudeness of their conception of love finds expression in the glibness with which each of them accepts the adequacy of the analogy between rope-making and love-making: two activities assumed to be on roughly equal levels of seriousness. Ametas's talk of binding and tying carries no overtones of permanence and constancy, and Thestylis's coyness is no more than a tactic in the game of dalliance. She soon invites him to take her in the knowledge that he cannot expect her to be 'constant'; and he responds eagerly with no qualms about the lack of commitment implied by a kiss 'within the hay'. Pastoral dialogues of this kind continued to be popular from the Elizabethan period through to Marvell's own day, though the simplicity of the earlier exchanges between two shepherds or shepherd and shepherdess was sometimes given an edge of 'metaphysical' wit by later poets.

Marvell, characteristically, exploits the gap between his own (and his reader's) awareness of life's complexities and the more naïve attitude of the inhabitants of the pastoral world. In 'Ametas and Thestylis Making Hay-ropes', the shepherd and shepherdess share the same low expectations of love, which are reflected in their uncritical use of imagery derived from their rustic occupation. Greater possibilities for irony are created when there is a disparity in sophistication between the two partners in a dialogue as well as between them and the reader. The hint for such a development is found in the question-and-answer, in which one speaker instructs a more simple companion. 'The Shepherd's Description of Love', for example, from the famous late-Elizabethan collection, *England's Helicon*, follows this pattern throughout:

> *Melibeus.* Shepherd, what's Love, I pray thee tell?
> *Faustus.* It is that Fountain, and that Well,
> Where pleasure and repentance dwell.

Other developments taken over by Marvell are the cut-and-thrust of a poem like Thomas Carew's 'A Pastoral Dialogue', which moves more dramatically than the song-like arrangement of the verses in 'Ametas and Thestylis Making Hay-ropes':

> *Cleon.* I dote not on thy snow-white skin.
> *Celia.* What then? *Cleon.* Thy purer mind.
> *Celia.* It lov'd too soon. *Cleon.* Thou hadst not bin
> So fair, if not so kind.
> *Celia.* Oh strange vain fancy! *Cleon.* But yet true.
> *Celia.* Prove it!

and the confutation of pastoral's oversimplified vision of the human lot in Sir Walter Ralegh's reply to Christopher Marlowe's celebrated invitation to love, 'The Passionate Shepherd to his Love', both printed in *England's Helicon*. Marlowe's shepherd offers the delights of 'Vallies, groves, hills and fields', and the entertainment afforded by pastoral idleness; Ralegh supplies a realistic perspective on these temptations, which brings with it the moral pressure associated with the *contemptus mundi* tradition:

If all the world and love were young,
And truth in every Shepherd's tongue,
These pretty pleasures might me move,
To live with thee, and be thy love.

Time drives the flocks from field to fold,
When Rivers rage, and Rocks grow cold,
And *Philomel* becometh dumb,
The rest complains of cares to come.

. . .

But could youth last, and love still breed,
Had joys no date, nor age no need,
Then these delights my mind might move,
To live with thee, and be thy love.

The contrast between hedonism and moralism is given a more precise focus and a more dramatic embodiment in Marvell's 'Clorinda and Damon'. It begins as a witty reversal of the pastoral seduction dialogue, with the shepherdess making advances to an unresponsive shepherd, but it soon becomes apparent that more than male coyness is at stake:

C. Damon, come drive thy flocks this way.
D. No, 'tis too late they went astray.
C. I have a grassy scutcheon spied,
Where Flora blazons all her pride.
The grass I aim to feast thy sheep:
The flowers I for thy temples keep.
D. Grass withers; and the flowers too fade.
C. Seize the short joys then, ere they vade,
Seest thou that unfrequented cave?
D. That den?
C. Love's Shrine.
D. But virtue's grave.
C. In whose cool bosom we may lie
Safe from the sun.
D. Not heaven's eye.

C. Near this, a fountain's liquid bell
Tinkles within the concave shell.
D. Might a soul bathe there and be clean,
Or slake its drought?

Clorinda, like Marlowe's passionate shepherd, speaks from within the pastoral world. She sees in the material scene around her signs of the bounty of the flower goddess, and opportunities for sensual pleasure afforded by the cave and the fountain. Her moral horizons are bounded by the simple imperative of the *carpe diem* formula: 'Seize the short joys then, ere they vade.' It is evident from Damon's replies that he is speaking from within a different set of assumptions. Each physical feature of the landscape mentioned by Clorinda is perceived symbolically by her companion. Her first line reminds him of the words in the Prayer Book about man's sinful condition: 'we have erred and strayed from thy ways, like lost sheep'. Grass calls to mind the biblical phrases 'All flesh is grass' and 'the grass withereth, the flower fadeth' (Isaiah 40, vv.6–8); the cave is the setting not for sexual consummation, but for spiritual death; the sun is interpreted as the all-seeing eye of God; and the stream becomes the cleansing waters of baptism. The shepherd receives his impressions of the natural world through a filter of Christian doctrine and imagery. No wonder Clorinda is bewildered and seeks an explanation:

C. What is't you mean?
D. These once had been enticing things,
Clorinda, pastures, caves, and springs.
C And what late change?
D. The other day
Pan met me.
C. What did great Pan say?
D. Words that transcend poor shepherds'
skill,
But he e'er since my songs does fill:
And his name swells my slender oat.
C. Sweet must Pan sound in Damon's note.
D. Clorinda's voice might make it sweet.
C. Who would not in Pan's praises meet?

CHORUS
Of Pan the flowery pastures sing,
Caves echo, and fountains ring.
Sing then while he doth us inspire;
For all the world is our Pan's choir.

The once pagan shepherd has had an encounter with Pan – the god of Nature who frequently appears in Renaissance pastorals as an allegorical substitute for Christ – and his whole way of seeing has been transformed. Although he is now a Christian, however, he still has the simple-mindedness of a shepherd. He lacks the 'skill' to relate the words of Christ and can only celebrate his new god in pastoral songs. He also lacks the insight to see that there is something unsatisfactory about Clorinda's instant conversion, as she joins him in a concluding hymn of praise. Her last two speeches are capable of different interpretations by the sophisticated reader who witnesses this little drama – just as Clora's tears were in 'Mourning': she may, in her simple way, be quite genuine in accepting her lover's new religion without anything more than his change of heart to base her own conversion on; or she may be more deviously going along with his strange new notions as a means of keeping her man. Either way, the depth of her spiritual commitment to the Christianized Pan is called in question. The detached observer may find a further insight into human behaviour and a further source of amusement in the eagerness with which Damon grasps at the chance to preserve his relationship with both his old mistress and his new god: 'Clorinda's voice might make it sweet.'

Each of Marvell's pastoral dialogues is built on the interaction of two fictional characters, although the exchanges between Clorinda and Damon are more dramatic than the very formal patterning of 'Ametas and Thestylis Making Hay-ropes'. 'A Dialogue between the Soul and Body' derives from a different genre and is quite different in effect. As Rosalie Osmond has demonstrated, dialogues between Body and Soul or a pair of personified abstractions were common in the Middle Ages and were revived, in verse and prose, during the seventeenth century. Marvell's poem owes something to this tradition, but also transcends it to become one of his most characteristic and brilliant exhibitions of wit and irony. The participants in the dialogue are each given two lengthy stanzas and seem to be directing their words at some third party, rather than engaging in dramatic confrontation with each other. The demonstrative pronouns in their opening couplets indicate that each is aware of the other's presence, however, and this makes for a comic tension throughout and a superb climactic gesture towards the end.

The tone of voice and the linguistic habits of the two speakers are subtly established in their initial complaints about their respective predicaments:

SOUL
O, who shall from this dungeon raise
A soul, enslaved so many ways,
With bolts of bones, that fettered stands
In feet, and manacled in hands.
Here blinded with an eye; and there
Deaf with the drumming of an ear,
A soul hung up, as 'twere, in chains
Of nerves, and arteries, and veins,
Tortured, besides each other part,
In a vain head, and double heart?

BODY
O, who shall me deliver whole,
From bonds of this tyrannic soul.
Which, stretched upright, impales me so,
That mine own precipice I go;
And warms and moves this needless frame
(A fever could but do the same),
And, wanting where its spite to try,
Has made me live to let me die,
A body that could never rest,
Since this ill spirit it possessed?

There is a note of either querulousness or sardonic humour in the reproachful, punning, and paradoxical expression of the Soul's captivity in the Body and the Body's possession by the Soul. Bones, feet, and hands themselves become the shackles with which the Soul is bolted, fettered, and manacled in its fleshly prison; the sense organs of eye and ear paradoxically hinder perception; and nerves, arteries, veins, head, and heart are instruments of restraint and torture. It is difficult to determine how far the cleverness with which the Soul develops its conceit of the Body as a dungeon is intended to be self-conscious and how far the contrived word play on feet and fetters, hands and manacles, on the ear-drum in line 6, and on the physical and moral connotations of 'vain' and 'double' in line 10 is part of a deliberate, wryly self-mocking rhetoric. The parenthetic 'as 'twere' in line 7 suggests that this might be the case, but on the other hand, the Soul may be one of those Marvellian speakers who are oblivious to the way in which their mode of expression betrays their self-absorbed and limited perspective.

The same ambivalence permeates the Body's reply. Rather than a single extended conceit, it consists of an itemized list of the consequences of the Soul's tyrannic power over matter. The Soul forces the flesh to walk upright, and therefore to be capable of falling in both a physical and a theological sense (lines 13–14); it animates the Body, and, along with warmth and motion, instils it with needs that did not trouble it in its inert state (lines 15–16); it informs it with life, and as an unavoidable corollary condemns it to undergo death (lines 17–18). The comic image of the Body impaled on the Soul, like a piece of meat on a skewer, and the witty notion of being liable to tumble over the precipice of itself, seem unlikely to be unintentional on the part of the speaker; and in particular, the ingenious syntactical pun in line 20 – is the Body possessed by the Soul as by a demon, or is the Soul possessed by the Body as an unwanted belonging? – hints at a rueful recognition that all its complaints are futile, since possessor and possessed are inextricably involved with each other as long as life lasts. But perhaps only poet and reader are alert to the comedy and the double meaning, and chuckle at the Body's obtuseness.

At this point, one speaker registers an awareness of what the other has said and the tension of debate enters into the alternation of speeches:

SOUL
What magic could me thus confine
Within another's grief to pine,
Where, whatsoever it complain,
I feel, that cannot feel, the pain,
And all my care itself employs,
That to preserve, which me destroys:
Constrained not only to endure
Diseases, but, what's worse, the cure:
And ready oft the port to gain,
Am shipwrecked into health again?

The Soul picks up the Body's sneer at the 'ill spirit' that possesses it, and brings a countercharge of sorcery against its antagonist. What but a maleficent spell could have caused the immaterial Soul to suffer all the afflictions that flesh is heir to? – pain, the struggle to survive, disease, and worst of all the recovery from sickness which prolongs its captivity in the physical world. Again, there is comedy – self-mocking or unconscious – in the indignant shrillness of line 24, 'I feel, that cannot feel, the pain', and in the reversal of a familiar image in the concluding couplet.

The next speech throws the idea of a cure and return to health back at the Soul, and, in a fine dramatic coup, drops into second-person address for the only time in the poem. As one critic puts it, 'here the Body turns sideways and points an accusing finger at the Soul' (Craze, p. 290):

BODY
But physic yet could never reach
The maladies thou me dost teach:
Whom first the cramp of hope does tear,
And then the palsy shakes of fear;
The pestilence of love does heat,
Or hatred's hidden ulcer eat;
Joy's cheerful madness does perplex,
Or sorrow's other madness vex;
Which knowledge forces me to know,
And memory will not forgo.
What but a soul could have the wit
To build me up for sin so fit?
So architects do square and hew,
Green trees that in the forest grew.

Physical diseases are nothing compared to the psychological and emotional torments that the Body is subjected to by the indwelling Soul – torments which can be neither ignored nor forgotten (lines 39–40). Cramp, palsy, pestilence, ulcer, madness: the very fact that the Body can legitimately describe the effects of hope, fear, love, hatred, joy, and sorrow in these terms reinforces the implications of lines 19–20 – that very often the contributions made by flesh and spirit to the complex human experience of being alive are hard to disentangle or distinguish.

Then, unexpectedly, the established symmetry of the poem is broken, and the Body is given an extra four lines to round off the dialogue (unless, as some scholars believe, the poem is incomplete, and lines 41–4 belong to a later, lost stanza). There is irony in the Body's accusation that only a soul could have 'wit' enough to design and construct out of lifeless matter a body so readily responsive to the temptations of the flesh. For, could any actions performed by the Body be regarded as sinful if it were not indwelt by a soul conscious of sin? And what of the ingenuity with which the Body has conducted its case? Where does its own wit derive from if not from the Soul? The further the ramifications of the argument are pursued, the more complex becomes the relationship between the two antagonists whose dearest wish is to dissociate themselves from each other. The simile of the final couplet shifts the terms of the debate from theology to art, and leaves us with another age-old and equally irresolvable dispute: whether Civilization or Nature is to be preferred. By raising this fresh controversy at the very end of the poem, Marvell seems to be reminding his readers of the academic status of any discussion which claims exclusive value for some aspect of life which can only be experienced in intricate conjunction with other and contradictory aspects. Taken to their logical conclusions, the arguments of both Body and Soul would lead to a rejection of life as it is known to humankind. The Body yearns for the condition of inert, inanimate matter; the Soul yearns to escape altogether from its incarnate existence into a realm of pure spirit. Neither is an option open to man.

The impulse to hold aloof or disentangle oneself from the complexities or the contaminating clutches of this world – in which the 'object vain' deludes the sight and the spirit languishes, fettered and manacled, in the dungeon of the flesh – motivates the reverie or debate in many of Marvell's poems. Behind it, in a number of them, lies the Christian dichotomy between the order of Nature, governed by the laws of the physical universe and tainted by Original Sin, and the order of Grace, informed and redeemed by the love of God. 'Clorinda and Damon' dramatizes the antagonism felt by the recently converted shepherd towards the natural realm of 'pastures, caves, and springs' which tempts him from his new path. But the Chorus which concludes his dialogue with Clorinda not only brings the two voices together in harmony, but also resolves the dichotomy by reconciling the two orders of Nature and Grace. 'Pastures', 'caves', and 'fountains' are all recognized as manifestations of the creating and sustaining divinity: 'For all the world is our Pan's choir.' In the three poems to be discussed in the rest of this chapter, no such resolution is attempted. The claims of Nature are firmly resisted in what are Marvell's most uncompromisingly Puritan formulations of human experience. As we might expect of this poet, however, they represent very different responses to the conflict between competing orders of reality and value, and draw upon the expressive resources of three quite distinct poetic genres.

'A Dialogue between the Resolved Soul and Created Pleasure' has been aptly described as 'Marvell's most fully conceived portrait of one particular kind of Puritan ethical attitude' (Friedman, p. 75). This attitude can best be summed up in the well-known words of Marvell's friend and colleague, John Milton: 'I cannot praise a fugitive and cloistered virtue, unexercised and unbreathed, that never sallies out and sees her adversary, but slinks out of the race, where that immortal garland is to be run for, not without dust and heat' (*Areopagitica* (1644)). Christian life is a perpetual warfare against the temptations of the world, the flesh, and the devil, but it is a war in which the true soldier of Christ will rejoice, because each success is a mark of his regenerate condition. It is important to confront the enemy, not avoid him, since, as Milton puts it later in the same passage: 'That virtue therefore which is but a youngling in the contemplation of evil, and knows not the utmost that vice promises to her followers, and rejects it, is but a blank virtue, not a pure.' Milton himself dramatized the resistance of the virtuous soul to 'the utmost that vice promises to her followers' in his early masque *Comus* (1634) and in his late epic *Paradise Regained* (1671). Marvell's dialogue is a lyric enactment and celebration of the same confident and assertive Puritanism.

The poem begins with the poet urging his Soul into the fray:

Courage, my Soul, now learn to wield
The weight of thine immortal shield.
Close on thy head thy helmet bright.
Balance thy sword against the fight.
See where an army, strong as fair,
With silken banners spreads the air.
Now, if thou be'st that thing divine,
In this day's combat let it shine:
And show that Nature wants an art
To conquer one resolvèd heart.

The Soul must be as yet a 'youngling in the contemplation of evil', like the fifteen-year-old Lady in *Comus*, since it is exhorted to 'learn' to 'wield' and 'balance' its spiritual weapons. Those weapons are 'the whole armour of God', borne by Spenser's Redcross Knight in Book I of *The Faerie Queene* and described by St Paul in the Epistle to the Ephesians: 'the shield of faith', 'the helmet of salvation', and 'the sword of the Spirit' (6, vv.10–17). The army of Created Pleasure, with its 'silken banners' seductively spread, is already drawn up opposite. The outcome of the battle is no foregone conclusion. Not all Christian warriors prove to be firmly 'resolved', and only 'if' this aspirant is truly 'that thing divine' – a saved soul – will it 'shine' in the ensuing combat in vindication of its status. Victory will not be a matter of merely personal achievement and private satisfaction; it will 'show', as an act of public witness, that strength is granted to the faithful Christian to withstand all the arts of Nature. 'This day's combat' takes on the air of a tournament, and spectators like the poet of this opening stanza and the later Chorus have a vested interest in the Soul's performance. The note of earnestness with which he encourages his champion is conveyed partly through the imperative verbs and the series of abrupt sentences, and partly through the metrical inversions which thrust the emphasis onto the first syllables of lines 1,3,4,5, and 7.

Metrical subtlety is one of Marvell's most effective devices for distinguishing the participants in the dialogue that follows. He alternates trochaic heptasyllabics (seven-syllable lines with stresses on syllables 1,3,5,7) for the temptations offered by Pleasure, with iambic tetrameters (eight-syllable lines with stresses on syllables 2,4,6,8) for the pithy but measured replies of the Resolved Soul:

PLEASURE
Welcome the creation's guest,
Lord of earth, and heaven's heir.
Lay aside that warlike crest,
And of Nature's banquet share:
Where the souls of fruits and flowers
Stand prepared to heighten yours.

SOUL
I sup above, and cannot stay
To bait so long upon the way.

PLEASURE
On these downy pillows lie,
Whose soft plumes will thither fly:
On these roses strewed so plain
Lest one leaf thy side should strain.

SOUL
My gentler rest is on a thought,
Conscious of doing what I ought.

PLEASURE
If thou be'st with perfumes pleased,
Such as oft the gods appeased,
Thou in fragrant clouds shalt show
Like another god below.

SOUL
A soul that knows not to presume
Is heaven's and its own perfume.

PLEASURE
Everything does seem to vie
Which should first attract thine eye:
But since none deserves that grace,
In this crystal view *thy* face.

SOUL
When the Creator's skill is prized,
The rest is all but earth disguised.

PLEASURE
Hark how music then prepares
For thy stay these charming airs;
Which the posting winds recall,
And suspend the river's fall.

SOUL
Had I but any time to lose,
On this I would it all dispose.
Cease, tempter. None can chain a mind
Whom this sweet chordage cannot bind.

CHORUS
Earth cannot show so brave a sight
As when a single soul does fence
The batteries of alluring sense,
And heaven views it with delight.
  Then persevere: for still new charges sound:
  And if thou overcom'st, thou shalt be crowned.

Having greeted the Soul under three titles which flatteringly define its privileged position in the hierarchical universe (lines 11–12), Pleasure seeks to entrap it in snares laid by each of the five senses in turn. The aim is to make the Soul abandon its prospects of glory as 'heaven's heir' in favour of the more immediate delights of the material world that can be commanded by a 'Lord of earth' as a result of being incarnated as 'creation's guest'. In contrast to the simple paganism of Clorinda and the somewhat priggish responses of Damon, both speakers in this dialogue display subtlety and wit. Pleasure's opening invitation to share in 'Nature's banquet' cleverly presents the indulgence of the sense of taste as a heightening of the Soul's own spiritual quality (lines 13–16); the Soul exposes the lavishness implied by the word 'banquet' with a curt monosyllabic reminder of the true destiny of the spirit: 'I *sup* above.' The conceit of flying upwards on 'soft plumes' cannot disguise the temptation to tactile luxury and idleness among the 'downy pillows' and rose-petals (line 19–22), and it is countered by a witty pun on the 'gentler rest' – both repose and support – afforded by thoughts of duty. The pleasures of the sense of smell are merged craftily with the aspiration to godhead – the sin of Satan (lines 25–8); the Soul rejects both the sensual and the moral temptation by pointedly rhyming 'perfume' with 'presume'. Sight is the occasion for an appeal to vanity, but the Soul is not to be deceived into valuing gross matter above the divine art which alone is the source of beauty (lines 31–6). The tempter has reserved till last the delights of sound, since these 'charming airs' are the most insubstantial and spirit-like of all sensual pleasures (lines 37–8). Music, too, has the added appeal of art, which claims to counteract the processes of time and impose permanence on the transient world (lines 39–40). The Soul seizes on the connotations of the word 'stay', and, while admitting the attractions of music, refuses to be either detained or sustained by any earthly thing in its urgent journey towards salvation. It closes this first round of the contest with a dismissal of its antagonist, and a graceful pun on the binding power of chords of music which is reminiscent of the compliment to the Fair Singer: 'Whose subtle art invisibly can wreathe / My fetters of the very air I breathe'. It is this element of courtly wit that prevents the laconic couplets of the Soul from sounding unpleasantly prim or self-satisfied in comparison with the more lyrical and expansive quatrains of Pleasure.

The Chorus applauds the Soul's performance so far (lines 45–8), but reminds us with another 'if' clause that the warfare against the world is unremitting, and that the true Puritan champion must 'persevere'. To 'be crowned' with Milton's 'immortal garland' is the reward of those who are resolute in overcoming all that Created Pleasure can bring against them (lines 49–50). Sure enough, the enemy musters its forces as 'new charges sound', and Beauty, Wealth, Power, and Knowledge enter the lists:

PLEASURE
All this fair, and soft, and sweet,
   Which scatteringly doth shine,
Shall within one beauty meet,
   And she be only thine.

SOUL
If things of sight such heavens be,
What heavens are those we cannot see?

PLEASURE
Wheresoe'er thy foot shall go
   The minted gold shall lie,
Till thou purchase all below,
   And want new worlds to buy.

SOUL
Were't not a price, who'd value gold?
And that's worth naught that can be sold.

PLEASURE
Wilt thou all the glory have
   That war or peace commend?
Half the world shall be thy slave
   The other half thy friend.

SOUL
What friends, if to my self untrue!
What slaves, unless I captive you!

PLEASURE
Thou shalt know each hidden cause;

And see the future time:
Try what depth the centre draws;
And then the heaven climb.

SOUL
None thither mounts by the degree
Of knowledge, but humility.

CHORUS
Triumph, triumph, victorious Soul;
The world has not one pleasure more:
The rest does lie beyond the Pole,
And is thine everlasting store.

For this new assault, the tempter changes his metre to alternating seven-syllable trochaics and six-syllable iambics, but the Soul remains faithful to its steady and confident iambic couplets. Indeed, its growing confidence is registered in the rhetorical questions and exclamations with which it begins to challenge and deride the assumptions upon which its opponent's appeals are based. Is the invisible world of spirit not superior to the world of visible beauty? Can anything of real value be bought and sold? No power is worth exercising except the self-control which will defeat Created Pleasure! The Faustian temptation – knowledge of the causes of physical phenomena, of the future, of the dimensions of the earth – is interpreted by this Puritan Soul as direct rivalry to God, as it is by Milton in Book VIII of *Paradise Lost*, and is dismissed in a final elegantly turned pun: the only 'degree' – step or learned qualification – which can raise a spirit to heaven is paradoxically that of 'humility'. The spectators break in once more to conclude the poem with a jubilant Chorus, in which the rewards of another world 'beyond the Pole' of the created universe are promised to this unyielding champion of otherworldly values.

If this version of Puritanism has something of the self-assured and combative ethical stance of Milton, 'On a Drop of Dew' offers a very different response to the dilemma posed by the antagonism between the orders of Nature and Grace. The kind of integrity celebrated in this curiously impersonal poem is preserved by avoiding the 'dust and heat' of trial in the world and would be condemned in Milton's terms as 'a fugitive and cloistered virtue'. A different approach to experience demands a different poetic mode, and Marvell turns from the dialogue form so appropriate for the dynamic interplay between opposing sets of values to the more static, pictorial qualities of the emblem. Strictly speaking, the emblem, as it was introduced into England by Geoffrey

Whitney in 1586 and flourished in the popular collections of Francis Quarles (1635), George Wither (1635), and Christopher Harvey (1647), consisted of an allegorical engraving accompanied by a motto and an interpretation in either verse or prose. The interpretation directed attention to significant details in the picture and then drew a moral lesson or religious truth from them. In time, the methods of the emblem books infiltrated the work of poets like George Herbert and Henry Vaughan, who replaced the graphic element completely with verbal description. Rowland Watkyns's volume *Flamma Sine Fumo* (1662) furnishes a convenient example:

> See how the careful Hen, with daily pain,
> Her young and tender Chickens doth maintain;
> From ravenous birds secure her young ones lie
> Under their mother's feather'd canopy:
> Thus his dear children God together brings,
> And still protects them with his gracious wings:
> The birds of prey God's Doves would soon devour,
> Did he not guard them with his watchful pow'r.

Though much more elaborate than this, Marvell's poem has the same basic structure. The first eighteen lines, governed by the command 'See', describe the drop of dew; the next eighteen lines, introduced by a 'So' that parallels Watkyns's 'Thus', apply the description to the human spirit. Marvell then adds a coda of four lines which effects the only kind of resolution possible for a soul that refuses to sally out and see her adversary.

The poem begins with a visually precise account of a drop of dew settling on the petals of a rose:

> See how the orient dew,
> Shed from the bosom of the morn
>   Into the blowing roses,
> Yet careless of its mansion new,
> For the clear region where 'twas born
>   Round in itself incloses:
>   And in its little globe's extent,
> Frames as it can its native element.

Already, however, Marvell's idiosyncratic handling of the emblem is evident: instead of keeping the two phases of the poem discrete as Watkyns did, he allows them to permeate each other, so that the opening description has symbolic colouring, and the subsequent interpretation continues to draw upon pictorial vocabulary. Associated with the east and a maternal morning in the first two lines, the dew cares nothing for its temporary dwelling-place among the 'blowing roses' – those familiar symbols of earthly transience. 'Born' in 'the clear region' above the earth, it remains self-contained, turning inwards, away from the new environment in which the purity it derives from its 'native element' is at risk of contamination.

The rest of the first section subtly develops the technique of simultaneous description and interpretation:

How it the purple flow'r does slight,
Scarce touching where it lies,
But gazing back upon the skies,
Shines with a mournful light,
Like its own tear,
Because so long divided from the sphere.
Restless it rolls and unsecure,
Trembling lest it grow impure,
Till the warm sun pity its pain,
And to the skies exhale it back again.

The verb of line 9 suggests an anthropomorphic reaction by the drop of dew: it is said to 'slight' its host flower, like a stand-offish visitor. But this is immediately shown to be an accurate metaphor for its physical characteristics – by means of surface tension it retains its spherical shape and is scarcely in contact with the petal on which it rests. Lines 11–14 exploit a conceit similar to that in 'Eyes and Tears': because the dewdrop is round like an eye, it can be said to be 'gazing'; and this leads to the idea that it is a tear dropped from itself in grief at being exiled from its true home. The word 'trembling' in line 16 need not in itself be anything more than a piece of minutely observed description – the movement of the flower on its stem makes the dew quiver; but in association with 'restless' and 'lest it grow impure', its psychological connotations are released. The sun which evaporates the dew and draws it back into the skies in lines 17–18 is barely to be distinguished imaginatively from the God who takes pity on the distressed soul and recalls it to its heavenly home.

In the manner of an emblem, the second phase of the poem makes a point-by-point application of the verbal picture painted in lines 1–18:

So the soul, that drop, that ray
Of the clear fountain of eternal day,
Could it within the human flow'r be seen,
Remembering still its former height,
Shuns the sweet leaves and blossoms green,
And recollecting its own light,
Does, in its pure and circling thoughts, express

The greater heaven in an heaven less.
In how coy a figure wound,
Every way it turns away:
So the world excluding round,
Yet receiving in the day,
Dark beneath, but bright above,
Here disdaining, there in love.
How loose and easy hence to go,
How girt and ready to ascend,
Moving but on a point below,
It all about does upward bend.

As the dew was shed from the morning skies into the roses, so the soul descended from the spiritual source of everlasting life – 'the fountain of eternal day' – to take up its lodging in the 'human flow'r'; as the dew slighted the roses, so the soul 'Shuns' the leaves and blossoms that metaphorically represent the human body; as the dew imitated the shape of the sphere that was its 'native element', so the soul creates 'in its pure and circling thoughts' a version of the perfect circle of heaven; as the dew trembled lest it be tainted by its earthly surroundings and gazed longingly back at the skies, so the soul excludes and disdains the material, sinful world and is 'in love' with the spiritual realm, to which it is always eager and prepared to reascend. The technique of blurring the linguistic boundaries between picture and application – which speaks of a drop of dew that can slight its host, gaze, mourn, be restless and tremble with fear, and of a soul that recollects 'its own light' (presumably an allusion to the way rays of light are refracted into the centre of a translucent globe), is 'Dark beneath, but bright above', and moves 'but on a point below' – is one more manifestation of Marvell's responsiveness to the complex interrelatedness of physical and spiritual in human experience and literal and metaphorical in human language.

In the final section of the poem, dewdrop and soul are completely identified in a further simile:

Such did the manna's sacred dew distill,
White and entire, though congealed and chill,
Congealed on earth: but does, dissolving, run
Into the glories of th' almighty sun.

Manna, the miraculous food that fell with the dew and sustained the Israelites in the wilderness, is related back by the introductory 'Such' to both the soul and the drop of dew. Each in its own way is 'congealed on earth', but each will return in time to the higher sphere from which it came, released from its unwilling sojourn in this world by the physical heat of the sun or the spiritual power of God.

The parallels between the drop of dew and the human soul are systematically pointed, and thus far the ideas contained in the poem are readily accessible. It is not so easy, however, to determine the attitude that is being adopted towards those ideas. The impersonal tones in which the speaker catalogues the characteristics and behaviour of the dew-soul give little away. The generalizing definite articles – '*the* orient dew', '*the* soul' – imply that this soul's response to the fact of incarnation is representative, as if the analogy with the drop of dew had the validity of a universal truth. And yet, as we have seen, both Milton and Marvell himself in 'A Dialogue between the Resolved Soul and Created Pleasure', could conceive of – and, indeed, applaud – a much more active method of asserting the soul's integrity, by overcoming rather than 'excluding' the world. Closer attention to the texture of the language of 'On a Drop of Dew' may bring to light a more ambivalent approach than the simple description-interpretation formula of the emblem usually imposes on human experience.

The 'blowing roses' (line 3) and the 'purple flow'r' (line 9) have traditional associations of beauty as well as transience; and the drop of dew's somewhat ungracious behaviour in ignoring ('careless', line 4) and slighting (line 9) the loveliness of the natural world created by God is even more sharply focussed in the soul's shunning of 'the sweet leaves and blossoms green' (line 23). Only if the fastidious overtones of the words 'slight' and 'Shuns' are suppressed can the dew-soul's rejection of the order of nature be unambiguously endorsed. Similarly, the pathos of the drop of dew – gazing mournfully back at its lost security (lines 11–12) and yearning for the maternal bosom (line 2) from which it has been cast out into the world – can seem self-absorbed, and even self-generated, if the implications of 'Like its own tear' are given their full value. Marvell's control of the elaborate metrical scheme reinforces this impression by allowing the conceit to be lingered over with sentimental indulgence in the shortest line of the poem (line 13). A laudable concern with maintaining its own integrity may be extracted from the line 'Trembling lest it grow impure' (line 16), but equally available is the suggestion of an unattractive and self-regarding timidity. Again, it is only possible to gloss the word 'coy' (line 27) as 'modest' – 'used here to suggest the chaste nature of the soul' (King, p. 32) – if its long history in amatory verse is deliberately ignored. If this *is* permitted to make its full contribution to the resonance of the poem, then it adds to the growing uneasiness with which we contemplate the soul's preoccupation with its own purity.

The dilemma posed by this soul's answer to the challenge of incarnate existence is neatly concentrated in line 38. To remain 'White and entire' while dwelling amidst 'the smoke and stir of this dim spot, / Which men call earth' (*Comus*, lines 5–6) is a noble spiritual ideal; but to achieve it at the cost of human spontaneity and warmth – to be 'congealed and chill' – may seem too high a price to pay. The soul is saved from corruption or the need to endure the 'dust and heat' of active resistance to the forces of Created Pleasure by the intervention of Grace in the last two lines of the poem. It may be part of Marvell's unspoken verdict that this soul finds its fulfilment in dissolution rather than resolution, and that its chilly aloofness is thawed by a divine warmth which draws it back into a communion where its carefully preserved individual being is lost in 'the glories of th' almighty sun'.

In contrast to the detached, neutral voice that describes and interprets the emblem in 'On a Drop of Dew', the voice created by the rhetorical strategy of 'The Coronet' speaks to us from the very toils of spiritual endeavour in the natural world. Firmly located in the pastoral scene, the shepherd-poet has determined, like the converted Damon, to fill his songs with the name of Christ. But he discovers, as other religious poets had before him, that the project of serving God through art has its pitfalls. George Herbert returned time and again to the question of how to write 'a true hymn', as he struggled with the problem pinpointed in a line from 'Jordan (II)': 'So did I weave my self into the sense.' The image of weaving a garland or coronet to present to Christ had a wide currency among religious poets of the seventeenth century as a means of expressing their preoccupation with the relationship between aesthetic and devotional practice. Herbert had fashioned a poem in a form which imitated both the subtle weaving together of words that constitutes the poet's art and the 'crooked winding ways' that lead man away from the straight path to God. Simplicity, rather than subtlety, he concludes, would produce a more fitting tribute of praise:

> A wreathed garland of deserved praise,
> Of praise deserved, unto thee I give,
> I give to thee, who knowest all my ways,
> My crooked winding ways, wherein I live,
> Wherein I die, not live: for life is straight,
> Straight as a line, and ever tends to thee,
> To thee, who art more far above deceit,

> Than deceit seems above simplicity.
> Give me simplicity, that I may live,
> So live and like, that I may know thy ways,
> Know them and practise them: then shall I give
> For this poor wreath, give thee a crown of praise('A Wreath')

In 'La Corona', John Donne had composed a sequence of seven sonnets linked together by the repetition of first and last lines to form a 'crown of prayer and praise'. In the opening sonnet, he had protested his 'sincerity' in the very act of working the idea of a coronet into an elaborate conceit:

> But do not, with a vile crown of frail bays,
> Reward my muse's white sincerity,
> But what thy thorny crown gained, that give me,
> A crown of glory, which doth flower always;
> The ends crown our works, but thou crown'st our ends.

Marvell's poem takes its cue both thematically and formally from the tradition to which these examples belong, but the pastoral perspective he brings to it encourages us to regard the speaker as a fictional character who is in the process of becoming aware of the difficulties endemic to the poetic genre he has chosen to adopt. In structure, 'The Coronet' consists of two eight-line units, followed by a contrasting ten-line unit. This cleverly preserves the overall balance of a sonnet, with its two quatrains and a sestet, while allowing the formal freedom and inventiveness that is the hallmark of the seventeenth-century devotional lyric. The opening movement – equivalent to the octave of a sonnet – gives a first-person narrative account of the shepherd's experience as religious poet:

> When for the thorns with which I long, too long,
>   With many a piercing wound,
>   My Saviour's head have crowned,
> I seek with garlands to redress that wrong:
>   Through every garden, every mead,
> I gather flowers (my fruits are only flowers),
>   Dismantling all the fragrant towers
> That once adorned my shepherdess's head.
> And now when I have summed up all my store,
>   Thinking (so I myself deceive)
>   So rich a chaplet thence to weave
> As never yet the King of Glory wore:
>   Alas, I find the serpent old
>   That, twining in his speckled breast,
>   About the flowers disguised does fold,
>   With wreaths of fame and interest.

Marvell, who usually favours simple stanzas built out of octosyllabic couplets, here rivals the virtuosity of the kind of lyric he has taken as his model. Regularity is played off against unpredictable variation, as each quatrain has a different arrangement of line lengths (10,6,6,10; 8,10,8,10; 10,8,8,10; 8,8,8,8) and what looks like an established pattern of rhyming (abba; cddc; effe) is broken in the fourth quatrain (ghgh). But this is not merely a gratuitous display of technical skill. It serves the same sort of expressive purpose as the weaving of words from line to line in Herbert's 'A Wreath' or of lines from sonnet to sonnet in Donne's 'La Corona'. The function here is to imitate the sinuous windings of the 'serpent old' whose corruption and all-pervading presence is discovered in lines 13–16 – the very quatrain which disrupts the rhyme-scheme. The syntactic movements that are articulated within this formal framework create a similar tension between pattern and disruption. The two long sentences which occupy lines 1–8 and 9–16 have precisely the same structure fitted to the same formal units. Subordinate clauses, introduced by 'When', 'And now when', occupy the first quatrain each time, and the suspense generated by thus delaying the main clause is released in the second quatrain. The focus shifts significantly, however, from the activities of the poet which have dominated the first three quatrains to the more sinister activities of the serpent in the fourth.

Unlike so many of Marvell's speakers, the shepherd-poet of 'The Coronet' is a critical commentator on his own shortcomings, although his awakening to moral insight is a gradual process enacted in the present-tense development of the poem. There is a painful acknowledgement of personal responsibility for the sufferings of Christ in the initial image of the crown of thorns and a sense of inadequacy in the parenthetic admission that he has nothing better than poems to offer – '(my fruits are only flowers)'. There is, as yet, however, no hint that the project mooted in lines 1–4 and undertaken in lines 5–8 is itself open to question. Only the alert Christian reader might wonder at the dubious doctrine lurking behind the assumption that *any* human gift can 'redress' the wounds borne by Christ to atone for human sin, and the attempt to make amends for past service of this world by the personal effort of 'dismantling' the works dedicated to a shepherdess. Another parenthesis in line 10 registers the chagrin of one who has become conscious that his dearest plans are doomed to failure on the very threshold of achievement. The alliteration, assonance, and rhythm that combine in the soaring climax of lines 11–12 embody the triumphant pride in artistic accomplishment which invalidates the enterprise as a devotional offering to Christ. Just as Herbert discovered that self was woven into the texture of the poem that should glorify God alone, so Marvell's shepherd learns that the worldly motives of fame and self-interest are inextricably bound up with the practice of his art.

The metrical intricacies of the first sixteen lines give way to the measured flow of decasyllabics, as the poet apostrophizes himself in a remorseful couplet, and then turns in humble supplication to the Saviour he had presumptuously intended to honour with a display of poetic skill:

> Ah, foolish man, that wouldst debase with them,
> And mortal glory, Heaven's diadem!
> But Thou who only couldst the serpent tame,
> Either his slippery knots at once untie;
> And disentangle all his winding snare;
> Or shatter too with him my curious frame,
> And let these wither, so that he may die,
> Though set with skill and chosen out with care:
> That they, while Thou on both their spoils dost tread,
> May crown thy feet, that could not crown thy head.

Paradoxically, the very skill that has betrayed him is still being employed in the brilliant evocation of Christ's rescue of the poet and the poem in lines 20–1. But the alternative remedy of the necessary sacrifice of an art that is irretrievable from the toils of original sin is already envisaged by the either/or syntax (lines 20–3). And even now, the shepherd cannot quite dismiss from his mind the self-satisfaction that human beings inevitably feel in the exercise of their talents. Is there not, in that wistful glance at 'my curious frame' and that final flicker of resentment at the need to reject a work 'set with skill and chosen out with care', a Marvellian acknowledgement that the Puritan solution to the problem of art in a fallen world is too drastic? After all, as the poem completes the circle from the crowning of Christ's head with thorns to the crowning of Christ's feet in the last line, a coronet of words *has* been woven out of the tangle of idealism and corruption that constitutes man's experience of life caught between the orders of Grace and Nature.

5

Innocence and experience

The poet who acknowledged the spirit's impulse to be free from enslavement in the bolts and fetters of the body, or to exclude the world completely and wait to be exhaled back to 'the clear region' above the imperfections and temptations of sublunary nature, was also realist enough to entertain serious doubts about the psychological and moral implications of that impulse. The mutual desire of the Body and Soul to untie what Donne called 'that subtle knot which makes us man' and the dewdrop soul's shunning of the 'sweet leaves and blossoms green' both have the ultimate effect of repudiating life. From the more strenuous Christian stance of 'A Dialogue between the Resolved Soul and Created Pleasure' and 'The Coronet', the sensuous delights and the flowers of this mortal world constitute an enemy to be vanquished or deceptive cover for the ensnaring serpent of vanity. But for many of the speakers in Marvell's poems, the primary aspect of created nature is not its power to corrupt but its subjection to the laws of time and change. Since 'we cannot make our sun / Stand still' and both 'honour' and 'lust' end up as 'dust' and 'ashes', one response of those who are not Puritanically resolved in their resistance to 'pleasures' is to 'tear' them 'with rough strife, / Thorough the iron gates of life' before it is too late. Another is to 'make impression upon time' by achieving – at whatever cost in suffering – such permanence as can be conferred by art: 'In a field sable a lover gules.'

In some of Marvell's most characteristic poems, however, the sound of 'Time's wingèd chariot' provokes an awareness not merely of the stark oppositions of life and death, of the beauty of youthful skin and the worms of the grave, but also of the more subtle qualitative contrast between the state of innocence and the state of experience and of the difficult passage from one to the other. In the poems to be considered in this chapter, we shall see Marvell, with his usual versatility, contemplating innocence through the eyes of experience, demonstrating the psychological refinements of a Cavalier rake, and dramatizing the consequences for innocent minds of an encounter with 'the world' that will not remain 'excluded'.

The idea of innocence had found its embodiment in 'The Gallery' and 'The Unfortunate Lover' in the artificial images of the pastoral tradition; in 'Young Love' and 'The Picture of Little T. C. in a Prospect of Flowers' the images are supplied by nature's own Golden Age of childhood. But the gap between child and adult provides a similar opportunity to that between shepherd and poet for exploiting different levels of awareness. 'Young Love' takes the form of direct address, but it is clear from the opening stanza that the poem is designed for the knowing amusement of other adults, not for the understanding of the little girl herself:

Come, little infant, love me now,
   While thine unsuspected years
Clear thine aged father's brow
   From cold jealousy and fears.

The whimsical flavour of this can best be appreciated by reading it alongside such 'grown-up' invitations to love as Jonson's 'Song. To Celia', with its cocky delight at outwitting the 'jealousy and fears' of a suspicious husband:

Why should we defer our joys?
Fame, and rumour are but toys.
Cannot we delude the eyes
Of a few poor household spies?

No 'household spies' need to be eluded when the mistress is too young to be suspected. The second half of the poem is based on a clever adaptation of the *carpe diem* formula:

5

Now then love me: time may take
   Thee before thy time away:
Of this need we'll virtue make,
   And learn love before we may.

Traditionally, the poet urges the reluctant lady to engage in 'the sports of love' with him, 'while we may', 'while we are in our prime'. But in this case, since the child has not yet reached her 'prime', and may never reach it, Time can only be outmanoeuvred if they 'learn love *before* we may'.

In 'The Picture of Little T. C. in a Prospect of Flowers' the archness of the first person invitation to love is avoided as we are called upon to share the poet's contemplation of a little girl in a garden, and the deeper resonances of myth replace the social ambience of 'Young Love', with its 'aged father' and 'nurse':

1

See with what simplicity
This nymph begins her golden days!
In the green grass she loves to lie,
And there with her fair aspect tames
The wilder flowers, and gives them names:
But only with the roses plays;
And them does tell
What colour best becomes them, and what smell.

This delightful image of the child chattering to the flowers in her solitary play is enriched with overtones from both classical and Christian versions of pastoral. The word 'nymph', although in the seventeenth century it was becoming no more than a poetic synonym for 'country girl' or 'virgin', could still retain its pagan connotations of 'nature-spirit', and the naming of the flowers was the prerogative of Eve in the Garden of Eden. As she 'begins her golden days', Little T. C. both relives in her own person and symbolizes for the experienced poet and reader that age of innocence through which we all pass. But already awareness of time has exerted its subtle pressure on the poem's vocabulary: the word 'begins', which betrays the transience of the phase of existence she is now enjoying, prompts the longer temporal perspective of stanza 2:

2

Who can foretell for what high cause
This Darling of the Gods was born!
Yet this is she whose chaster laws
The wanton Love shall one day fear,
And, under her command severe,
See his bow broke and ensigns torn.
Happy, who can
Appease this virtuous enemy of man!

When her 'golden days' are over, a mature T. C. will fulfil her heroic destiny by imposing her 'laws' of chastity upon the licentious freedom of Cupid. The movement from the realm of innocent play to the realm of moral imperatives is marked by the shift from pastoral to epic, from the 'simplicity' of the 'green grass' to the military metaphors appropriate to the service of a 'high cause'. The last two lines suggest that her severity is directed only at the '*wanton* Love' and that her hostility to the male sex in general may one day be pacified by some 'happy' man. But the speaker himself has no stomach for the contests of adult passion, whatever their outcome, and makes a first person appearance to negotiate a truce before battle is joined:

3

O, then let me in time compound,
And parley with those conquering eyes;
Ere they have tried their force to wound,
Ere, with their glancing wheels, they drive
In triumph over hearts that strive,
And them that yield but more despise.
Let me be laid,
Where I may see thy glories from some shade.

The military images are carried over from stanza 2, but they now express the arrogance of a woman aware of her sexual power rather than the authority of aggressive virtue – more the cruel lady of Petrarchanism than the Resolved Soul. Her 'conquering eyes' will actively test their capacity to 'wound' the hearts of admiring males, and their 'glancing wheels' (with a pun on chariot-wheels) will either drive over their victims 'in triumph' or treat them with contempt. Recoiling from this somewhat forbidding vision, the poet seeks the safe obscurity of 'some shade', from which he may observe the 'glories' of T. C.'s womanhood without endangering himself.

After this disturbing excursion into the future, it is a relief to be brought back to the pre-sexual innocence of the child among the flowers:

4

Meantime, whilst every verdant thing
Itself does at thy beauty charm,
Reform the errors of the spring;
Make that the tulips may have share
Of sweetness, seeing they are fair;
And roses of their thorns disarm:
But most procure
That violets may a longer age endure.

The introductory 'Meantime', however, keeps the vision of the 'golden days' firmly within the confines of temporal process, and the green world where Little T. C. plays with the roses is now perceived in terms of its own inherent imperfections: the tulips have no fragrance, roses have thorns, and violets fade all too quickly. That final detail casts its shadow over the concluding stanza:

5

But, O young beauty of the woods,
Whom Nature courts with fruits and flowers,
Gather the flowers, but spare the buds;
Lest Flora angry at thy crime,
To kill her infants in their prime,
Do quickly make the example yours
And, ere we see,
Nip in the blossom all our hopes and thee.

The poem which began so buoyantly closes on the sombre reflection that death may cut short the progress towards the 'glories' of maturity foretold in stanzas 2 and 3. The same thought had occurred in 'Young Love', but there it merely provoked a witty refashioning of the *carpe diem* argument. Here, it is thrown up naturally and unavoidably by Marvell's pursuit of the far-reaching implications of the images he placed before us in stanza 1. That sense of foreboding which colours the time-conscious adult's perception of a child at play is extended, by the 'we' of the penultimate line, to all those who were invited to look at the picture of Little T. C. in a prospect of flowers. And the poignancy is intensified if we include in our response the knowledge that 'T. C.' was probably Theophila Cornewall, born in 1644 to friends of the Marvell family whose previous daughter of the same name had died in infancy. This information also gives added point to the phrase 'Darling of the Gods' in stanza 2, which is a translation of 'Theophila'.

Looking back, we realize that this meditation on 'simplicity' is, paradoxically, one of Marvell's most complex and carefully crafted works of art. Besides the striking changes of tone and time-perspective, there is an almost imperceptible modulation from address to the reader in stanzas 1 and 2 to address to Little T. C. herself in stanzas 4 and 5, which is subtly effected as we pass from 'those conquering eyes' to 'thy glories' in the course of the middle stanza. Even after this formal transition, however, the appeal of stanza 4 ('Reform the errors of the spring') and the warning of stanza 5 ('Gather the flowers, but spare the buds' – another quizzical glance at the *carpe diem* advice) are not spoken aloud, as it were, for T. C. to hear. They still seem to be part of the reverie of one watching from a distance, whose lament for the imperfections and transitoriness of created nature cannot carry across the gulf that separates him – and us – from the mind of a child not yet a prey to the longings, dissatisfactions, and fears that knowledge and experience bring.

The voice of experience speaks in very different accents in 'Daphnis and Chloe', and the kind of innocence displayed by Chloe bears little resemblance to the 'simplicity' of T. C. We are back in the Cavalier world of 'Mourning', where nothing can be taken at face value and the game of love is played according to subtle conventions. Even the choice of names in this decadent comedy of manners is a sophisticated joke. It is not just that the pastoral associations of 'Daphnis' and 'Chloe' have the same deliberate incongruity as 'Clora' and 'Strephon' in 'Mourning': the pairing of these particular names sets up more precise literary echoes. *Daphnis and Chloe* is the title of a prose romance, composed originally in Greek in the third century A.D., but translated into various European languages during the sixteenth and seventeenth centuries, which tells the story of two foundlings who grow up together in a pastoral setting and develop an adolescent passion for each other without understanding its nature or knowing how to consummate it. The author, probably named Longus, misses no opportunity for ironic, but sympathetic, humour, as he describes the young lovers' quest for the art of satisfying their natural instincts.

Marvell also plays off art against nature, although the naïvety of *his* Daphnis and Chloe is of a more questionable variety and the ironies are cynical rather than sympathetic:

1

Daphnis must from Chloe part:
Now is come the dismal hour
That must all his hopes devour,
All his labour, all his art.

2

Nature, her own sex's foe,
Long had taught her to be coy:
But she neither knew t'enjoy,
Nor yet let her lover go.

3

But with this sad news surprised,
Soon she let that niceness fall,
And would gladly yield to all,
So it had his stay comprised.

4

Nature so herself does use
To lay by her wonted state,
Lest the world should separate;
Sudden parting closer glues.

The narrative situation is set out economically in the first stanza, though what necessity lies behind the repeated 'must' and frustrates the hopes, labour, and art of the lover remains unexplained. Chloe, playing the coquette by instinct rather than by art – ironically 'taught' to be 'coy' by Nature – is swept off balance by the unexpected 'news' that Daphnis is leaving and quickly signals her willingness to surrender. In this, too, she is behaving naturally, since the union of the sexes is the mechanism which guarantees that 'the world' under Nature's governance will not 'separate' or disintegrate. The 'wonted state' or dignity of Nature, like the 'niceness' of Chloe's reluctance, is soon laid aside when the gratification of the sexual urge is put seriously at risk. The narrator's lofty amusement at the inept coyness of Chloe (clearly inexperienced in these matters) and the undignified haste of her capitulation is communicated partly by the flippant choice of words ('this sad news', 'glues') and partly by the jaunty trochaic rhythm, which requires a slight pause between the strong beats that open and close each line. The air of superiority is reinforced by the tendency to make Chloe's behaviour an occasion for philosophizing on the ways of Nature, who is said to be 'her own sex's foe' because she teaches women to delay the pleasure that awaits them in the sexual act, and whose apparent inconsistency is explained away in stanza 4. This is reminiscent of the Cavalier poets' practice of conducting intellectual analyses of aspects of the psychology or philosophy of love. Sir John Suckling, for example, gives reasons why the satisfaction of physical lust seems to defeat its own purposes:

> Fruition adds no new wealth, but destroys,
> And while it pleaseth much the palate, cloys;
>
> . . .
>
> 'Tis expectation makes a blessing dear,
> Heaven were not heaven, if we knew what it were.
>
> ('Against Fruition')

And Thomas Carew, in a poem which may have provided the model for Marvell's unusual stanza form in 'Daphnis and Chloe', examines the effects of separation on the intensity of desire:

> Yet though absence for a space
> Sharpen the keen appetite,
> Long continuance doth quite
> All love's characters efface:

For the sense not fed denies
  Nourishment unto the mind,
  Which with expectation pin'd,
Love of a consumption dies.
('Separation of Lovers')

The hedonistic conception of love found in this kind of Caroline lyric – which is much preoccupied with the pleasures of the 'palate' and the keenness of the 'appetite' – informs Marvell's account of the parting of his inexperienced lovers.

As we might expect from a poem in the male-orientated Cavalier mode, Chloe's sudden change of heart is merely the prelude to a lengthy analysis of the much more interesting predicament in which Daphnis now finds himself. The narrator continues the story, with the wry smile of an old campaigner who knows a thing or two about the art of seduction that cannot be learnt from books:

5

He, well-read in all the ways
By which men their siege maintain,
Knew not that the fort to gain,
Better 'twas the siege to raise.

6

But he came so full possessed
With the grief of parting thence,
That he had not so much sense
As to see he might be blessed.

But by the time it has dawned on Daphnis that Chloe is offering no further resistance, it is too late:

7

Till Love in her language breathed
Words she never spake before,
But than legacies no more
To a dying man bequeathed.

8

For, alas, the time was spent,
Now the latest minute's run
When poor Daphnis is undone,
Between joy and sorrow rent.

9

At that 'Why', that 'Stay, my Dear',
His disordered locks he tare;
And with rolling eyes did glare,
And his cruel fate forswear.

10

As the soul of one scarce dead,
With the shrieks of friends aghast,
Looks distracted back in haste,
And then straight again is fled,

11

So did wretched Daphnis look,
Frighting her he lovèd most.
At the last, this lover's ghost
Thus his leave resolvèd took.

Running through this group of stanzas is a burlesque treatment of the well-worn conceit that parting from the beloved is like dying. Donne had used it more than once, in 'The Legacy' ('When I died last, and, dear, I die / As often as from thee I go'); in 'The Expiration' ('So, so, break off this last lamenting kiss, / Which sucks two souls, and vapours both away, / Turn thou ghost that way, and let me turn this'); and in the opening stanza of 'A Valediction: Forbidding Mourning', the hushed and tender tones of which seem to be deliberately coarsened in the melodramatic reworking of the simile in Marvell's tenth stanza:

As virtuous men pass mildly away,
   And whisper to their souls, to go,
Whilst some of their sad friends do say,
   The breath goes now, and some say, no:

So let us melt, and make no noise . . .

The contrast with Donne's solemn, steady-paced iambic lines helps one to appreciate how much Marvell's trochaics contribute to that note of worldly mockery that keeps the reader at arm's length from the 'cruel fate' of the 'poor' and 'wretched' Daphnis.

The next thirteen stanzas, comprising almost half the poem, are occupied by Daphnis's parting complaint to Chloe, which assembles a variety of ingenious conceits to express the reasons – psychological and aesthetic – for his refusal to take advantage of her readiness to 'yield to all'. The kinship with the philosophical hedonism of Suckling and Carew is evident in a stanza which sums up the particular dilemma of Daphnis in abstract terms:

16

'Absence is too much alone:
Better 'tis to go in peace,
Than my losses to increase
By a late fruition.'

His fastidious self-denial finds more concrete expression in the parting–dying analogy, which spills over from the narrative in increasingly dubious images of execution (stanza 14), cannibalism (stanza 18), and necrophilia (stanza 19). The most memorable of all Daphnis's attempts to formulate his objections to the last-minute satisfaction offered by Chloe probably contains the seed of the whole poem:

22

'Gentler times for love are meant:
Who for parting pleasure strain
Gather roses in the rain,
Wet themselves, and spoil their scent.'

This striking conceit almost certainly derives from some lines in Suckling's *Aglaura* (Act III, scene i), in which the heroine asks her husband to defer the consummation of their marriage until his life is no longer in danger:

Gather not roses in a wet and frowning hour,
They'll lose their sweets then, trust me they will, Sir.
What pleasure can Love take to play his game out,
When death must keep the stakes?

It looks as if Marvell took up the challenge of fashioning a new narrative context for this subtle psychological insight – one of social comedy rather than heroic tragedy – in which the imminence of death would be reduced to nothing more than the self-dramatizing hyperbole of love-poetry.

With a melodramatic 'Fate, I come', Daphnis concludes his long aria of self-justification and farewell, and the narrator completes the story with one final flourish of the dominant metaphor:

25

At these words away he broke;
As who long has praying li'n,
To his headsman makes the sign,
And receives the parting stroke.

But this is not quite the end. Marvell's narrator still has to draw an appropriately worldly moral from the tale of his latter-day Daphnis and Chloe:

26

But hence, virgins, all beware;
Last night he with Phlogis slept;
This night for Dorinda kept;
And but rid to take the air.

27

Yet he does himself excuse;
Nor indeed without a cause:
For, according to the laws,
Why did Chloe once refuse?

The young man whose inexperience in the tactics of seduction was mocked in stanzas 5 and 6, and whose fastidiousness robbed him of victory at the eleventh hour, has since become a practised philanderer. If we are shocked at the revelation of stanza 26 – if we, like Chloe, are to be included among the 'virgins' who are unfamiliar with the ways of the world – then we fall victim to the final sneer of stanza 27: are we so unsophisticated as to be ignorant of the 'laws' by which the modern libertine plays the game of love? What we have no means of assessing, of course, is Marvell's attitude to the philosophy that the poem endorses in its concluding question. Arrogant cynicism is merely one more of the perspectives available in his poetry to those who look upon innocence with the eyes of experience.

The title of 'The Nymph Complaining for the Death of her Fawn' places the poem within two distinct literary traditions: the pastoral complaint and the lament for the death of a pet. The mock-solemn tributes to Lesbia's sparrow and Corinna's parrot by the Roman poets Catullus and Ovid had given rise to a number of Renaissance imitations; and among the many complaints of love-sick or forsaken shepherds in *England's Helicon*, there are also several by 'nymphs' who have been betrayed. The combination of these two kinds of poem enables Marvell to dispense with the filter of an adult consciousness and afford us direct access to an unsophisticated mind. Whereas Little T. C., the 'little infant' of 'Young Love', and even in her own way the inexperienced Chloe, were all examples of innocence observed, the Nymph speaks for herself:

The wanton troopers riding by
Have shot my fawn, and it will die.
Ungentle men! They cannot thrive –
To kill thee! Thou ne'er didst alive
Them any harm: alas, nor could
Thy death yet do them any good.
I'm sure I never wished them ill;
Nor do I for all this; nor will:
But if my simple prayers may yet
Prevail with heaven to forget

Thy murder, I will join my tears
Rather than fail. But, O my fears!
It cannot die so. Heaven's King
Keeps register of everything:
And nothing may we use in vain.
E'en beasts must be with justice slain,
Else men are made their deodands.
Though they should wash their guilty hands
In this warm life-blood, which doth part
From thine, and wound me to the heart,
Yet could they not be clean: their stain
Is dyed in such a purple grain,
There is not such another in
The world, to offer for their sin.

It is evident at once that this is the voice of a child. The very simple diction and syntax and the broken octosyllabic couplets create a convincing idiom for the expression of the pain, bewilderment, and indignation of a young mind trying to come to terms with an act of gratuitous violence. The act itself is recorded in the disbelieving monosyllables of line 2, and what follows is a turmoil of conflicting responses. After her first shocked recognition that all men do not deserve the respectful title of 'gentle men', the nymph strives to make sense of what has happened. There should be understandable motives for human actions, but she can find none in this case: neither profit nor provocation. The thought that she never 'wished them ill' causes a little tremor of unfamiliar feeling and the halting movement of line 8 delicately captures her momentary struggle as she dispels resentment: 'Nor do I . . .; nor will.' Like a good Christian girl, she prays for the forgiveness of those who have committed wrong. But although she knows that she must not feel personally vengeful, it is comforting to call up the image of a God who does not let such deeds go unnoticed. The belief that 'E'en beasts must be with justice slain' reinstates the moral order of the universe that seemed to be put in jeopardy by the irrational and 'wanton' crime. All life is sacred, and if beasts which cause the death of human beings are legally forfeit to the Crown ('deodands' being the technical term for them), then the reverse is also true: men who slay beasts must be forfeit to 'Heaven's King'. Recalled from these speculations to the unalterable fact of the 'warm life-blood' flowing from the wound, the nymph is reluctant to contemplate the mercy that Christian doctrine holds out to the murderers ('murder' is the strong word that she herself uses in line 11). In the confusion of her grief, she draws on language associated with the sacrifice of Christ to express her horror at the unforgivable violation of the fawn's harmless life. The idea of blood that cleanses and the allusion in lines 23–4 to one who dies for the sin of others are better seen as indicative of the nymph's troubled effort to reconcile this outrage with her religious beliefs, than as evidence that the poet intends some covert equivalence between the fawn and Christ. None of the allegorical interpretations that have been offered by critics is wholly satisfying, and the care Marvell takes to invest the nymph's manner of speaking with individuality encourages us to attend to the psychological rather than the symbolic significance of details.

And indeed, psychological interest quickens as the lament of a child for a dying pet merges into the complaint of a forsaken maiden. The nymph is older than we thought, and her reaction to the wounding of the fawn begins to seem less excessive as more of her story comes to light:

> Unconstant Sylvio, when yet
> I had not found him counterfeit,
> One morning (I remember well),
> Tied in this silver chain and bell
> Gave it to me: nay, and I know
> What he said then: I'm sure I do.
> Said he, 'Look how your huntsman here
> Hath taught a fawn to hunt his *dear*.'
> But Sylvio soon had me beguiled.
> This waxèd tame, while he grew wild,
> And quite regardless of my smart,
> Left me his fawn, but took his heart.

The 'wanton troopers' were not the first to ride by and disrupt the peace of her world. She has been 'beguiled' and abandoned, like many another nymph, but her counterfeit lover was no shepherd, in spite of his pastoral name. His gift of a fawn tied in a 'silver chain and bell' is not that of a simple rustic, nor is the studied wit of the conceit of the huntsman and the pun on dear/deer in the speech that she repeats with such touching exactness. But this is not a conventional tale of a milkmaid seduced by an aristocrat. The nymph, after all, knows about such things as 'deodands', and is to speak later of a golden vial and a marble statue. So the contrast between her naïve language in lines 29–30 and the artifice of Sylvio's reported words is to be taken as a means of dramatizing the difference in experience, not a difference in social class, between the two.

The details of the affair remain vague. Whatever the implications of the phrases 'soon had me beguiled' and 'he grew wild' may be, the important fact is that Sylvio deserted the nymph 'quite regardless' of her suffering. Whether or not she is conscious of her pun on heart/hart, the neat balance of line 36 emphasizes the rôle of the fawn as a substitute for the unfaithful lover. Consoling herself with this playmate, she retreats from the pain of desertion:

> Thenceforth I set myself to play
> My solitary time away
> With this: and very well content,
> Could so mine idle life have spent.
> For it was full of sport; and light
> Of foot, and heart; and did invite
> Me to its game; it seemed to bless
> Itself in me. How could I less
> Than love it? O I cannot be
> Unkind, t'a beast that loveth me.
>   Had it lived long, I do not know
> Whether it too might have done so
> As Sylvio did: his gifts might be
> Perhaps as false or more than he.
> But I am sure, for ought that I
> Could in so short a time espy,
> Thy love was far more better than
> The love of false and cruel men.

The fawn was 'full of sport', like Sylvio, but the game it invited her to had none of the latent danger of the sexual hunt. A cry of painful incomprehension is extorted from her in lines 45–6 as the thought of Sylvio's unnatural cruelty ('Unkind' contains both meanings) breaks in upon her memories of the natural growth of her tenderness for the fawn in response to its devotion to her. What sort of world is it in which simple love can be treated with brutal indifference? Her brush with that world has left its mark on her, however, and she can entertain doubts even about the fidelity of the fawn. 'Had it lived long' – if it had grown up – would its innocent affection have been transformed into complex and demanding passion? Would it too have grown 'wild'? Turning from this unsettling glimpse of the possible effects of time, the nymph takes refuge in the more secure antithesis between the loyalty of an animal and the unpredictable love of 'false and cruel men' – a phrase which gathers up her experience of the 'Unconstant Sylvio' and the 'Ungentle men'.

That is the last we hear of the distressing activities of 'men', as the nymph concentrates for the rest of the poem on the fawn and her relationship with it:

With sweetest milk, and sugar, first
I it at mine own fingers nursed.
And as it grew, so every day
It waxed more white and sweet than they.
It had so sweet a breath! and oft
I blushed to see its foot more soft,
And white (shall I say than my hand?)
Nay, any lady's of the land.
It is a wondrous thing, how fleet
'Twas on those little silver feet.
With what a pretty skipping grace,
It oft would challenge me the race:
And when 't had left me far away,
'Twould stay, and run again, and stay.
For it was nimbler much than hinds;
And trod, as on the four winds.

Having fed it with her own hands, the nymph has become totally engrossed in the creature's qualities of sweetness, softness, and whiteness, fleetness, grace, and nimbleness. It is no longer merely a memento of lost love, to be valued because it was a gift from Sylvio, but is cherished and admired for its own sake. Psychologically, it has provided both a distraction from the hurt of Sylvio's betrayal and an outlet for the girl's need to love.

In the next paragraph, the symbolic colouring derived from the Song of Solomon has led some critics in the direction of allegory, following the traditional Christian interpretation of the *hortus conclusus* (the 'enclosed garden' of the Old Testament text) as the Virgin Mary, the Church, or the Soul, and the hart that feeds among the lilies as Christ, the bridegroom of the Soul. Others have invoked the classical *hortus mentis* (the 'garden of the mind') and the mediaeval *jardin d'amour* (the 'garden of love', where Cupid dwells with his mother, Venus). The roses and lilies belong equally to the religious and the erotic traditions, as symbols variously of youth, passion, purity, beauty, and death. Consistent allegorical reading is difficult to sustain, however, and the main effect of the passage's richly allusive texture is to intensify the nymph's introspective withdrawal after the shock of Sylvio's defection:

I have a garden of my own
But so with roses overgrown,
And lilies, that you would it guess
To be a little wilderness.
And all the springtime of the year
It only lovèd to be there.

Among the beds of lilies, I
Have sought it oft, where it should lie;
Yet could not, till itself would rise,
Find it, although before mine eyes.
For, in the flaxen lilies' shade,
It like a bank of lilies laid.
Upon the roses it would feed,
Until its lips e'en seemed to bleed:
And then to me 'twould boldly trip,
And print those roses on my lip.
But all its chief delight was still
On roses thus itself to fill:
And its pure virgin limbs to fold
In whitest sheets of lilies cold.
Had it lived long, it would have been
Lilies without, roses within.

This enclosed springtime garden of innocent delight was both a place and a state of mind, in which there was such harmony between creature and environment that they were scarcely distinguishable: the fawn lost among the banks of lilies and its lips bleeding with the juice of rose-petals. Complete identity might have been achieved – 'Lilies without, roses within' – if the idyll had not been broken by the incursion of the 'wanton troopers', just as the nymph's present escape into memory is ended by the harsh reality that asserts itself in the phrase repeated from line 47: 'Had it lived long.'

Remembrance of happy times past offers only a temporary respite from the pain of living, and the nymph must face the inevitable conclusion of the event with which her complaint began:

O help! O help! I see it faint:
And die as calmly as a saint.
See how it weeps. The tears do come
Sad, slowly dropping like a gum.
So weeps the wounded balsam: so
The holy frankincense doth flow.
The brotherless Heliades
Melt in such amber tears as these.
I in a golden vial will
Keep these two crystal tears; and fill
It till it do o'erflow with mine;
Then place it in Diana's shrine.

The tears, 'slowly dropping' from the eyes of the expiring fawn, are gradually converted by the girl's imagination into precious and sacred relics, to be preserved in the shrine of Diana, goddess appropriately of both the hunt and chastity. The consolation of art, which can transform grief and loss into beauty and permanence, is condensed into a single matchless couplet (lines 99–100), as Marvell invokes the myth of the daughters of Helios from Book II of Ovid's *Metamorphoses*. Mourning at the tomb of their brother, Phaethon, they became rooted to the spot as poplar trees and the resin that oozed from their bark was hardened into beads of amber by the sun.

Meanwhile, the fawn has slipped quietly out of this life – 'vanished' to a pastoral heaven where innocence finds a lasting home – and the nymph makes plans to immortalize both it and her own sorrows in art:

> Now my sweet fawn is vanished to
> Whither the swans and turtles go;
> In fair Elysium to endure,
> With milk-white lambs, and ermines pure.
> O do not run too fast: for I
> Will but bespeak thy grave, and die.
> First my unhappy statue shall
> Be cut in marble; and withal,
> Let it be weeping too – but there
> The engraver sure his art may spare,
> For I so truly thee bemoan,
> That I shall weep though I be stone:
> Until my tears (still dropping) wear
> My breast, themselves engraving there.
> There at my feet shalt thou be laid,
> Of purest alabaster made:
> For I would have thine image be
> White as I can, though not as thee.

The reference to her own death need not be taken literally, as a premonition of the fatal effects of bereavement or an intimation of suicide. These concluding lines embody a psychological resistance to the bitter knowledge that innocence cannot 'endure', rather than a serious determination to die. Throughout the poem, the nymph has sought to distance herself from the actualities of an ungentle, unconstant, and unkind world forced upon her consciousness by the 'warm life-blood' flowing from the wounded fawn and the 'wild' and 'regardless' behaviour of Sylvio. Better to dream of a private garden overgrown with symbolic roses and lilies and an Elysium of 'milk-white lambs, and ermines pure' than to face the conflicting claims of passion and purity or the unyielding fact of death; better to think about precious drops of 'holy frankincense' or 'amber' seeping from a tree, or the cool beauty of crystal, than the tears of pain and distress extorted from a creature that one loves; better to indulge the fantasy of becoming a weeping statue (like Niobe, turned to marble by grief for her dead children and husband), than to undergo the difficult process of adjusting to the reality of loss. With its 'pure virgin limbs' folded in 'whitest sheets of lilies cold', and now about to be transmuted into 'purest alabaster', the fawn has assumed the status of an emblem, very similar in significance to the manna – 'White and entire, though congealed and chill' – in 'On a Drop of Dew'. But this is a dramatic complaint, not an emblem poem, and interest is centred in the speaker whose imagination effects the metamorphosis of fawn into symbol, not in the symbolic qualities of the fawn as such. In 'The Nymph Complaining for the Death of her Fawn', Marvell does not meditate on innocence or the fate of innocence, as he did in 'Young Love' and 'The Picture of Little T. C. in a Prospect of Flowers'; instead, he renders with great sensitivity and sympathy the psychological measures taken by a young mind to protect itself from the moral and emotional demands made upon it by a complex and imperfect world.

With the four poems developed around the figure of the Mower, we come to Marvell's most sustained and richly human treatment of the cost and necessity of making the transition from the state of innocence to the state of experience. As in the previous poem, the voice we hear is that of the innocent protagonist, though a more sophisticated intelligence keeps ironic watch over the proceedings and materializes in the form of a narrator in 'Damon the Mower'. There is some disagreement about whether the four poems should be read independently or as a group, but the majority of critics consider that they form a coherent sequence in the order in which they were originally printed in 1681. Indeed, it can be argued that their full significance is only released by attending to the process of disorientation that transforms the confident champion of pastoral values in 'The Mower against Gardens' into the alienated dealer of death in 'The Mower's Song'. There has also been disagreement about the degree of seriousness with which the Mower and his predicament should be approached. Is he to be seen primarily as a figure of fun, who comically conceives of himself as 'a big shot in the rustic world' (Cullen, p.187); or is he to be accorded mythic stature, as 'Marvell's symbol of fallen man, the lowest of the angels and the highest of the beasts' (Tayler, p. 163) or, more portentously, 'the Clown as Death' (Empson, p. 106)? It would certainly be a mistake to overlook the comic elements in these poems, and yet the issues raised by the dilemma and demeanour of the Mower are by no means trivial. The very fact that he is a mower, rather than the traditional shepherd, opens up new vistas on the pastoral world and complicates the kind of perceptions available to the genre.

In the first poem in the group, the Mower takes a stand in the age-old debate about man's right to interfere with the processes of Nature. He begins with a narrative account, in the past tense, of the consequences for the vegetable kingdom of mankind's fall into sin:

> Luxurious man, to bring his vice in use,
> Did after him the world seduce,
> And from the fields the flowers and plants allure,
> Where nature was most plain and pure.
> He first enclosed within the gardens square
> A dead and standing pool of air,
> And a more luscious earth for them did knead,
> Which stupified them while it fed.
> The pink grew then as double as his mind;
> The nutriment did change the kind.
> With strange perfumes he did the roses taint,
> And flowers themselves were taught to paint.
> The tulip, white, did for complexion seek,
> And learned to interline its cheek:
> Its onion root they then so high did hold,
> That one was for a meadow sold.
> Another world was searched, through oceans new,
> To find the *Marvel of Peru*.

Having himself been seduced from his prelapsarian innocence, man set about enticing the plants from the fields into the sinister enclosure of the garden, where they could be refashioned in his own corrupt image. The methods and achievements of the art of horticulture are interpreted by the Mower as instances of the contamination of the 'plain and pure' by a variety of human vices: gluttony (lines 7–8); duplicity (lines 9–10); the vanity of cosmetics (lines 11–14). The reference to the economic absurdities of the tulip mania, which was at its height in Holland in the 1630s (lines 15–16), and the hyperbolical claim that the exploration of the Americas was motivated by the quest for an exotic plant (lines 17–18), vividly suggest the distorted system of values associated with the advent of the garden and what it signifies of man's relation to his environment. With its chronological sweep from the seduction of the old 'world' after the Fall (line 2) to the hunt for treasures in the New World (line 17), this first movement of the poem traces the spread of Art's empire over Nature – a Mower's view of the history of civilization.

In the second movement, he takes up the sexual metaphor of the opening couplet (where 'Luxurious' has its seventeenth-century meaning of 'lecherous') and reveals, with a growing sense of moral outrage, the scandalous perversions and mutilations that the gardener's art has introduced into the orchard:

> And yet these rarities might be allowed
>   To man, that sovereign thing and proud,
> Had he not dealt between the bark and tree,
>   Forbidden mixtures there to see.
> No plant now knew the stock from which it came;
>   He grafts upon the wild the tame:
> That th' uncertain and adulterate fruit
>   Might put the palate in dispute.
> His green seraglio has its eunuchs too,
>   Lest any tyrant him outdo.
> And in the cherry he does nature vex,
>   To procreate without a sex.

Effecting a skilful transition from the past tense of historical narrative to the present tense of contemporary satire in the course of a single couplet (lines 23–4), the Mower condemns such practices as budding (lines 21–2) and grafting (lines 23–4), which produce the monstrosities of hybrid fruit (lines 25–6) and stoneless cherries (lines 29–30). Behind lines 27–30, there appears to be a submerged pun on the word 'stone', a common synonym for 'testicle' in Marvell's day. The enclosed garden has now degenerated into a seraglio (harem), and the cherries 'without a sex' are the stoneless eunuchs, whose very existence frustrates nature's procreative purposes. It has been suggested that Marvell may have taken his hint for the whole poem from the horticultural imagery in a passage in Thomas Randolph's 'Upon Love, fondly refused for Conscience' Sake', which is composed in the same unusual couplets of alternate decasyllabic and octosyllabic lines:

> If the fresh Trunk have sap enough to give
>   That each insertive branch may live;
> The Gardener grafts not only Apples there,
>   But adds the Warden and the Pear,
> The Peach, and Apricock together grow,
>   The Cherry, and the Damson too.
> Till he hath made by skilful husbandry
>   An intire Orchard of one Tree.

So lest our Paradise perfection want,
We may as well inoculate as plant.

Never one to borrow mindlessly, however, he has contrived a context in which both verse-form and image serve an argument diametrically opposed to Randolph's libertine philosophy. Closer in spirit to the Mower's contrast between 'plain and pure' Nature and the 'uncertain and adulterate' results of Art is Ben Jonson's celebration of country life in 'To Sir Robert Wroth' (also in couplets of mixed iambic pentameter and tetrameter):

How blessed art thou, canst love the country, Wroth,
Whether by choice, or fate, or both;
And, though so near the city, and the court,
Art ta'en with neither's vice, nor sport:

. . .

But canst, at home, in thy securer rest,
Live, with unbought provision blessed;
Free from proud porches, or their gilded roofs,
'Mongst lowing herds, and solid hoofs:

. . .

Such, and no other, was that age, of old,
Which boasts to have had the head of gold.
And such since thou canst make thine own content,
Strive, Wroth, to live long innocent.

But whereas Wroth represents an ideal that was attainable within the real world of Jacobean society – the moral and economic security of a country gentleman, who could resist the temptations of court and city and choose to make his own 'content' on his estate – Marvell's Mower is a fictional instrument for probing the perplexities of the human condition and inhabits a metaphorical realm where gardens, not cities, embody the ills of civilization.

Marvell's complex strategy emerges more clearly in the third and final movement of the poem:

'Tis all enforced, the fountain and the grot,
While the sweet fields do lie forgot:
Where willing nature does to all dispense
A wild and fragrant innocence:
And fauns and fairies do the meadow till,
More by their presence than their skill.
Their statues, polished by some ancient hand,
May to adorn the gardens stand:
But howsoe'er the figures do excel,
The gods themselves with us do dwell.

The Mower does not subscribe to the widespread Christian belief that 'Both beasts and plants' were directly affected by the Fall of Adam, 'cursed in the curse of man' (Donne, *The First Anniversary*, line 200). Beyond the confines of the corrupt gardens of civilization, Nature still flourishes in all its pristine innocence – not tainted by 'strange perfumes', but 'wild and fragrant', and paradoxically cultivated without the intervention of art (lines 35–6). The Mower, speaking out of the golden world of pastoral – where 'fauns and fairies', and even the 'gods themselves', are still real presences – has all along dissociated himself from the world of postlapsarian experience. The 'us' of the final line contrasts pointedly with the dismissive 'they' of line 15 and seals his refusal to acknowledge identity with the race of 'Luxurious man', 'that soveriegn thing and proud' (line 20). But Marvell and his readers are well aware that no human being can evade either the consequences of the Fall or the exercise of that authority over the rest of created nature entailed by the possession of reason: man is both 'Luxurious' and 'sovereign', and a human being can no more opt out of the dilemmas posed by his complex endowments than the Body or the Soul can sustain existence on earth independently.

Similar issues arise in meditating on the picture of Little T. C. The child instinctively expresses her sovereignty in taming the wilder flowers, just as she will later confront her own fallen nature by imposing laws of chastity on the 'wanton Love'. But in the last two stanzas, the speaker recognizes the limits of her authority. The injunction to grant 'sweetness' to the tulips and disarm roses of their thorns may look less fanciful in the light of the horticultural modifications of nature vilified by the Mower, but T. C. must beware of provoking the flower-goddess, Flora, by wielding her power thoughtlessly. Art may be used beneficently to 'reform the errors of the spring', or it may be used irresponsibly to frustrate the ends of Nature; Nature, on her side, may 'court' or 'kill' the human creatures who are invested by their reason with dominion over her, but who, at the same time, cannot transcend the material dimension of their being which renders them her subjects. It is the obliviousness to all such complexities that casts a mantle of irony over the performance of the historian-philosopher whose voice is heard in 'The Mower against Gardens'. Only the title reminds us that this voice belongs to one whose very occupation disqualifies him from setting up as spokesman for Nature and scourge of Art.

In the second poem of the sequence, 'Damon the Mower', the

distance between knowing reader and naîve speaker, always implicit in pastoral, is formally established by the tone of a narrator who invites us to adopt an ironic attitude towards the ensuing monologue:

1

Hark how the Mower Damon sung,
With love of Juliana stung!
While everything did seem to paint
The scene more fit for his complaint.
Like her fair eyes the day was fair,
But scorching like his am'rous care.
Sharp like his scythe his sorrow was,
And withered like his hopes the grass.

The theatrical and literary qualities of Damon's recital are insisted upon: the 'scene' is appropriate to the 'complaint' of a love-sick swain, as if painted especially for the occasion, and a series of similes elaborates on the apparent correspondence between the condition of the lover and the physical surroundings.

When Damon is allowed to speak in the first person, it looks as if the unstable relation between concrete phenomena and states of mind in those introductory similes – which expressed the inward sorrows of the Mower in terms of the sharpness of the scythe and then, inversely, the physical condition of the mown grass in terms of his subjective hopes – was designed to be indicative of the Mower's difficulty in distinguishing between internal and external categories of experience:

2

'Oh what unusual heats are here,
Which thus our sunburned meadows sear!
The grasshopper its pipe gives o'er;
And hamstringed frogs can dance no more.
But in the brook the green frog wades;
And grasshoppers seek out the shades.
Only the snake, that kept within,
Now glitters in its second skin.

3

'This heat the sun could never raise,
Nor Dog Star so inflame the days.
It from an higher beauty grow'th,
Which burns the fields and mower both:
Which mads the dog, and makes the sun
Hotter than his own Phaëton.
Not July causeth these extremes,
But Juliana's scorching beams.

4

'Tell me where I may pass the fires
Of the hot day, or hot desires.
To what cool cave shall I descend,
Or to what gelid fountain bend?
Alas! I look for ease in vain,
When remedies themselves complain.
No moisture but my tears do rest,
Nor cold but in her icy breast.'

The description of the effects of excessive heat on the creatures of the countryside in stanza 2 derives from Virgil's Second Eclogue, one of the major models for pastoral complaint and the chief source of Marvell's poem:

Cruel Alexis, do you care nothing for my songs? Have you no pity for me? You will end by driving me to death. This is the hour when even cattle seek the coolness of the shade; when even the green lizard lies hidden in the thorny brake; when Thestylis brews a fragrant soup of pounded garlic and wild-thyme for the reapers wearied by the scorching heat. Yet I am wandering in the paths that you have trod, under the burning sun, while the orchards echo to the harsh cicadas' notes and mine.

The 'heats' of the Mower's complaint, however, are 'unusual', and are not to be attributed to such natural causes as the sun or the Dog Star, which was held to be responsible for the 'dog-days' of July and August, the hottest part of the year. They originate in human passion, and have more in common with the fires which consumed the love-lorn Cyclops of Ovid's *Metamorphoses* than with the Mediterranean sun that beat down upon Virgil's lizards and reapers: 'For I am burning with love, and its flame scorches me more fiercely when I am spurned. I feel as if I were carrying Etna, flames and all, within my breast, and you, Galatea, do not care at all!' (Book XIII). But whereas the Cyclops acknowledged that the seat of discomfort was in his own breast, Damon tries to locate it in something outside himself, and to universalize its effects: in a hyperbole as comic in its extravagance as the Cyclops's internal volcano, 'Juliana's scorching beams' are said to burn 'the fields and mower both'. This way of formulating his experience is a desperate manoeuvre to preserve that sense of personal harmony with Nature expressed in 'The Mower against Gardens'. If he can hold on to the belief that both he and the fields are the victims of Juliana, he can protect himself from the recognition that any correspondence between the heat which sears the meadows and silences the grasshoppers and the 'am'rous care' which scorches him from within is a figment of his own imagination: that the heat raised by the July sun and the heat raised by Juliana are separate and totally unconnected phenomena, which only accidentally coincide in his perception of outward and inward realities. By stanza 4, however, the Mower who disowned any kinship with 'Luxurious man' has been brought to admit a distinction between himself and the natural denizens of the countryside: frogs and grasshoppers can find relief from the dog-days in the brook and the shades, but the inflamed lover is denied recourse to the 'cool cave' and 'gelid fountain' of pastoral. Like Adam, he has been dispossessed of the landscape of his former innocence.

The simple offerings appropriate to a simple world make no impression on the 'icy breast' of Juliana:

5

'How long wilt thou, fair shepherdess,
Esteem me, and my presents less?
To thee the harmless snake I bring,
Disarmèd of its teeth and sting;
To thee chameleons, changing hue,
And oak leaves tipped with honey dew.
Yet thou, ungrateful, hast not sought
Nor what they are, nor who them brought.'

Her 'ungrateful' indifference to both gifts and giver (lines 39–40) seems to clarify for the Mower the threat to his self-esteem and even his sense of identity which is the most disturbing feature of the onset of experience. He turns in bewilderment from his obsession with Juliana to an attempt to salvage the conception of himself and his place in the scheme of things that her coming has put in jeopardy:

6

'I am the Mower Damon, known
Through all the meadows I have mown.
On me the morn her dew distills
Before her darling daffodils.
And, if at noon my toil me heat,
The sun himself licks off my sweat.
While, going home, the evening sweet
In cowslip-water bathes my feet.

7

'What, though the piping shepherd stock
The plains with an unnumbered flock,
This scythe of mine discovers wide

More ground than all his sheep do hide.
With this the golden fleece I shear
Of all these closes every year.
And though in wool more poor than they,
Yet am I richer far in hay.

8

'Nor am I so deformed to sight,
If in my scythe I lookèd right;
In which I see my picture done,
As in a crescent moon the sun.
The deathless fairies take me oft
To lead them in their dances soft:
And, when I tune myself to sing,
About me they contract their ring.'

The immediate source of the Mower's affirmation of his material prosperity and the attractiveness of his person is Virgil's Second Eclogue:

Alexis, you despise me. You do not even ask what sort of man I am, what flocks I may possess, how rich I am in snowy milk. Yet a thousand lambs of mine range the Sicilian hills; summer and winter I have fresh milk in plenty . . . Nor am I as ill-favoured as all that. Down by the sea the other day, I saw myself reflected when the dying wind had left the water calm.

But the comedy of Damon's self-important air, as he compares his wealth with that of mere shepherds and peers at his reflection in the curved blade of his scythe, is more in the spirit of Theocritus, whose amorous Cyclops admires the beauty of his shaggy beard and single eye in the calm sea and boasts of the abundance of his flocks and cheeses in Idyls VI and XI, or of Ovid, who had fun with the equally grotesque posturing of his Cyclops:

All these sheep are mine, and I have many more, roaming the valleys. Many are sheltering in the woods, and many penned in the caves at home. Were you to ask, I could not tell you how many there are. It is the mark of a poor man, to count his flocks . . . Assuredly I know what I look like; quite recently I saw my reflection in the clear water, and I liked what I saw.

(*Metamorphoses*, XIII)

Nevertheless, Damon is not merely comic. The bravado of his forlorn attempt to sustain an untenable view of his own significance is both absurd and poignant to the poet and his readers, who have long since shed the comforting illusions of innocence. We know, as the price of our experience, that the present tense of the verbs in these three stanzas is a piece of self-deception: the Mower is trying to prolong a sense of relationship with Nature which only existed in his imagination and which is already firmly in the past. Each of the instances he offers of Nature's care for him in stanza 6 can be explained in a rational, non-animistic way. The Morn does not single him out for special favours – he just happens to be there when the dew is being distilled upon the earth; the Sun does not lick off his sweat – he just happens to be warmed by the sun that shines on all indiscriminately; the cowslip-water does not lovingly bathe his feet – the action of walking through the fields shakes the moisture from the flowers. He is projecting upon the inanimate surroundings his own need to believe that he belongs and is cared for.

The scythe, which is the mark of the Mower's sovereignty over Nature and which was ignored in the previous poem, is given prominence by Marvell's adaptation of his classical sources. It begins to acquire symbolic connotations as the instrument which distinguishes the Mower from the traditional shepherd of pastoral, laying bare ('discovering') things hidden from mere minders of sheep in stanza 7 and providing him with a means of self-scrutiny in stanza 8. In lines 61–4, Damon presents an image of himself as artist, performing those very activities of dancing and singing which were prevented among the creatures of the 'sunburned meadows' in stanza 2. The 'deathless fairies' are akin to the 'fauns and fairies' of 'The Mower against Gardens'. The epithet is significant: the forces of natural continuity which the fairies represent are indeed 'deathless', but death will soon intrude upon Damon's consciousness and remove him from the position he likes to imagine himself occupying at the centre of the fairy ring (line 64).

In the very next stanza, he confesses that he has been indulging a dream of the vanished past:

9

'How happy might I still have mowed,
Had not Love here his thistles sowed!
But now I all the day complain,
Joining my labour to my pain;
And with my scythe cut down the grass,
Yet still my grief is where it was:
But, when the iron blunter grows,
Sighing, I whet my scythe and woes.'

The meadows of pastoral innocence sprout hurtful thistles and become the setting for the painful labour that has been part of the curse of Adam since the Fall. The scythe, the instrument of discovery, is also an instrument of destruction which cuts down the grass; and, with a glance at the myth of the succeeding Ages of Gold, Silver, and Iron, it is the iron scythe that shears the 'golden fleece' from the meadows of the pastoral idyll. (Marvell elsewhere associates iron with what is imperfect and hostile in this world. Fate drives 'iron wedges' between the hopeless lovers of 'The Definition of Love'; the Coy Mistress is told that pleasures must be torn roughly through 'the iron gates of life'.)

The narrator then breaks in to describe the effect of the Mower's 'woes' upon his behaviour:

10

While thus he threw his elbow round,
Depopulating all the ground,
And, with his whistling scythe, does cut
Each stroke between the earth and root,
The edgèd steel by careless chance
Did into his own ankle glance;
And there among the grass fell down,
By his own scythe, the Mower mown.

There is a comic aspect to this event, emphasized in the patness of the final phrase. But there is also something disturbing in the brutal abandon and indifference conveyed by the diction ('threw', 'depopulating') and the sound, particularly of the second couplet, in which the blade can be heard swishing through the air and slicing remorselessly through the living substance of the grass. The Mower falls in the very act of destroying – a tragi-comic example of the fate of 'man, that sovereign thing and proud'. He is permitted a dramatic curtain speech in which, like the Nymph, he looks to death as the only answer to the pain of an experience that renders the simple remedies of pastoral ineffective:

11

'Alas!' said he, 'these hurts are slight
To those that die by love's despite.
With shepherd's-purse, and clown's-all-heal,
The blood I staunch, and wound I seal.
Only for him no cure is found,
Whom Juliana's eyes do wound.
'Tis death alone that this must do:
For Death thou art a Mower too.'

Damon's predicament is given its most moving and economical

expression in 'The Mower to the Glow-worms'. This graceful lyric, which records the Mower's melancholy resignation to his irremediable estrangement from nature, carefully accommodates syntax to poetic form. A vision of pastoral harmony is sustained through three quatrains, with their repeated pattern of apostrophe followed by relative clause, only to be dissipated by the main clause of the poem's single sentence at the beginning of stanza 4 and the flurry of explanatory conjunctions in the last three lines ('Since . . . ,' 'For . . . ,' 'That . . . '):

1

Ye living lamps, by whose dear light
The nightingale does sit so late,
And studying all the summer night,
Her matchless songs does meditate;

2

Ye country comets, that portend
No war, nor prince's funeral,
Shining unto no higher end
Than to presage the grass's fall;

3

Ye glow-worms, whose officious flame
To wandering mowers shows the way,
That in the night have lost their aim,
And after foolish fires do stray;

4

Your courteous lights in vain you waste,
Since Juliana here is come,
For she my mind hath so displaced
That I shall never find my home.

In a world blessed by the gentle shine of the glow-worms, art, politics, and morality are all 'disarmed' of their 'teeth and sting', like the 'harmless snake' of 'Damon the Mower': no poet wearily burns the midnight oil, no state is shaken by war or change of monarch, no wanderer from the true path is lost forever in the darkness. But the 'courteous lights' of a sympathetic universe cannot rescue a mind disorientated by the fires kindled by Juliana. The Mower knows that he will never again be at home in that innocent landscape where the nightingale meditates her 'matchless songs' and only the grass falls.

In 'The Mower's Song', Damon pursues the insight that some

displacement of the mind is responsible for his alienation from the natural scene. No longer able to maintain the image of himself as the centre round which the fairies of unspoiled nature 'contract their ring', and forced to recognise the disharmony of body and mind in the very different wounds inflicted by the scythe and Juliana's eyes, he attempts to come to terms with what has happened to him:

1

My mind was once the true survey
Of all these meadows fresh and gay,
And in the greenness of the grass
Did see its hopes as in a glass;
When Juliana came, and she
What I do to the grass, does to my thoughts and me.

When he was at one with the pastoral world – when he could confidently claim that 'the gods themselves with *us* do dwell' – his mind was a 'true survey' of its surroundings, like 'an accurately measured, artistically coloured estate map, made to scale by a skilled surveyor' (Craze, p. 153). External facts and internal facts – 'grass' and 'hopes' – reflected each other. Such sympathy between man and nature lies at the heart of the pastoral genre's interpretation of human existence. Spenser's Colin Clout finds comfort in the correspondence between his love-lorn state and the bleakness of the winter landscape in the January eclogue of *The Shepheardes Calender*: 'Thou barren ground, whom winter's wrath hath wasted, / Art made a mirror to behold my plight.' And the lover in the tenth of Sidney's *Certain Sonnets* finds his pain 'engraved' on the rocks and hills and laments, in an image that Marvell may have recalled specifically here: 'Like late mown meads, late cut from joy I live.' This way of experiencing man's relationship with his environment is concentrated into a single line in which Spenser's shepherd addresses his 'feeble flock': 'With mourning pine I; you with pining mourn.'

The 'once' of the opening line of 'The Mower's Song' sadly acknowledges the breakdown of this kind of relationship. While the man languishes with grief, the meadows continue to flourish:

2

But these, while I with sorrow pine,
Grew more luxuriant still and fine,
That not one blade of grass you spied,
But had a flower on either side;
When Juliana came, and she
What I do to the grass, does to my thoughts and me.

3

Unthankful meadows, could you so
A fellowship so true forgo,
And in your gaudy May-games meet,
While I lay trodden under feet?
When Juliana came, and she
What I do to the grass, does to my thoughts and me.

Although the pastoral harmony is broken, however, the rhetorical mechanism of pastoral as a literary genre is still in working order: Damon remains naïvely unaware of implications which experience makes available to poet and readers. There is unperceived irony in the phrase 'fellowship so true'. Damon intends 'true' to mean 'constant', as in 'true love'; but the word picks up the 'true' of the first line of the poem, and may suggest to the detached observer that neither the mind's 'survey' of the meadows nor the meadows' 'fellowship' with the Mower ever had the truth of objective facts: both were constructs of the Mower's imagination, which remained true only as long as he could maintain belief in them. There is a telling contrast between the first line of stanza 3 and line 39 of 'Damon the Mower'. In the earlier poem, Damon had complained that it was Juliana who was 'ungrateful'; here, he lays the blame for his suffering on the 'Unthankful meadows'. In neither case does he fully understand that the real cause of the disruption that he is experiencing lies in himself, in his own inability to sustain his innocent view of himself and his place in created nature.

With the petulance of a thwarted child, he resorts to retaliatory violence:

4

But what you in compassion ought,
Shall now by my revenge be wrought:
And flow'rs, and grass, and I and all,
Will in one common ruin fall.
For Juliana comes, and she
What I do to the grass, does to my thoughts and me.

Asserting his power over the rest of creation, with a wantonness expressed in the indiscriminate listing of victims in the third line, Damon throws in his lot with 'Luxurious man' and ensures that his fall will become 'common'. The Nymph withdrew inwards from the sting of experience; the Mower, 'with love of Juliana stung', reacts more aggressively: but both these representatives of innocence fail to adapt to the complexities of postlapsarian living and look instead towards the solace of death:

5

And thus, ye meadows, which have been
Companions of my thoughts more green,
Shall now the heraldry become
With which I will adorn my tomb;
For Juliana comes, and she
What I do to the grass, does to my thoughts and me.

The Mower's tomb will be marked by the heraldry of the meadows – wreaths of mown grass – a rustic equivalent to the Nymph's statue of herself and the companion of *her* happier days. But even this sombre close to his drama is not free of the irony that clings to the figures of pastoral. For Damon, the phrase 'thoughts more green' refers to the time when his mind was a 'true survey' of the 'meadows fresh and gay'; for the reader it may suggest something nearer to Cleopatra's 'My salad days, when I was green in judgement'. The greenness of innocence can be regarded from another perspective as the greenness of inexperience: a state upon which the adult mind may look with a mixture of nostalgia, amusement, and perhaps – with Shakespeare's queen of Egypt – even a touch of contempt.

Read as a group, in the order of their first printing, the Mower poems do deliver up a coherent meaning in the terms of their own pastoral myth. At the start of his career, like Little T. C. and the Nymph, Damon is absorbed in and defined by his relationship with the physical setting; the intervention of Juliana turns his world upside down, and he ends by recognizing, but not being reconciled to, the bitter lessons of experience – that mind and body ('my thoughts and me') draw him in opposite directions and that his unified vision of Self and Nature has been shattered beyond hope of restoration. In learning those lessons, he often arouses indulgent laughter, but it seems inadequate to describe 'Damon the Mower' as 'an ironic and witty examination of the contradictions and absurdities of the amorous mind', and to praise Marvell merely for insights into 'the psychology of love' that he discovers in the tradition of the 'comic amorous pastoral' (Cullen, p. 191). For although 'Juliana–Eros' functions primarily as disdainful mistress in the fable of an innocent who is dislocated from his universe 'by the impact of frustrated sexual experience' (Nevo, pp. 18–19), her influence can be taken as symptomatic of disturbances in the very fabric of seventeenth-century life for which the traumas of awakening sexuality are a convenient and powerful paradigm. One critic has seen 'political implications' in the 'beliefs about the interdependence of natural growth and legitimate sovereignty' that lie behind the Mower's denunciation of gardens (Friedman, p. 127); and another detects a parody of radical polemics in his invective against the practices of horticulture (King, ' "The Mower against Gardens" and the Levellers'). (It is worth recalling at this point that the Nymph's peace was disrupted by the intrusion of 'wanton *troopers*' – a word recorded in the Oxford English Dictionary as first being used in print in 1640 with reference to the soldiers of the Scottish Covenanting army, and thereafter associated particularly with the parliamentary Ironsides. At least one critic considers that the poem is based on some actual incident involving a girl of royalist sympathies during the Civil Wars (Craze, p. 70).)

The Mower poems contain no such overt indications of contemporary relevance, but it should not be forgotten that pastoral itself could reverberate with political significance without sacrificing its rich powers of generalization. Peter L. Smith has pointed out that in the figures of Tityrus and Meliboeus – the happy rustic and the farmer dispossessed by Roman politics – Virgil establishes a symbolic opposition between 'cool, shaded repose' and the 'hot, dusty world of homeless yearning'. His article deserves quoting at some length, because of the interesting gloss it supplies on Marvell's borrowings in 'Damon the Mower':

> *Libertas* is symbolically opposed to *servitium*; peace, to civil discord. The underlying basis for this contrast is the recurring suggestion that leisure, relaxation, freedom, and peace are all to be found in the shade, whereas exile, anxiety, slavery, and discord are exposed to the pitiless glare of the sun . . . Like the lovesick Corydon of Eclogue 2, who is there the only living creature forced to endure the blazing midday sun (*Ecl.* 2. 8–13), Meliboeus seems to feel that the unattainable shade would soothe his restlessness and torment.
> (p. 300)

The contrast between Virgil's Meliboeus and Tityrus is like that between Jonson's Sir Robert Wroth, 'at home' in the 'securer rest' of his family estate, and the straying Mower, who will 'never find' his 'home'.

As we shall see in the next chapter, Marvell's preoccupation with innocence and experience, nature and art, was by no means confined to the psychology of sex. Being the product of a period of upheaval very similar to Virgil's, it would be surprising if the plight of his most richly imagined pastoral persona were not symbolic of the plight of the individual in mid-seventeenth-century England, made uncomfortable by the 'blazing midday sun' of political and religious – not to mention scientific – revolution, and wandering dispossessed of traditional certainties in the 'hot, dusty world of homeless yearning'.

6

Action and retirement

Climb at Court for me that will
Tottering favour's pinnacle;
All I seek is to lie still.
Settled in some secret nest,
In calm leisure let me rest,
And far off the public stage
Pass away my silent age.
Thus when without noise, unknown,
I have lived out all my span,
I shall die, without a groan,
An old honest Country man.
Who exposed to others' eyes,
Into his own heart ne'er pries,
Death to him's a strange surprise.

These measured, self-assured lines, translated into laconic heptasyllables from the Second Chorus of Seneca's Latin tragedy, *Thyestes*, express the same impulse to hold aloof from the world and maintain one's own personal integrity which informs 'On a Drop of Dew' and 'The Mower against Gardens', but place it in a different context and give it a different emphasis. Seneca had distilled in this famous passage a widespread philosophical ideal of self-knowledge cultivated far from the haunts of ambitious and busy men – an ideal which depended on neither the religious conviction that the soul will one day return to 'the clear region where 'twas born' nor the pastoral contrast between naïvety and sophistication. A temperamental preference for 'calm leisure' is dignified as a moral choice of the contemplative obscurity of a country life rather than the active pursuit of fame and favour. It is evident from what we know of Marvell's life, as well as from what can be inferred from his poetry, that the perennial debate about the competing values of contemplation and action – retirement from the world in order to perfect the self and engagement with the world in order to serve society – was one which had more than academic significance for him.

He seems to have been a man whose natural inclination to follow the scheme of life embodied in the Senecan Chorus was periodically disturbed by the demands made upon his moral and imaginative faculties by the progress of the great drama being acted out during the middle decades of the seventeenth century. Indeed, it may even be the case that the very lines which apparently endorse a deliberate seclusion from political affairs actually contain a veiled declaration of allegiance to the 'Country' in opposition to the 'Court', these being the names of the parties which emerged in the course of Charles II's reign. Such an interpretation depends on assigning a fairly late date to the translation, but there is evidence – generously made available to me by Mrs E. E. Duncan-Jones – to suggest that the first couplet owes its phrasing to a passage on page 112 of *The Causes of the Decay of Christian Piety*, a work thought to be by Richard Allestree, which was published in 1667.

Some of the poems to be dealt with in this and the following chapters have a much more explicit connection with contemporary politics and in particular with the two men whose careers gave a sharper focus to Marvell's consideration of the rival claims of the active and contemplative lives and who came to perform complex functions in the moral universe of his poetry. As Lieutenant-General and Commander-in-Chief of the military forces at a time when the army was the supreme power in the land and the nature of the state was being transformed from monarchy to republic, Oliver Cromwell and Thomas Lord Fairfax were 'exposed to others' eyes' at the very centre of 'the public stage'. Cromwell was prominent at the trial of Charles I and instrumental in gathering signatures on the death-warrant; Fairfax played no part in the proceedings in Westminster Hall and his absence was made conspicuous by the disturbance caused when his wife shouted 'Oliver Cromwell is a traitor' from one of the galleries and had to be hustled out at musket-point. Cromwell took up the burden of directing the political as well as the military fortunes of his country in the new and challenging circumstances of the 1650s; in 1650, Fairfax resigned his command of the army and the political responsibilities that went with it, and withdrew to his estates in Yorkshire. Such contrasting behaviour at such a crisis in the national drama invested the two great men with symbolic status, and they function largely as representative examples in the poems that Marvell wrote at this time. And yet, in spite of his habitual air of detachment, it is difficult to avoid the conclusion that Marvell's objective analysis of the moral and political problems posed by Fairfax and Cromwell – both of whom he came to know personally between 1650 and 1657 in his capacity as tutor to Mary Fairfax and William Dutton – also forced upon him an assessment of his own position.

The critical controversy over what that position might have been in the crucial years before and after the beheading of the king in

January 1649 is still unresolved. In default of any independent evidence as to Marvell's political orientation in this period, inferences can only be drawn from the poems. Five of them can be dated with some degree of accuracy. The commendatory verses, 'To His Noble Friend Mr Richard Lovelace, upon His Poems', were printed along with contributions by thirteen others in the first edition of *Lucasta* in the early summer of 1649, although allusions in the text suggest that they were composed some time early in the previous year. 'An Elegy upon the Death of My Lord Francis Villiers' commemorates a young nobleman who was killed fighting for the king in one of the skirmishes of the Second Civil War on 7 July 1648. It was ascribed to Marvell in a manuscript note by George Clarke (1660–1736) and printed by Margoliouth as an appendix to the edition of 1927. Although it can be strongly supported on internal grounds, however, the ascription has failed to command universal assent. Another elegy, 'Upon the Death of the Lord Hastings', was first published in *Lachrymae Musarum*, a collection of verse tributes to the Earl of Huntingdon's young son and heir, who died of smallpox on 24 June 1649. The composition of 'An Horatian Ode upon Cromwell's Return from Ireland' can be dated precisely to the months of June and July 1650, between the end of Cromwell's Irish campaign in May and the start of his Scottish campaign on 22 July. There is less certainty about the fifth poem, which is a satire on the poet and dramatist, Thomas May, who died on 13 November 1650. It seems logical to assume that a poem entitled 'Tom May's Death' was written in the weeks immediately following the event, but it was not printed until 1681 in *Miscellaneous Poems*, and some critics have argued for a date in the 1660s, or even denied Marvell's authorship altogether. The reasons for this uneasiness about the dating and authenticity of 'Tom May's Death' are bound up with a deduction that has commonly been made from the earlier group of poems. Richard Lovelace, Lord Francis Villiers, and the family of Lord Hastings – together with the majority of the contributors to *Lucasta* and *Lachrymae Musarum* – were supporters of the king. The assumption has been that if, in Pierre Legouis's words, 'a man is known by the company he keeps' (p. 14), then Marvell's sympathies were with the Royalists in the late 1640s. Since many commentators regard 'An Horatian Ode' as evidence of a shift of support towards Cromwell or at least as non-partisan in its political affiliation, the apparent disparagement of the parliamentary cause and the obvious contempt directed at Tom May for deserting the king and throwing in his lot with the rebels, in a poem written only a few months after the Ode, call Marvell's own consistency and probity into question. The alternatives are to interpret the Ode itself as essentially royalist in tenor (a view put forward tentatively by Newton ('Further Notes', pp. 125–33)); to defend Marvell as the kind of loyalist whose allegiance is granted not to a person, or even to a particular system, but to the current working institutions of government, provided the institutions they replace have effectively ceased to exist (Wallace); or to refuse to admit the Villiers elegy (called by Margoliouth the 'one unequivocally royalist utterance' attributed to Marvell) to the canon, and argue that the other poems in the group do not preclude a steady, if undemonstrative, sympathy for the cause of Parliament, which hardened into active commitment later on (Chernaik). There is not room to rehearse all the arguments here or to discuss more than the famous Ode in any detail, but it will be useful to draw attention to passages in the poems on Lovelace and May for the light they throw on Marvell's attitude to the relation between the poet and the politics of the age he lives in.

The commendatory verses for *Lucasta* begin with a contrast between 'Our times' (the late 1640s) and 'That candid age' (the 1630s), when Lovelace first made his mark in Cavalier circles at Oxford and the two poets probably became acquainted at Cambridge:

Sir,
Our times are much degenerate from those
Which your sweet muse with your fair fortune chose,
And as complexions alter with the climes,
Our wits have drawn the infection of our times.
That candid age no other way could tell
To be ingenious, but by speaking well.
Who best could praise had then the greatest praise,
'Twas more esteemed to give than wear the bays:
Modest ambition studied only then
To honour not herself but worthy men.
These virtues now are banished out of town,
Our Civil Wars have lost the civic crown.
He highest builds, who with most art destroys,
And against others' fame his own employs.
I see the envious caterpillar sit
On the fair blossom of each growing wit.

The word 'candid' (*candidus* means 'white' in Latin) indicates that a fall from innocence has occurred in the years since Lovelace's 'sweet muse' first gained him entry into the community of poets. The aesthetic and moral values which held that community together – implied in the phrase 'speaking well' and symbolized by the granting of 'the bays' as a recognition of poetic excellence – have given way to malicious rivalry and envy. The 'wits' of the present age are no longer 'candid' (frank and unbiased in their judgements), but have been infected by the spirit of faction bred in the country at large by the Civil Wars.

The intrusion of the world of politics into the world of art is presented in more specific detail in the second paragraph:

> The air's already tainted with the swarms
> Of insects which against you rise in arms:
> Word-peckers, paper-rats, book-scorpions,
> Of wit corrupted, the unfashioned sons.
> The barbèd censurers begin to look
> Like the grim consistory on thy book;
> And on each line cast a reforming eye,
> Severer than the young presbýtery.
> Till when in vain they have thee all perused,
> You shall, for being faultless, be accused.
> Some reading your *Lucasta* will allege
> You wronged in her the House's Privilege.
> Some that you under sequestration are,
> Because you writ when going to the war,
> And one the book prohibits, because Kent
> Their first petition by the author sent.

Before a licence to print could be issued, *Lucasta*, like all books, had to pass under the eyes of 'the barbèd censurers' established by a Parliamentary Ordinance of June 1643. The reimposition of censorship after the freedom gained by the abolition of the repressive Court of the Star Chamber in 1641, together with the new tyranny over conscience wielded by the 'grim consistory' of the Presbyterians which replaced the Episcopacy in 1643, are merely the most conspicuous manifestations of the general distortion of aesthetic judgement by political prejudice. Lovelace's poems will not get a fair hearing from the party hacks – the 'Word-peckers, paper-rats, book-scorpions' – who condemn the work because the author is 'under sequestration' for unrepentant royalism and because he had dared to present to the House of Commons a petition in support of the king from the men of Kent in 1642. There is no need to interpret the dislike of the parliamentary licensers and the 'young presbýtery' as evidence that Marvell shared Lovelace's political allegiance at the time he composed the poem, since John Milton, who has never been suspected of Royalism, was also openly antagonistic to the Printing Ordinance and the Presbyterians in *Areopagitica* (1644) and 'On the New Forcers of Conscience under the Long Parliament' (1646). Indeed, the main point that Marvell is making in these verses is strengthened if it is assumed that he was himself not committed to the royal cause, whether or not he was actively opposed to it. At a time when the 'unfashioned sons' of 'wit corrupted' allow factional interests to colour their literary judgements, he retains the impartiality of 'that candid age', in which 'worthy men' were honoured by their fellow poets according to their merits, not their party. The attitude which emerges, then, is that ideally the poet should strive to remain uncompromised by the conditions that prevail in the grubby arena of politics – 'So the world excluding round' and maintaining his artistic principles 'white and entire', like the soul in 'On a Drop of Dew'.

Such views might well have appeared appropriate in early 1648, to a man who had only recently returned from an extended continental tour, which had kept him out of England throughout the years of armed conflict. But between then and November 1650, when Thomas May died, the situation had been radically altered by the brutalities of the Second Civil War, the trial and execution of the king, and the ascendancy of Cromwell as the strong man in whom hopes of stable government rested. The death of a writer who, in contrast to the faithful Lovelace, had notoriously deserted his royal master in the 1640s to become official apologist for the rebellion in *The History of the Parliament of England* (1647) and *A Breviary of the History of the Parliament of England* (1650), seems to have stimulated Marvell to a reassessment of the poet's responsibilities. He imagines the ghost of Tom May being denied admittance to 'the learned throng' presided over by Ben Jonson in the Elysian fields:

> 'Far from these blessed shades tread back again
> Most servile wit, and mercenary pen,
> Polydore, Lucan, Alan, Vandal, Goth,
> Malignant poet and historian both.' (lines 39–42)

Like Polydore Virgil and Lucan, both of whom wrote partisan histories, May has prostituted his talent for mercenary ends; and like the Alani, Vandals, and Goths, his activities have been destructive of civilized values. Motivated by resentment at being passed over by the king for the post of poet laureate when Jonson died in 1637, May has exacerbated the factional bitterness that has torn the nation apart, as the rivalry of the Guelphs and Ghibellines divided the city of Florence:

> 'But thee nor ignorance nor seeming good
> Misled, but malice fixed and understood.
> Because some one than thee more worthy wears
> The sacred laurel, hence are all these tears?
> Must therefore all the world be set on flame,

> Because a gázette-writer missed his aim?
> And for a tankard-bearing muse must we
> As for the basket, Guelphs and Ghib'llines be?' (lines 55–62)

Whereas Jonson 'knew not neither foe nor friend' (line 29), May has fomented discord by exerting his 'servile wit' in the cause of one party against another. Since this seems to be the main burden of the charge against him, it is unlikely that Marvell's own poem should be read, as it often has been, as an equally partisan condemnation of May's betrayal of the royal cause as such.

In the lines that follow, Marvell sets out a model for the true artist's way of conducting himself amidst the confusions of a revolutionary period:

> 'When the sword glitters o'er the judge's head,
> And fear has coward churchmen silencèd,
> Then is the poet's time, 'tis then he draws,
> And single fights forsaken virtue's cause.
> He, when the wheel of empire whirleth back,
> And though the world's disjointed axle crack,
> Sings still of ancient rights and better times,
> Seeks wretched good, arraigns successful crimes.
> But thou, base man, first prostituted hast
> Our spotless knowledge and the studies chaste,
> Apostatizing from our arts and us,
> To turn the chronicler to Spartacus.
> Yet wast thou taken hence with equal fate,
> Before thou couldst great Charles his death relate.'
> (lines 63–76)

The poet's rôle is not to enter the fray and lend – or sell – his voice to one side or the other, but to stand above faction and fight 'forsaken virtue's cause'. While other men lose sight of the moral principles that transcend particular struggles for control of empire, it is his duty to keep the vision of 'ancient rights and better times' alive and to remind his compatriots that good is good, even though 'wretched', and crimes are crimes, even though 'successful'. Just as the Mower is the spokesman for the 'wild and fragrant innocence' of the unspoiled meadows, where the 'gods themselves' dwell 'with us', so Ben Jonson speaks here on behalf of those genuine poets whose 'spotless knowledge' and 'chaste studies' have been 'prostituted' by Tom May. To turn Jonson himself into a propagandist for a specific political cause is to make him guilty of the very apostasy against 'our arts and us' that he lays at May's door; to set him up as champion of the king against 'the chronicler to Spartacus', the instigator of the revolt of slaves in ancient Rome, is to miss the entire thrust of Marvell's indictment of May and the conception of the poet's task that he is in the process of elaborating. The significant issue for Jonson, as the representative of impartial art, is that May only chronicled the successes of Parliament from a partisan point of view and avoided the moral complexities that an attempt to relate 'great Charles his death' would have entailed. It was precisely these complexities that Marvell had felt himself compelled to confront a few months earlier in 'An Horation Ode'.

It is hardly a surprise to find the poet who preferred to keep his 'silent judgement' and 'lie still' in 'some secret nest' responding to that compulsion with very mixed feelings:

> The forward youth that would appear
> Must now forsake his muses dear,
> Nor in the shadows sing
> His numbers languishing.
> 'Tis time to leave the books in dust,
> And oil the unusèd armour's rust:
> Removing from the wall
> The corslet of the hall.

Although first person pronouns are studiously avoided, the phrasing of these introductory lines betrays the reluctance ('would' and 'Must') and the regret ('forsake' and 'dear') that colour the poet's call to put aside 'muses' and 'books' in favour of commitment to the world of action. Nevertheless, the apparent antipathy to the very notion of a 'forward youth', presumptuous as well as eager in his desire to 'appear' and make his mark on 'the public stage', is counterbalanced by a hint of disdain for the continued cultivation of 'numbers languishing' in the secluded safety of 'the shadows'. No longer comfortable with one mode of life, the speaker is resistant to the alternative urged by circumstances. ''Tis time' to take some new initiative, but what was it in the circumstances of early summer 1650 that made it imperative to act 'now'? To answer this question, and to understand the nature of the crisis that lies behind what many regard as Marvell's greatest achievement as a poet, it is necessary to look more closely at developments in the political situation since the death of the king in January 1649.

In the months following the regicide, the monarchy and House of Lords were abolished and a new Commonwealth declared. The 'Rump' Parliament, consisting of those members of the Commons who still held their seats after Colonel Pride had excluded opponents of the army from the House in December 1648, retained the prerogative of making laws, but executive power was vested in a Council of State drawn from M.P.s and senior army officers. Delays in calling new elections and reforming the franchise angered the democratic elements in the army, and a Leveller revolt in May was severely put down by Fairfax and Cromwell. The government had to contend with enemies abroad as well as opponents at home, and in August Cromwell sailed for Ireland to meet the threat of a military alliance between Catholics and royalists. Meanwhile controversy was raging over an oath of loyalty to the republic which was imposed on all civilian office-holders, clergy, and army officers in October and extended to all adult males in January 1650, in an attempt to secure recognition of the legitimacy of the new regime. The back of Irish resistance was broken in the autumn of 1649 by the brutal massacres at Drogheda and Wexford, though the subjugation of Ireland was not completed till 1652 under Cromwell's successors, Ireton and Ludlow. Cromwell himself was recalled to England in the spring of 1650 and was soon to take over as Commander-in-Chief from Fairfax, who refused to lead a campaign against the Scots and Charles II. His return must have been anticipated by friends and foes alike with uncertainty and misgiving. The security of the young republic depended upon his ruthless efficiency as a soldier, but as he came back from one successful military expedition to undertake another, many must have wondered how he would use the political power that was being consolidated with each new victory. It is not difficult to imagine that for both former Royalists and moderate supporters of Parliament who were shocked by the turn events had taken over the past two years, the decision being forced upon their consciences by the Oath of Engagement to the Commonwealth would have found its focus in the figure of the new commander of the army.

The opening metaphors of Marvell's 'Ode' bear witness to the moral pressure exerted upon each individual by the questions about the country's future precipitated by Cromwell's return from Ireland. It is no longer enough to bewail the passing of the 'candid age' before the Civil Wars and turn away fastidiously from the tainted world of politics. ''Tis time' for the poet, in his own way, to 'oil the unusèd armour's rust' and face the painful ambiguities of the present. Any serious stock-taking must begin with Cromwell, and there was no need to have been committed to the king's lost cause to harbour ambivalent feelings about this indispensable and dangerous man.

The linking word 'So' carries the psychological tensions of the first eight lines through into the initial attempt to establish a perspective on a career which seems to demonstrate the very process of emergence from the shadows of private life advocated by the poet:

> So restless Cromwell could not cease
> In the inglorious arts of peace,
> But through adventurous war
> Urgèd his active star.
> And, like the three-forked lightning, first
> Breaking the clouds where it was nursed,
> Did thorough his own side
> His fiery way divide.
> (For 'tis all one to courage high
> The emulous or enemy:
> And with such to inclose
> Is more than to oppose.)
> Then burning through the air he went,
> And palaces and temples rent:
> And Caesar's head at last
> Did through his laurels blast.
> 'Tis madness to resist or blame
> The force of angry heaven's flame.

Cromwell is the man of action, in the light of whose achievements the 'arts of peace' appear to be as 'inglorious' as the 'numbers languishing' that must be forsaken by the 'forward youth'. The impression created by the imagery is of a natural force, doing violence to itself and everything that tries to contain it. Regard for the bonds of human affection (implied in the metaphor 'nursed') and party loyalty (one of the connotations of 'his own side') could no more impede its progress than respect for the institutions of state and church ('palaces and temples'). Even the sacred office of kingship (represented by the laurel which was the symbol of the imperial authority of the Roman Caesars and commonly believed to be proof against lightning) could afford Charles I no protection.

As in so many of his poems, Marvell was reshaping something he had read to a quite different end, and it is particularly interesting to discover that the major source for 'An Horatian Ode' was a translation of Lucan's *Pharsalia* by none other than Thomas May, which had been published originally in 1627 and reprinted in 1631, 1635, and 1650. Lucan's account of the Roman civil wars had an obvious relevance for Marvell's generation, in an age when history was largely conceived as a storehouse of examples to be applied in the interpretation of more recent events. In Lucan's historical epic, Julius Caesar is the villain whose reckless destruction of the traditional liberties of Rome is motivated by selfish ambition and vainglory. Marvell's account of

Cromwell owes something to both Lucan's Latin and the following extract from May's English version:

> but in Caesar now
> Remains not only a great General's name,
> But restless valour, and in war a shame
> Not to be Conqueror; fierce, not curbed at all,
> Ready to fight, where hope, or anger call
> His forward Sword; confident of success,
> And bold the favour of the gods to press:
> O'erthrowing all that his ambition stay,
> And loves that ruin should enforce his way:
> As lightning by the wind forced from a cloud
> Breaks through the wounded air with thunder loud,
> Disturbs the Day, the people terrifies,
> And by a light oblique dazzles our eyes,
> Not Jove's own Temple spares it.

And yet, for all the features that they have in common – from the sense of a personal purpose that co-operates impatiently with destiny (pressing 'the favour of the gods' and urging 'his active star') to the image of lightning bursting from the clouds – the overall effects of the two passages are quite different. May's loose pentameter couplets, with their run-on lines and frequent caesuras, accumulate the details of a damning portrait of a proud and cruel soldier who enjoys the havoc caused by his rise to power. Marvell's verse advances unhurriedly in alternating octosyllabic and hexasyllabic couplets, each couplet metrically self-contained and each pair of couplets embracing a single sentence. It is as if the mind pauses to allow each new fact or idea to settle into place before the next is brought forward for consideration. This impression is reinforced by the interruption of the narrative in order to reflect upon the political lessons of Cromwell's career. There is a moral challenge in both his triumph over rivals in the parliamentary ranks (lines 15–16) and his elimination of the king (lines 23–4), but the matter-of-fact ''Tis' which introduces the narrator's comments on these actions in lines 17 and 25 recognizes the realities that override orthodox scruples. It is only natural for a man of 'courage high' – exceptional in character and therefore not bound by conventional rules – to find the constraints imposed by competitors in his own party (the 'emulous') even more irksome than the obstacles placed in his path by enemies. And if it is as pointless to condemn his behaviour in dividing a 'fiery way' through 'his own side' as it would be to pass moral judgement on the lightning for rending the clouds, it is equally mad to 'resist or blame' the inevitable climax of blasting

'Caesar's head'. Acceptance of natural and political facts is not the same as approval, however, and only if 'angry heaven' is interpreted as the righteous wrath of the Christian God can the poem so far be read as a celebration rather than an appraisal of Cromwell's impact upon history. Marvell may be remembering Marchamont Needham's contribution to the Engagement controversy in a pamphlet of 1650 entitled *Case of the Commonwealth of England stated or the Equity Utility and Necessity of a submission to the present Government* – 'It must needs be . . . madness to strive against the stream for the upholding of a power cast down by the Almighty' – but the classical decorum of the 'Ode', which carefully avoids Christian references elsewhere, makes it unlikely that lines 25–6 are intended to confirm Commonwealth propaganda rather than recognize a political *fait accompli*.

It is above all, perhaps, Marvell's extension of May's concluding simile that distinguishes his approach to his subject from that of the source-passage in *Pharsalia*. The fierce, bold, and ambitious Caesar remains on the plane of human endeavour, and is therefore open to ethical evaluation; the phenomenon of Cromwell, pursuing its 'fiery way' and 'burning through the air', seems to be beyond the reach of approbation or 'blame'. But the analogy of lightning provides only one means of formulating a response to Cromwell's story, and with his usual agility at avoiding oversimplification, Marvell shifts his perspective to the human qualities of his poem's protagonist and the moral implications of his success:

And, if we would speak true,
Much to the man is due,
Who, from his private gardens, where
He lived reservèd and austere,
As if his highest plot
To plant the bergamot,
Could by industrious valour climb
To ruin the great work of time,
And cast the kingdoms old
Into another mould.
Though justice against fate complain,
And plead the ancient rights in vain:
But those do hold or break
As men are strong or weak.
Nature, that hateth emptiness,
Allows of penetration less:
And therefore must make room
Where greater spirits come.
What field of all the Civil Wars,

Where his were not the deepest scars?
And Hampton shows what part
He had of wiser art,
Where, twining subtle fears with hope,
He wove a net of such a scope,
That Charles himself might chase
To Carisbrooke's narrow case.

The first line clearly registers the poet's concern to weigh up all aspects of the situation; and in what follows the process of emergence from 'the shadows' is recapitulated once more. Although there is nothing reprehensible in living 'reservèd and austere' in 'his private gardens', 'industrious valour' cannot rest content with schemes to 'plant the bergamot' – commonly known as 'the pear of kings', a nice play on words which gives edge to the phrase 'highest plot' – but must fulfil itself by uprooting monarchy, that 'great work of time'. An image derived from the iron foundry (lines 35–6) effectively distances Cromwell's later achievements from his earlier horticultural pursuits, and suggests that the arts required to refashion the state are more strenuous than the 'inglorious arts of peace'. In the lengthiest of his commentaries on the narrative (lines 37–44), the speaker reveals an ability to come to terms with the harsh facts of experience which is in sharp contrast to the pious evasiveness of the Nymph's insistence that 'E'en beasts must be with justice slain.' His unsentimental acknowledgement of the realities of political power was already available in the equally terse wording of May's translation – 'the sword's power all right / Confounds by force' – and the same ideas were to be set out systematically a year later by Thomas Hobbes in *Leviathan*: 'The Obligation of Subjects to the Sovereign, is understood to last as long, and no longer, than the power lasteth, by which he is able to protect them.' Hobbes's theory of sovereignty is based on a materialistic conception of natural law, and Marvell shows himself to be a man of his time in drawing support for his political realism from the laws of physics. Just as Nature abhors a vacuum and does not permit two objects to occupy the same space (lines 41–2), so Charles I must cede his position in the state when the 'greater spirit' of Cromwell moves towards it (lines 43–4).

Returning to his survey of recent history, the poet finds evidence of Cromwell's superiority in the combination of physical and mental powers expected of the complete Renaissance man. On the field of battle, he gave 'the deepest scars'; and his 'wiser art' was demonstrated in the skill with which he was commonly (though erroneously) believed to have tricked Charles I into fleeing from his detention at Hampton Court to Carisbrooke Castle on the Isle of Wight, where he would be much more securely in the power of the army.

The specific references to Hampton and Carisbrooke lead from the abstractions of 'industrious valour' and 'ancient rights' into the direct evocation and analysis of the event which – to Marvell's scorn – Thomas May had balked at in *A Breviary of the History of the Parliament of England*:

That thence the royal actor borne
The tragic scaffold might adorn:
  While round the armèd bands
  Did clap their bloody hands.
He nothing common did or mean
Upon that memorable scene:
  But with his keener eye
  The axe's edge did try:
Nor called the gods with vulgar spite
To vindicate his helpless right,
  But bowed his comely head,
  Down, as upon a bed.
This was that memorable hour
Which first assured the forcèd power.
  So when they did design
  The Capitol's first line,
A bleeding head where they begun,
Did fright the architects to run;
  And yet in that the State
  Foresaw its happy fate.

For many readers, the tribute to the dignity with which Charles I went to the block is the emotional heart of the poem. Whether or not they betray Marvell's own deeper allegiance, which is being painfully discarded as the force of Cromwell's claims gathers momentum, these lines certainly serve to maintain the complexity of the demands made by the recent past on the sympathy and moral values – let alone the political commitment – of contemporary Englishmen. While there is no need, as some critics have done, to take the theatrical metaphors of 'royal actor' and 'memorable scene' as critical of Charles, the graceful composure of his final performance on the 'tragic scaffold' – so beautifully conveyed in the image of lines 63–4 – is a telling contrast to the more impetuous and assertive heroism of the man who 'Urgèd his active star' with 'industrious valour'. It is Marvell's extraordinary ability to forge such universal symbols of human behaviour and experience out of the particular historical moment –

without falsifying the complexities of that moment for those who are living through it – that raises the 'Ode' so far above other examples of occasional political poetry.

The second half of the passage turns from the 'memorable scene' itself to the significance of 'that memorable hour' for the future of the country – the repeated word marking a transition from the perspectives of aesthetic taste and human sympathy to that of practical politics. There is no blinking the fact that the republic is based on a 'forcèd power' and that the death of the king was necessary to assure the position of the usurpers. But just as the unearthing of a man's head during the excavations for a new temple of Jupiter was taken as an omen of the success of the Roman state, so the 'bleeding head' of Charles is the foundation upon which the English Commonwealth will be reared to greatness. In classical texts there is no suggestion that the head was 'bleeding' or that the architects fled from the portent in terror. The effect of adding these details is to reinstate the realism that was in danger of being sentimentalized away in the picture of the king bowing 'his comely head / Down, as upon a bed'. The architects of the Commonwealth are right to tremble at the step they have taken, even though that step may have been dictated by political necessity and may be vindicated by the 'happy fate' that lies in store for England.

The poem has now reached its turning-point. Marvell has completed his review of the past and taken full account of both 'ancient rights' and 'successful crimes', without 'apostatizing' from Jonson's art of the true poet and becoming merely 'the chronicler to Spartacus' like Tom May. He has not pretended that it is easy to establish an attitude to what has happened or that there is no challenge to moral complacency or human sensibility in recognizing – as he seems to do in the second half of the 'Ode' – that the best hope for the future lies in Cromwell. Some of the tension inevitably goes out of the poetry, now that a resolution has been reached in the struggle to accept that 'ancient rights' are not absolute, but 'do hold or break / As men are strong or weak', and that it is quite possible to pity 'helpless right' while admiring the 'greater spirit' that overthrows it. But although the tone changes from exploratory to celebratory, there is still keen scrutiny of Cromwell's conduct on his return to the political centre after a prolonged absence:

And now the Irish are ashamed
To see themselves in one year tamed:
    So much one man can do,
    That does both act and know.
They can affirm his praises best,

And have, though overcome, confessed
  How good he is, how just,
  And fit for highest trust:
Nor yet grown stiffer with command,
But still in the Republic's hand:
  How fit he is to sway
  That can so well obey.
He to the Commons' feet presents
A kingdom, for his first year's rents:
  And, what he may, forbears
  His fame, to make it theirs:
And has his sword and spoils ungirt,
To lay them at the public's skirt.
  So when the falcon high
  Falls heavy from the sky,
She, having killed, no more does search
But on the next green bough to perch,
  Where, when he first does lure,
  The falc'ner has her sure.

Many critics, remembering only the massacre at Drogheda, have detected irony at Cromwell's expense in the invocation of Irish testimony to his goodness and justice. But, as Wallace points out, it is the fitness for 'highest trust' displayed in his administrative capacity as Lord Lieutenant of Ireland, rather than his ruthlessness as a general, that is affirmed by those he has overcome. Marvell may well have had in mind contemporary reports that 'the Lord Lieu. hath so gallant a Discipline of his forces, that where his Lordship comes, he doth much get into the affections of the people' and that 'the Gentlemen and Commonalty of *Ireland* do generally comply and submit to the Lord Lieutenant's orders' (Wallace, p. 86).

Irony has also been suspected in the expressions 'Nor yet' and 'still' (lines 81–2), which are taken to imply doubts about Cromwell's willingness to remain 'in the Republic's hand'. Though an undercurrent of ambivalence need not be entirely suppressed here, the rhetorical tide seems to be flowing in the opposite direction, so that 'still' primarily has its common seventeenth-century meaning of 'always' and the force of 'Nor yet' is to refute the fears of those who expected the worst when the great soldier returned. For Cromwell has done nothing to shake the constitutional arrangements that prevailed in the summer of 1650 – arrangements accurately described in lines 85–90 and illustrated in the simile of the falcon: Cromwell embodies the executive power of the state, but holds it as the agent of the legislature (the Commons), which in turn derives its authority from the people. His military might ('his sword'), and both the 'fame' and the 'spoils' he has won with it, are laid at 'the Commons' feet' and 'the public's skirt' in symbolic gestures of subservience. But there is no denying that the stability of the system depends upon the sword, and therefore, Marvell implies, the country is fortunate that it is wielded by a man with a reputation for goodness and justice. The inadequacy of the falcon image in this respect enhances by contrast the magnanimity of Cromwell, whose submission to Parliament and people is an act of moral choice, whereas the obedience of bird to falconer is merely a conditioned response to training.

Marvell's clear-eyed analysis of the present situation also glances at possible future developments: the man who can 'so well obey' would be 'fit to sway' – fit to bear the 'highest trust' of supreme personal authority if the occasion arose. But for the moment, it is his rôle as military champion of the republic, rather than as potential dictator, that engrosses the poet's imagination:

What may not then our isle presume
While Victory his crest does plume?
  What may not others fear
  If thus he crowns each year?
A Caesar, he, ere long to Gaul,
To Italy an Hannibal,
  And to all states not free
  Shall climactéric be.
The Pict no shelter now shall find
Within his parti-coloured mind,
  But from this valour sad
  Shrink underneath the plaid:
Happy, if in the tufted brake
The English hunter him mistake,
  Nor lay his hounds in near
  The Caledonian deer.

The dream of a Protestant crusade to free France and Italy from the yoke of Roman Catholicism (lines 97–104) was actually being entertained in some quarters. Cromwell himself is reported to have remarked to one of his officers, 'Were I as young as you, I should not doubt, ere I died, to knock at the gates of Rome.' But Marvell's syntax betrays his scepticism about this dream even as he voices it – 'What may not . . . While . . .? What may not . . . If . . . ?' – and his classical allusions do not let us forget that any grand scheme of conquest may meet with either Caesar's success or Hannibal's ultimate failure. Nevertheless, there is nothing tentative about the prophecy of easy victory against Scotland (lines 105–12). No doubt many Englishmen who otherwise had serious reservations about Cromwell would have shared Marvell's enthusiasm at the prospect of swift defeat for a troublesome and untrustworthy neighbour. Exultant chauvinism affects the texture of the poetry, however, as moral and linguistic complexity are sacrificed in the glib image of the 'Caledonian deer' (possibly Charles II) pursued by the 'English hunter', and in the word play of 'parti-coloured', which exploits the supposed derivation of Pict from the Latin verb *pingere* ('to paint') and the tartan costume of the Highlanders ('the plaid') for narrowly satiric purposes.

Fortunately, the poem does not come to rest on this note, and Marvell's concluding apostrophe to Cromwell tempers the heroic vision with a pragmatic warning that the 'forcèd power' will survive only with continued military backing:

> But thou, the Wars' and Fortune's son,
> March indefatigably on,
>   And for the last effect
>   Still keep thy sword erect:
> Besides the force it has to fright
> The spirits of the shady night,
>   The same arts that did gain
>   A power, must it maintain.

Some of the moral tension also returns with the grim reminder of the cost in human life of casting 'the kingdoms old / Into another mould'. Cromwell will need the power ascribed to the naked sword in classical literature in order to keep at bay the 'spirits of the shady night' – the ghosts of the executed monarch and of those who died in the Civil Wars, which may well be imagined haunting him like the victims of Shakespeare's Richard III before the Battle of Bosworth Field. But the 'arts' of the exceptional man 'That does both act and know' have so far proved adequate to the task of sustaining the moral and military integrity of the new state, and Marvell allows the tone of admiration to dominate these closing lines.

It remains to consider briefly the significance of the epithet 'Horatian' in the title of the 'Ode'. The poet Horace had written a number of odes celebrating the victories of Caesar Augustus and the peace his rule brought to a Roman empire that had been torn apart by civil wars. But Horace was no 'servile wit, and mercenary pen'. Realist enough to know that men must adapt to the times, he could value the stability assured by autocracy without repudiating the ideals of the republican cause for which he had once taken up arms against the future Emperor Augustus. His urbane stance as the guardian of civilized tradition in a world changing under the impact of political necessity provided Marvell with a model for his measured – and some would say ambivalent, or even ironic – endorsement of Cromwell. And the lines on Charles I's death may owe a more specific debt to Ode 37 of Book I, in which Horace calls upon his companions to rejoice at Octavian Caesar's defeat of Cleopatra – the 'wild Queen' who sought to bring 'ruin to the Empire' – only to conclude with a noble tribute to her moral victory over her Roman captors by 'a finer style of dying'. There is one vital difference, however, between 'An Horatian Ode' and the poems it imitated: many of Horace's odes were public statements – the *Carmen Saeculare* was even commissioned by Augustus; Marvell's was never published in his lifetime and can hardly have been intended for the eyes of Cromwell himself. For all its rhetorical appeal to an audience at the beginning and its address to Cromwell at the end, it is essentially a private poem. But while the 'Ode' is by no means a straightforward panegyric to 'heaven's viceregent' (Berthoff, p. 60) and still less 'a sermon on the divine mission of Cromwell' (Friedman, p. 256), Marvell's Horatian poise should not be mistaken for 'an almost inhuman aloofness' (Legouis, p. 14), which results in a work of 'complete detachment and uncommittedness' (Leishman, p. 13). Its tensions and ambiguities are those of a mind engaging, reluctantly at first, with material that tests inherited values and conceptions, and arriving eventually at an accommodation with the disquieting circumstances that provoked it.

That this accommodation, reached at a moment of particular crisis in the nation's history, had not hardened into a firm commitment to the new order of things is evident from the different emphasis some five or six months later in 'Tom May's Death'. For, although Marvell had certianly not been guilty of prostituting his art in the interests of faction, the references to 'forsaken virtue's cause' and Spartacus, and the description of the true poet as one who 'Sings still of ancient rights and better times', suggest that he had had to suppress more of himself than was comfortable in responding so positively to the 'greater spirit' of 'restless Cromwell' and was undergoing a reaction. And whether or not his political opinions were influenced by his subsequent employment at Nun Appleton, it is clear that the example of Lord Fairfax's withdrawal from public life encouraged the side of his temperament which loved 'the shadows'. The poems he addressed to Fairfax, however, contrive to celebrate the values associated with retirement without ignoring the contrary moral and psychological pull towards active involvement.

'Upon the Hill and Grove at Bilbrough' takes as its subject one of the former general's rural haunts, and appropriately adopts an emblematic method which invites the reader to 'see' and 'learn', in contrast to the more dynamic narrative method of 'An Horatian Ode', with its opening injunction to 'appear':

1

See how the archèd earth does here
Rise in a perfect hemisphere!
The stiffest compass could not strike
A line more circular and like;
Nor softest pencil draw a brow
So equal as this hill does bow.
It seems as for a model laid,
And that the world by it was made.

2

Here learn, ye mountains more unjust,
Which to abrupter greatness thrust,
That do with your hook-shouldered height
The earth deform and heaven fright,
For whose excrescence, ill-designed,
Nature must a new centre find,
Learn here those humble steps to tread,
Which to securer glory lead.

The 'perfect hemisphere' of Bilbrough and the rugged outlines of 'mountains more unjust' have obvious analogues in human society, where some men practise the restraint characterized in the image of the 'stiffest compass' and others thrust themselves 'to abrupter greatness'. It is tempting to suspect something more specific behind this comparison and to read a rebuke to Cromwell's impatience with 'the inglorious arts of peace' into the adjuration to be content with the 'securer glory' of humility. The conceit that the hill might have served as a model for the creation of the spherical universe is developed in the second stanza into an adverse comment on the disorientating effect of those who deform the earth and frighten heaven with their unnatural aspiration. Like the Mower, whose mind has been 'so displaced' that he will never find his home – and like a nation that loses its moral and political bearings when the 'great work of time' is ruined by violent revolution – Nature itself must seek 'a new centre' because the 'ill-designed' contours of the mountains have distorted the circular perfection of the original world.

In the next stanza, the landscape becomes expressive of a human personality – graciously hospitable, courteous, and generous in its concern for the welfare of inferiors:

3

See what a soft access and wide
Lies open to its grassy side;
Nor with the rugged path deters
The feet of breathless travellers.
See then how courteous it ascends,
And all the way it rises bends:
Nor for itself the height does gain,
But only strives to raise the plain.

This technique of emblematic description had been developed by Sir John Denham in *Cooper's Hill*, one of the most influential poems of the 1640s. Marvell took his cue from the following passage, but with greater poetic tact he avoided the explicitness with which Denham identifies the true subject of his flattery:

With such an easy, and unforc'd Ascent,
Windsor her gentle bosom doth present:
Where no stupendous Cliff, no threatening heights
Access deny, no horrid steep affrights,
But such a Rise, as doth at once invite
A pleasure, and a reverence from the sight.
Thy Master's Emblem, in whose face I saw
A friend-like sweetness, and a King-like awe;
Where Majesty and love so mixed appear,
Both gently kind, both royally severe.

Marvell maintains the integrity of the descriptive mode in stanza 4, while managing to convey both the public eminence which Fairfax shares with the hill and the contrast with more ambitious men, who dare heaven like the famous peak in the Canary Islands:

4

Yet thus it all the field commands,
And in unenvied greatness stands,
Discerning further than the cliff
Of heaven-daring Tenerife.
How glad the weary seamen haste
When they salute it from the mast!
By night the Northern Star their way
Directs, and this no less by day.

Standing in 'unenvied greatness', because he has chosen to lay aside his powerful position in the state, the man who once commanded the field in a military sense remains an inspiration to his countrymen, just as Bilbrough Hill is a beacon to 'weary seamen'.

The poet now turns from the hill to the clump of trees on its summit and for the first time introduces direct references to Lord Fairfax and his wife, who belonged to the Vere family:

5

Upon its crest this mountain grave
A plume of agèd trees does wave.
No hostile hand durst ere invade
With impious steel the sacred shade
For something always did appear
Of the great Master's terror there:
And men could hear his armour still
Rattling through all the grove and hill.

6

Fear of the Master, and respect
Of the great Nymph, did it protect,
Vera the Nymph that him inspired,
To whom he often here retired,
And on these oaks engraved her name;
Such wounds alone these woods became:
But ere he well the barks could part
'Twas writ already in their heart.

The echo of his rattling armour is a timely reminder of the 'great Master's' ability to strike 'terror' into the hearts of enemies; and the information that 'he often here retired' to be with his wife subtly suggests that the fiercer attributes of the soldier have always been complemented and fed by the domestic and private aspects of his personality. (In the Latin epigram 'In Duos Montes', also addressed to Fairfax, Marvell associates him with a similar combination of contrasting qualities represented by Almscliff and Bilbrough Hill:

The former stands untamed with towering stones all about;
  The tall ash tree circles the pleasant summit of the other.
On the former, the jutting stone stands erect in stiffened ridges:
  On the latter, the soft slopes shake their green manes.

...

That is lofty, steep, uneven, and arduous:
  This is sloping, gentle, soft, and pleasing.
Nature joined dissimilar things under one master.)

The Petrarchan conceit that the name of 'the great Nymph' was already engraved in the hearts of the trees before Fairfax could cut it in their barks leads to an extended passage of personification:

7

For they ('tis credible) have sense,
As we, of love and reverence,
And underneath the coarser rind
The genius of the house do bind.
Hence they successes seem to know,
And in their Lord's advancement grow;
But in no memory were seen,
As under this, so straight and green;

8

Yet now no further strive to shoot,
Contented if they fix their root.
Nor to the wind's uncertain gust,
Their prudent heads too far intrust.
Only sometimes a fluttering breeze
Discourses with the breathing trees,
Which in their modest whispers name
Those acts that swelled the cheek of fame.

After the typically wry glance at the fancifulness of the literary device – ' 'tis credible' – Marvell proceeds to use it very subtly to broach the issue of Fairfax's decision to give up his public career. Since the trees embody the genius or guardian spirit of the family, they are responsive to the 'successes' that lead to 'their Lord's advancement', and under this particular head of the house have grown 'straight and green' as never before. But like him, they have become wary of the 'uncertain gust' that blows through the world of ambitious striving and are happy to 'fix their root' in this secluded spot. All the same, the past is not easily forgotten and 'their modest whispers' cannot quite disguise a hint of nostalgic pride in naming 'Those acts that swelled the cheek of fame'.

That hint is then taken up by the trees in the nearest approach the poem makes to a critical view of Fairfax's retirement:

9

'Much other groves', say they, 'than these
And other hills him once did please.
Through groves of pikes he thundered then,
And mountains raised of dying men.
For all the civic garlands due
To him, our branches are but few.

Nor are our trunks enow to bear
The trophies of one fertile year.'

The 'branches' and 'trunks' of the grove he has retreated to are made to seem poor compensation for the 'civic garlands' and 'trophies' that he might have continued to win in 'one fertile year' in the 'other groves' of action. Somewhere in the background lies the thought that the hero is honoured by the community he has served: to give up winning garlands and trophies is to give up serving the state. But having tactfully distanced himself from such reflections by the witty expedient of a clump of talking trees, the poet is able to intervene in his employer's defence and conclude the poem with an astute compliment to his moral character:

10
'Tis true, ye trees, nor ever spoke
More certain oracles in oak.
But peace, (if you his favour prize):
That courage its own praises flies.
Therefore to your obscurer seats
From his own brightness he retreats:
Nor he the hills without the groves,
Nor height, but with retirement, loves.

The physical properties of the hill and grove at Bilbrough – which can literally both raise to prominence and conceal from view – are cleverly exploited to catch the complex personality of a man whose achievements are paradoxically enhanced by his modest retreat 'from his own brightness'.

Although an admonitory tone breaks in at the end of both 'An Horatian Ode' and 'Upon the Hill and Grove at Bilbrough' – 'But thou, the Wars' and Fortune's son'; 'But peace, (if you his favour prize)' – and although there are undercurrents which subvert any tendency towards simple panegyric, Marvell is careful to preserve an impersonal stance and to avoid disturbing the surface decorum of the narrative and emblematic modes. Formally, both poems are objective appraisals of the choices exemplified in Cromwell's climb to glory and Fairfax's retirement to 'obscurer seats'. 'The Garden' – whether or not it belongs to the Nun Appleton years, as most critics assume – contributes to the same debate, but divorces it from the context of politics and presents a case for the contemplative life in the guise of a first-person experience. 'Eyes and Tears', 'To His Coy Mistress', and 'The Mower's Song' should serve to warn us, however, that 'I' in Marvell's poetry is a rhetorical device for exploring the possibilities of literary traditions, rather than a vehicle for autobiography. And indeed, 'The Garden' is the richest and most brilliantly orchestrated of all his lyrics, drawing with extraordinary wit and delicacy upon a wide spectrum of literary genres and philosophical ideas. Poems on such subjects as the country life, retirement, contemplation, and solitude (including three with the title 'The Garden' by James Shirley, Joseph Beaumont, and Abraham Cowley) abounded in the middle decades of the century, and reflected a variety of attitudes – sensual, aesthetic, moral, and religious – to the ideal of withdrawing from the cares of active life.

Marvell's poem needs to be approached initially in the light of what Maren-Sofie Røstvig has called the *beatus ille* tradition, from the words which open Horace's Second Epode with an apostrophe to the happy man who enjoys the blessings of rural obscurity and tranquillity. The conception of the Happy Man, safe in his peaceful haven from the pressures of court and city, has obvious affinities with pastoral. But as developed by seventeenth-century translators and imitators from passages in the Latin works of Horace, Virgil, Claudian, Seneca, and Martial, the *beatus ille* poem differed from pastoral in one important respect: the speaker was not a naïve shepherd or mower, but a man or woman of taste and sophistication who, like Fairfax, had the wisdom to reject the busy world for a more truly satisfying way of life. The contrast which usually remains implicit in pastoral becomes a major feature of poems like Thomas Randolph's 'An Ode to Mr. Anthony Strafford to hasten him into the Country' or Katherine Philips's 'A Country Life':

> How sacred and how innocent
>   A country-life appears,
> How free from tumult, discontent,
>   From flattery or fears!

In 'To Retiredness', Mildmay Fane's contentment derives largely from an awareness of what he has left behind:

> Thus out of fears, or noise of War,
> Crowds, and the clamourings at Bar;
> The Merchant's dread, th' unconstant tides,
> With all Vexations besides;
> I hug my Quiet, and alone
> Take thee for my Companion,
> And deem in doing so, I've all
> I can True Conversation call.

Edward Benlowes concludes his long metaphysical poem, *Theophila*, with two cantos entitled 'The Sweetness of Retirement' and 'The Pleasure of Retirement'. A supporter of the king like Fane, he speaks for many defeated royalists who sought refuge and solace in the countryside:

> Thus go we, like the heroes of old Greece,
> In quest of more than golden fleece,
> Retreating to sweet shades, our shatter'd thoughts we piece.
> (Canto XII, stanza 21)

Fane's volume of poetry, *Otia Sacra*, was printed in 1648, and *Theophila*, though not published until 1652, was being circulated in manuscript before 1650. The two poets were presumably acquainted, since Benlowes sent a presentation copy of *Theophila* to Fane; and Fane was the brother-in-law of Lord Fairfax. Marvell was certainly familiar with Benlowes's work and would most probably have had access to *Otia Sacra* during his time at Nun Appleton. His employer was himself occupied with a manuscript volume of translations from the Bible, which he called 'The Employment of my Solitude', and a collection of poems, which he called 'The Recreations of my Solitude'.

Reverberations from the works of such writers echo through the first two stanzas of 'The Garden':

1

> How vainly men themselves amaze
> To win the palm, the oak, or bays,
> And their uncessant labours see
> Crowned from some single herb or tree,
> Whose short and narrow vergèd shade
> Does prudently their toils upbraid,
> While all flow'rs and all trees do close
> To weave the garlands of repose.

2

> Fair Quiet, have I found thee here,
> And Innocence, thy sister dear!
> Mistaken long, I sought you then
> In busy companies of men.
> Your sacred plants, if here below,
> Only among the plants will grow.
> Society is all but rude,
> To this delicious solitude.

The pun in the exclamatory 'How vainly' has the function of establishing both a tone of voice and a point of view. It first of all passes moral judgement on those who feed their vanity by seeking acclaim for their achievements in war ('the palm'), public service ('the oak'), or the arts ('bays'). Such a judgement condemns the motives, but not the activities. The alternative meaning, however, denounces the activities themselves as futile, and implies that the speaker is judging the whole world of active endeavour according to some superior code of values. This second attitude is the one adopted in many *beatus ille* poems, and is responsible for the view that Quiet and Innocence are to be found (if at all on earth) *only* 'among the plants'. The 'uncessant labours' and 'toils' of men like Cromwell, who have no option but to 'march indefatigably on', are mocked (upbraided) by the inadequacy of their reward – a wreath woven from the leaves of 'some single herb or tree'. It would be more prudent of them to avoid the snares (another meaning of 'toils') of public life and be content with 'the garlands of repose'. But, as in stanza 8 of 'Upon the Hill and Grove at Bilbrough', the idea of prudence ('wise discernment') cannot quite be purged of its more negative overtones ('politic calculation'). In fact, ironic amusement pervades the speaker's presentation of the familiar *beatus ille* arguments. To pretend that men exert themselves to win a crown of leaves for the sake of the shade it affords, rather than for the honour it confers, is whimsically comic. To feign surprise that quiet and innocence are to be found not 'in busy companies of men', but in the seclusion of a garden, is a piece of false naïvety. And the concluding paradox that society – civilization itself – is almost uncivilized in comparison with the delights of solitude wittily exposes the premise on which the poetic cult of solitude rests: that to enjoy it man must renounce his human citizenship. Once again, Marvell has contrived to express both the attitudes inherent in a genre and his reservations about them at one and the same time.

In the next two stanzas, he plays with the genre identified by Frank Kermode as that of 'the naturalist paradise' (p. 229). The vision of a golden time when lovers could follow their sexual inclinations free from all stain of guilt is summed up in Lovelace's 'Love Made in the First Age':

> Love, then unstinted, love did sip,
> And cherries pluck'd fresh from the lip,
>   On cheeks and roses free he fed;
> Lasses like Autumn plums did drop,
> And Lads indifferently did crop
>   A flower and a maidenhead.

Instead of merely supplying metaphors for human behaviour, the plants themselves offer an example to the hesitant mistress in Thomas Stanley's 'Love's Innocence':

See how this Ivy strives to twine
Her wanton arms about the Vine,
And her coy lover thus restrains,
Entangled in her amorous chains;
See how these neighb'ring Palms do bend
Their heads, and mutual murmurs send,
As whisp'ring with a jealous fear
Their loves, into each other's ear.
Then blush not such a flame to own
As like thy self no crime hath known;
Led by these harmless guides, we may
Embrace and kiss as well as they.

This kind of libertinism was countered by poems which explicitly banished sex from the landscape of retirement. In 'The Garden', for example, James Shirley is determined that 'No woman here shall find me out.'

Marvell, too, seeks the garden as a refuge from women, but takes the ingenious step of transferring his affections to the trees:

3

No white nor red was ever seen
So am'rous as this lovely green.
Fond lovers, cruel as their flame,
Cut in these trees their mistress' name.
Little, alas, they know, or heed,
How far these beauties hers exceed!
Fair trees! wheres'e'er your barks I wound,
No name shall but your own be found.

4

When we have run our passion's heat,
Love hither makes his best retreat.
The gods, that mortal beauty chase,
Still in a tree did end their race.
Apollo hunted Daphne so,
Only that she might laurel grow.
And Pan did after Syrinx speed,
Not as a nymph, but for a reed.

The idea of carving the trees' own names in their bark takes the wit of stanza 6 of the Bilbrough poem one step further towards conscious absurdity; and the comic effect is reinforced by the puns on 'heat' (ardour or a course in a race) and 'race' (a contest of speed or a family line), and by the solemn assurance that the true purpose of the gods' pursuit of Daphne and Syrinx was to metamorphose them into the 'lovely green' which is so much more attractive than the white and red of female beauty.

Up to this point, Marvell has been distilling into more concise terms the argument of his own Latin poem, 'Hortus'. He now abandons both his Latin text and the mode of half-facetious argument for a sustained lyrical evocation of the garden experience:

5

What wondrous life in this I lead!
Ripe apples drop about my head;
The luscious clusters of the vine
Upon my mouth do crush their wine;
The nectarene, and curious peach,
Into my hands themselves do reach;
Stumbling on melons, as I pass,
Ensnared with flowers, I fall on grass.

6

Meanwhile the mind, from pleasure less,
Withdraws into its happiness:
The mind, that ocean where each kind
Does straight its own resemblance find,
Yet it creates, transcending these,
Far other worlds, and other seas,
Annihilating all that's made
To a green thought in a green shade.

7

Here at the fountain's sliding foot,
Or at some fruit-tree's mossy root,
Casting the body's vest aside,
My soul into the boughs does glide:
There like a bird it sits, and sings,
Then whets, and combs its silver wings;
And, till prepared for longer flight,
Waves in its plumes the various light.

There is a remarkable thickening of texture and deepening of tone as a bold reorientation is effected. The emphasis on retreat gives way to a celebration of the 'wondrous life' enjoyed in the garden. In generic terms, the Horatian, Petrarchan, and Ovidian contexts of the first four stanzas are replaced by a context of Christian Platonism. Although the ideas and images in these three stanzas have been traced to sources in works by ancient, mediaeval, and Renaissance philosophers and theologians, the basic concepts of Neoplatonism on which they draw were widely diffused in the intellectual climate of the age and had already made their influence felt in the evolution of the retirement poem.

Fundamental to all branches of Platonic thought is the belief in two worlds – the world of Being and the world of Becoming. The latter, the material world which is apprehended by the senses and subject to time and decay, is merely a copy of the former, the realm of eternal and unchanging Ideas, which can only be apprehended by the intellect. These Ideas or Forms are the perfect archetypes – the true reality – of which all the individual things in the world of Becoming are imperfect shadows. The distinction between the material and the ideal bred contradictory attitudes towards both the inferior world of created nature and the human senses through which it is mediated. On the one hand, following Plato's *Phaedo*, matter could be regarded as gross and contaminating, a prison and a temptation to the soul that is forced to endure life 'here below' (a phrase with Platonic connotations from stanza 2 of 'The Garden'). This ascetic view prevails in some of Marvell's lyrics, particularly the more Puritan ones, in which 'the object vain' elicits only tears of complaint from the perceiving eyes, the Resolved Soul stoutly defends itself against the 'batteries of alluring sense', and the fastidious dewdrop-soul timidly slights 'the purple flow'r' and shuns 'the sweet leaves and blossoms green' of its bodily tenement. On the other hand, following Plato's *Timaeus*, the material world could be valued as a faithful reflection of the higher realm, in which real beauty and goodness were made apprehensible to man through his senses. This view lies behind the Mower's delight in the 'sweet fields' tended by the 'fauns and fairies' of unspoiled nature and the claim that pastures, caves, and fountains all sing of Pan's glory at the end of 'Clorinda and Damon'.

The goal of human existence for the Platonist is to rise above the temporal shadows and contemplate eternal reality. The ascetic waits for the release of the soul by death and practises an arduous self-discipline; the alternative route is to trust the senses and allow the soul to be drawn up in ecstasy towards the Idea of Beauty which informs the myriad manifestations of beauty in created nature. Spenser develops a Christianized version of the Platonic ascent in 'An Hymn of Heavenly Beauty':

> The means, therefore, which unto us is lent
> Him to behold, is on his works to look,
> Which he hath made in beauty excellent,
> And in the same, as in a brazen book,
> To read enregistered in every nook
> His goodness, which his beauty doth declare;

For all that's good is beautiful and fair.

Thence gathering plumes of perfect speculation
To imp the wing of thy high flying mind,
Mount up aloft, through heavenly contemplation,
From this dark world, whose damps the soul do blind,
And, like the native brood of Eagle's kind,
On that bright Sun of glory fix thine eyes,
Clear'd from gross mists of frail infirmities.
(lines 127–40)

This progress from sensual perception ('on his works to look') via mental activity (the 'perfect speculation' of the 'high flying mind') to spiritual contemplation (fixing the eyes of the soul on 'that bright Sun of glory') parallels the structure of the experience pursued in stanzas 5, 6 and 7 of 'The Garden'. Other mid-century retirement poets besides Marvell – though not all from a Neoplatonic perspective – were fascinated by the relationship of man's body and his higher faculties, and especially by the mind's responsiveness to its material surroundings. In her aptly titled poem, 'A Reverie', Katherine Philips is content to indulge the play of 'Fancy' stimulated by the natural setting:

The beauteous quiet of a summer's day,
A brook which sobb'd aloud and ran away,
Invited my repose, and then conspir'd
To entertain my Fancy thus retir'd.

Spiritual improvement, rather than pleasure, is sought from the sights and sounds of the countryside by the more sober Rowland Watkyns in 'The Poet's Soliloquy':

It is my comfort to escape the rude
And sluttish trouble of the multitude:
Flowers, rivers, woods, the pleasant air and wind,
With Sacred thoughts, do feed my serious mind.

Closer to Marvell is the philosopher and poet, Henry More, who has a Platonist's ambivalence about the beauties of nature – enjoying, but soon tiring of the superficial delights offered by the 'secret shade far moved from mortal's sight', where he has laid his 'wandering limbs' on 'the cool grass':

The place a while did feed my foolish eye
As being new, and eke mine idle ear
Did listen oft to that wild harmony
And oft my curious phansie would compare

How well agreed the Brook's low muttering Base,
With the birds' trebles perch'd on higher place.

But sense's objects soon do glut the soul
Or rather weary with their emptiness;
So I, all heedless how the waters roll
And mindless of the mirth the birds express,
Into my self 'gin softly to retire
After hid heavenly pleasures to enquire.
('Cupid's Conflict', lines 31–42)

Edward Benlowes, having recorded in Canto XII of *Theophila* the philosophical musings that result when the flowery earth 'doth us gently woo, / On her embroider'd mantle to / Repose', goes on in Canto XIII to describe a religious experience inspired by the natural scene:

Where roots of Nature, flow'rs of Grace,
And fruits of Glory bud. A glimpse of Heav'n the place.

This the Spring-Garden to spiritual eyes,
Which fragrant scent of gums outvies;

. . .

What ecstasy's in this delicious grove!
(stanzas 22–6)

Marvell expertly guides his poem into the Christian Platonist stream of retirement poetry by means of a transitional passage on the 'wondrous life' of the senses. Stanza 5 evokes the first stage of the ascent to ecstasy, but it is also the climax of the burlesque of the naturalist paradise begun in stanzas 3 and 4. The metaphors of 'Love Made in the First Age', which equate the pleasures afforded by cherries, roses, and plums with the pleasures afforded by women, and the amorous behaviour of ivy, vine, and palms in 'Love's Innocence', are wittily adapted into a vision of sensual fulfilment unsullied by the libertinism of Lovelace and Stanley: gratefully submitting to the seductive attentions of the vegetable world, the poet may stumble, be ensnared, and fall – but unlike that other Fall in another Garden, this fall 'on grass' incurs no guilt and has no dire consequences. Other poets in both the libertine and Platonic traditions had dwelt on the physical enjoyment to be had in a 'delicious grove', but Marvell's lines vibrate with a richly imagined sensuousness which is distinctively his own. Tactile qualities, in particular, are brilliantly conveyed by the images themselves and by alliteration ('Ri*p*e a*pp*les dro*p*'; '*l*us*c*iou*s* *cl*uster*s* . . . *c*ru*sh*'; '*m*y *m*outh'), assonance ('l*u*scious cl*u*sters . . .

cr*u*sh'), and the syntax which delays the verb 'reach' until the end of its couplet in order to imitate the action described.

The Platonic contemplator, however, is eventually glutted by feeding his 'foolish eye' with 'sense's objects', and like More retires into himself to seek 'hid heavenly pleasures'; or as Benlowes puts it, 'To gadding Sense we shut the door; / Rich in our mind alone' (Canto XII, stanza 38). Marvell's speaker also withdraws from the 'pleasure less' of the senses to the 'happiness' of the mind – implying some qualitative difference between the conditions denoted by the terms 'pleasure' and 'happiness'. But the introductory word 'Meanwhile' indicates simultaneous not successive activities: the body has not been abandoned for the mind, and still has a contribution to make to the experience of stanza 6. The operations of the mind are manifold. According to Platonist epistemology, it contains innate ideas of everything in the material realm – just as the ocean was supposed to contain counterparts to all the species that existed on land – and so can recognize the objects presented to it by the senses. It also has the faculty of bringing into being ideas that have no parallel in the world known to the senses – imaginary 'worlds' and 'seas' of its own creating. For Sir Philip Sidney, in his famous Elizabethan defence of poetry, it is the cultivation of this dimension of the mind that distinguishes the art of the poet from other intellectual disciplines:

> Only the poet, disdaining to be tied to any such subjection, lifted up with the vigour of his own invention, doth grow in effect into another nature, in making things either better than Nature bringeth forth, or, quite anew, forms such as never were in Nature. (*An Apology for Poetry* (1595))

But there is a price to be paid for the creative miracle performed by the mind: it involves the annihilation of 'all that's made', a transcending of the resemblances of this world, among which we live out our earthly lives. Like the 'delicious solitude' of stanza 2, the withdrawal into that garden of the mind where the process of artistic creation takes place may entail a retreat from the responsibilities of everyday life. The ambivalence at the heart of Platonism – and at the heart of each of Marvell's explorations of the problem posed by the alternatives of action and retirement – lodges in the ambiguous connotations of 'all that's made'. If created nature, including everything implied by the phrase 'busy companies of men', is merely an insubstantial shadow-play, then art or ecstasy are not an escape but an approach to the real. If 'all that's made', including human history, is a book in which men can read the workings of divine providence, then to transcend or annihilate it by the power of imagination – to 'sing . . . numbers languishing' – is open to the charge of escapist self-indulgence. Such oppositions are not permitted to assert themselves here, however, as harmony rather than discord is established in the richly evocative image of 'a green thought in a green shade'. Marvell often dramatizes the disjunction between the human creature and the hostile or indifferent universe of space and time: the 'opposition of the stars' prevents the consummation of an impossibly ideal love; the Mower can find no remedy for his 'hot desires' in 'cool cave' or 'gelid fountain'; the lover urges his Coy Mistress to an act of desperate resistance to the 'slow-chapped power' of time. In 'The Garden', he makes his most concerted attempt to heal the breach and restore that apprehension of unity – between body and mind, man and environment – the loss of which sent the Mower wandering in homeless exile. Many ingenious and esoteric explanations of the line 'To a green thought in a green shade' have been devised, but however much it may resonate with symbolic meanings, its extraordinary hold over the imagination comes from the simple conjunction of thought and shade, internal and external modes of reality, simply expressed in monosyllables. The force of 'Meanwhile' is now apparent. Mind and senses are interdependent, mysteriously fused in a moment of vision: thought taking its colour from the body's perception of the surroundings and the surroundings receiving value as they assume the status of an idea in the human mind.

In stanza 7, Marvell draws upon traditional features of the experience of the 'Hortulan saints' – Maren-Sofie Røstvig's name for poets like More and Fane, who sought 'the vision of ultimate reality' (p. 133) in the contemplative quiet of a garden or a rural retreat. The figure of the soul as a bird was a commonplace of Neoplatonic writing. So, too, was the image of the 'various light' into which the one light of the godhead is dispersed among the creatures of this world. And the 'mossy root' of a tree was a favourite location for the garden-mystic's spiritual ecstasies. But even as Marvell uses these images to enact the ascent from lower to higher realms of being, his natural scepticism about any such attempts to transcend the complexities of the human condition begins to reassert itself. His bird-soul has some of the self-absorption and self-satisfaction of the speakers in 'Eyes and Tears' and 'A Definition of Love', as it 'whets, and combs its silver wings'. Not yet 'prepared for longer flight' – whether the final departure from the body in death, a mystical union with the One, or a poetic flight of greater ambition – it is happy to wave 'in its plumes the various light', simultaneously reflecting the beauty of Nature and showing off its own. It is as if, after the deeper involvement and sense of union with Nature in stanza 6, the speaker regains his detached and slightly amused perspective on the excesses of literary raptures (like Benlowes's 'glimpse of Heav'n') and offers us his own series of variations on the conventional images of ecstatic transcendence.

The change of tense in stanza 8 signals a return to wry reflection, as the poet compares the garden experience to the pleasures of solitude in that earlier 'garden-state' (both a condition of being and a political economy) which has hovered at the edge of our consciousness ever since the poem began:

8

Such was that happy garden-state,
While man there walked without a mate:
After a place so pure, and sweet,
What other help could yet be meet!
But 'twas beyond a mortal's share
To wander solitary there:
Two paradises 'twere in one
To live in paradise alone.

In his lyric meditation, 'The Garden', Joseph Beaumont had been 'haunted with the thought of that / Heaven-planted Garden', now lost; and Abraham Cowley, in his, was to hit upon the same idea as Marvell – that God gave Adam a garden 'as the chief Help and Joy of human life . . . first, ev'n before a Wife'. Marvell's tone is lighter, however, and accepts with good grace – and a humorous glance at the Book of Genesis – that mortal man must make the best of the 'helpmeet' provided for him in the descendants of Eve.

The 'How well' which brings us back into the actual garden of the here-and-now contrasts pointedly with the 'How vainly' of stanza 1, and confirms the reconciliation with the facts of life in time towards which the speaker has been leading us:

9

How well the skilful gardener drew
Of flowers and herbs this dial new,
Where from above the milder sun
Does through a fragrant zodiac run;
And, as it works, the industrious bee
Computes its time as well as we.
How could such sweet and wholesome hours
Be reckoned but with herbs and flowers!

The 'skilful gardener' may be taken as the Creator himself (recalling Francis Bacon's remark that 'God Almighty first planted a garden'), in which case 'this dial new' refers to the whole realm of nature; or the reference may be confined to the specific garden, with its floral sundial, in which the poet has been musing. Whichever meaning is uppermost, the images of 'fragrant zodiac' and 'industrious bee' combine to express an acceptance of man's lot as a labourer among the transient 'flowers and herbs' of a postlapsarian world. The hours spent in a garden of contemplation (symbolic or real) are 'sweet and wholesome': they do give us a respite in which, in Benlowes's words, we can 'piece' our 'shatter'd thoughts'. But just as the bee cannot avoid computing time along with the sweetness it gathers from 'thyme' (a pun sanctioned by the parallel Latin text of 'Hortus'), so we cannot escape for more than a brief interlude from the demands of that 'public stage' where history is made and the passing years are reckoned with the rise and fall of kingdoms, rather than with 'herbs and flowers'. Wistfully, and in a mood of gentle irony, Marvell tempers his age's dream of re-entering a lost garden of innocence and repose with the relentless knowledge that, for all its attractions, solitude is not a practical substitute for society, and an existence simplified by the exclusion of business and sex and the processes of time is 'beyond a mortal's share'.

The discovery of the New World had for a while seemed to open up the possibility of realizing that dream. There, across the Atlantic, where ancient fables had placed the Fortunate Isles and the Garden of the Hesperides, were lands of unspoiled natural abundance where European man might make a fresh start. The Bermudas, also known as the 'Somers Islands' from Sir George Somers who was shipwrecked there on his way to the plantation in Virginia in 1609, had been celebrated as an earthly paradise in a poem by Edmund Waller published in 1645:

> Bermudas, walled with rocks, who does not know?
> That happy island where huge lemons grow,
> And orange trees, which golden fruit do bear,
> The Hesperian garden boasts of none so fair;
> Where shining pearl, coral, and many a pound,
> On the rich shore, of ambergris is found.
>
> . . .
>
> With candied plantains, and the juicy pine,
> On choicest melons, and sweet grapes, they dine,
> And with potatoes fat their wanton swine.
> Nature these cates with such a lavish hand

Pours out among them, that our coarser land
Tastes of that bounty, and does cloth return . . .

. . .

Heaven sure has kept this spot of earth uncursed,
To show how all things were created first.
('The Battle of the Summer Islands')

Juan Bermudez had discovered the islands in 1515, but it was the English who colonized them in the seventeenth cenury. The spirit which inspired some of the early settlers is demonstrated in *A Plaine and True Relation of the Goodness of God towards the Sommer Ilands, written by way of exhortation, to stirre up the people there to praise God* (1621) by Lewis Hughes, Puritan minister to the islanders: 'Consider also the goodness of God, in reserving and keeping these Islands, ever since the beginning of the world, for the English Nation, and in not discovering them to any, to inhabit but to the English.'

Marvell's acquaintance with the Bermudas was not limited to such poetic and religious idealizations. John Oxenbridge, in whose household he lived as tutor to William Dutton, had sought refuge there from the persecution of Puritans under Archbishop Laud in the 1630s, and served on the London Commission for the Government of the Bermudas during Marvell's residence with him. Members of the Trott family, for whom Marvell was to write epitaphs, were shareholders in the Company set up to exploit the islands' resources, and the poet himself later sat on a parliamentary committee of inquiry into the affairs of the settlement. Recently, critics have been at pains to point out that historical realities, which must have been familiar to Marvell, had long since exploded the myth of a paradise where nature and man could flourish in divinely mediated harmony. Early reports of the rich supply of ambergris and pearls proved to be exaggerated and the human community was subject to the same religious and political tensions as the mother country. How far such knowledge should be allowed to colour a reader's response to 'Bermudas' is not easy to determine:

Where the remote Bermudas ride
In the ocean's bosom unespied,
From a small boat, that rowed along,
The listening winds received this song.
'What should we do but sing his praise
That led us through the watery maze,
Unto an isle so long unkown,
And yet far kinder than our own?

Where he the huge sea-monsters wracks,
That lift the deep upon their backs,
He lands us on a grassy stage,
Safe from the storms, and prelate's rage.
He gave us this eternal spring,
Which here enamels everything,
And sends the fowl to us in care,
On daily visits through the air.
He hangs in shades the orange bright,
Like golden lamps in a green night,
And does in the pom'granates close
Jewels more rich than Ormus shows.
He makes the figs our mouths to meet,
And throws the melons at our feet,
But apples plants of such a price,
No tree could ever bear them twice.
With cedars, chosen by his hand,
From Lebanon, he stores the land,
And makes the hollow seas, that roar,
Proclaim the ambergris on shore.
He cast (of which we rather boast)
The gospel's pearl upon our coast,
And in these rocks for us did frame
A temple, where to sound his name.
Oh let our voice his praise exalt,
Till it arrive at heaven's vault:
Which thence (perhaps) rebounding, may
Echo beyond the Mexique Bay.'
 Thus sung they, in the English boat,
An holy and a cheerful note,
And all the way, to guide their chime,
With falling oars they kept the time.

The central portion of the poem is 'sung' by the only group of voices among Marvell's gallery of dramatic mouthpieces. This is significant, because the song is modelled on the biblical psalms which were a prominent feature of public worship in the Reformed churches and which were a major influence in shaping the collective identity of those Puritans who – like Lewis Hughes – saw a special rôle for themselves and the English nation in the working out of God's providential purposes. The words that rise from the 'small boat' echo the Psalmist's recurring paean of praise and gratitude for the direct care that the Lord takes of his chosen people. It is the emphasis on the active intervention of God, who is the subject of almost all the main verbs in lines 9–32, that makes this evocation of natural plenty so different from otherwise similar passages in 'The Battle of the Summer Islands' and stanza 5 of 'The Garden'. The singers are confident that this isle 'so long unknown' has been reserved as a haven for them from the dual dangers of the sea and religious intolerance (lines 5–12), and that all their needs, physical (lines 13–28) and spiritual (lines 29–32), are anticipated. The parenthesis in line 29 – '(of which we rather boast)' – sounds like an explicit rebuke to men of Waller's kind, who were evidently less interested in the gospel than in the material value of the 'shining pearl' and the 'many a pound' of ambergris 'on the rich shore', or in the commercial opportunities for trading the fruits that Nature poured out 'with such a lavish hand'. The other parenthesis in line 35 – '(perhaps)' – can hardly have the sceptical force attributed to it by some critics, since it belongs inside a song characterized by a firm faith in the supreme and benevolent power of God. It is truer to the Puritan psychology of the singers to see it as a proper reluctance to presume upon God's intentions concerning their own part in spreading the Reformation across 'the Mexique Bay' into Roman Catholic territories. The mixture of tenses in the psalm of thanksgiving subtly establishes the attitude of these exiles to the divine control of their destiny: the God who 'led' them safely from their former island home, 'gave' them 'this eternal spring', and 'cast' the gospel's pearl upon their coast had long ago prepared this new home for them – 'in these rocks . . . *did frame* / A temple'; provision continues to be made for them in the present by the God who 'sends' them fowl, 'hangs' oranges in the trees, and 'plants' priceless apples; the future – in which the witness of their praise '(perhaps) . . . may' be used by God to further his will – is also best left in his hands. Through their religious faith, these men feel at home in a universe that is neither indifferent nor hostile. They are in permanent possession of that sense of well-being and harmony – of 'fellowship' with nature, to use Damon's word – which is irretrievably lost to the Mower and accessible only in privileged moments to the speaker of 'The Garden'.

But such faith, as the history of the Bermudas settlement had sadly demonstrated, is difficult to sustain in a world constantly threatened with disruption by 'wanton troopers' and 'Juliana's scorching beams'. Perhaps this is why the song comes to us from far away, where 'the remote Bermudas' ride like ships at anchor, 'unespied' in the vast expanse of 'the ocean's bosom', and emanates mysteriously from 'a small boat' to an audience of 'listening winds'. The concluding quatrain grounds the vision of paradise in the more familiar reality of an 'English boat' and a note that is reassuringly 'cheerful' as well as 'holy'. As their oars and voices rise and fall in perfect unison 'all the way', however, these Puritan pilgrims recede into the distance to become emblems of that longed-for harmony of mind and body, man and nature, which preoccupied so many in an age which was to find its greatest artistic expression in an epic entitled *Paradise Lost*.

7

Paradise's only map

During two years or so as tutor to Mary Fairfax, Marvell had the opportunity both to ponder the implications of a great man's decision to retreat 'from his own brightness' and also to experience for himself a more extended period of withdrawal from 'the busy companies of men' than that afforded by the 'sweet and wholesome hours' spent in a garden. *Upon Appleton House*, the longest of his non-satirical poems, brings together the objective panegyric mode of 'Upon the Hill and Grove at Bilbrough' and the subjective lyric mode of 'The Garden' in what is gradually being recognized as his most sustained and richly imagined evocation of those complex relationships between mind and body, self and world, art and nature, which constitute the human creature's perception and assessment of the physical, moral, spiritual, social, political, and literary dimensions of reality. It belongs to a tradition of poetic celebrations of the houses of eminent men which has been traced back to classical times (Allen, pp. 119–24; Leishman, pp. 253–60), and which was given a new lease of life in the seventeenth century as a means of honouring the values associated with the country estates of the English aristocracy and gentry. Ben Jonson's 'To Penshurst', which set the pattern for later writers, begins by contrasting the unpretentious architecture of this 'ancient pile' with the ostentation of the new age –

> Thou art not, Penshurst, built to envious show,
> Of touch, or marble; nor canst boast a row
> Of polished pillars, or a roof of gold –

and goes on to catalogue the excellences of the 'walks', the 'Mount', the 'copse', the 'lower land', the 'middle grounds', the 'ponds', and the 'orchard'. In this well-ordered setting, the virtues of a feudal way of life still flourish: loyalty and grateful service on the part of 'the farmer, and the clown' and bounty and hospitality on the part of the lord. The children of the noble household 'have been taught religion' and can learn from their parents' example the 'mysteries of manners, arms, and arts'. House and family together stand as a bulwark against contemporary materialism in Jonson's closing lines:

> Now, Penshurst, they that will proportion thee
> With other edifices, when they see

Those proud, ambitious heaps, and nothing else,
May say, their lords have built, but thy lord dwells.

This method of praising a benefactor by praising the style of his house, the management of his estate, and the generosity of his house-keeping was continued by Thomas Carew and Robert Herrick, and provided a suitable vehicle for Marvell's most elaborate compliment to the Fairfax family.

The earlier view that *Upon Appleton House* is 'uneven, muddled' (Bradbrook and Lloyd Thomas, p. 38) has been challenged by critics who have admired the 'remarkable display of architectonic virtuosity' (Hodge, p. 141), in which the 'progress is logical and systematic, the transitions clearly marked, the balance exact' (Røstvig, in Friedenreich, p. 255). Whether or not one is convinced by Røstvig's analysis of lines 81–680 into blocks of twenty-five stanzas arranged in a 'pattern of interlinked circles', it is evident that the poem does have a carefully designed thematic structure derived from its much briefer Jonsonian model. Stanzas 1–10 are concerned with the house itself; stanzas 11–35 with an incident from the heroic past of the Fairfax family; stanzas 36–46 with the gardens and with the character of the current master; stanzas 47–81 with a tour of the estate beyond the gardens; stanzas 82–93 with praise of Mary, to whom, as an only child, the future of both the estate and the Fairfax line will be entrusted; and stanzas 94–7 with the symbolic status of the 'lesser world' of Nun Appleton as 'paradise's only map'.

It is in the long interlude from stanza 47 to stanza 81, during which panegyric gives way to lyric and the poet's persona emerges as observer and protagonist in a first-person encounter with nature, that the country house poem 'grows into something new and different' (Hibbard, p. 169). Marvell developed this section out of Jonson's cursory survey of the environs of Penshurst by exploiting another poetic topic that had come into its own in the first half of the seventeenth century. Pastoral in origin, the description of the sights and sounds enjoyed in the course of a day's walk in the countryside had been utilized by Milton in 'L'Allegro' and 'Il Penseroso', by Lovelace in 'Aramantha', and by Benlowes in the last two cantos of *Theophila*. Marvell's speaker follows precisely the same route as Lovelace's heroine, from flower-garden to meadows and thence into the wood and down to the river-side. Within the compass of one ideal day at Nun Appleton, however, seasons pass (the grass is mown, tedded, 'piled in cocks', and carted away; the flood-waters of the Wharfe rise and recede), while events from the universal history of mankind (the Fall, the Exodus, Noah's Ark) and the recent civil wars in England are metaphorically enacted. This fluid treatment of time is symptomatic of the imaginative processes at work in a poem which plays tricks with the eye's perception of the material world, effects disorientating shifts of style and of visual and mental perspective, and renders uncertain the distinctions between subject and object, image and reality, literary and literal orders of truth.

There has been a certain amount of debate as to which house Marvell was familiar with, since it is known that some time in the 1640s or 1650s the original Nun Appleton – modest in size and partly built from the stones of a neighbouring nunnery – was replaced by a more imposing brick structure. Unless poetic licence was allowed to distort the facts in the interest of either irony or flattery, the 'sober frame' which stimulated the descriptive and meditative ingenuities of the first ten stanzas must have been the earlier building:

1

Within this sober frame expect
Work of no foreign architect,
That unto caves the quarries drew,
And forests did to pastures hew,
Who of his great design in pain
Did for a model vault his brain,
Whose columns should so high be raised
To arch the brows that on them gazed.

The conventional scorn for 'envious show' is the occasion for a series of observations on the disfigurement of the natural landscape (in a couplet that recalls the conclusion of 'A Dialogue between the Soul and Body'), the aspiration and creative agony of the architect, and the response of the spectator, whose eyebrows are raised both in the physical act of gazing upwards and in astonished disapproval at the vanity of such a 'great design'.

In stanza 2, Nature administers an apt reproof to the vaulting ambition manifested in the 'unproportioned dwellings' of mankind: 'The low-roofed tortoises do dwell / In cases fit of tortoise shell.' At Nun Appleton, in salutary contrast, a sense of both physical and moral proportion prevails:

4

But all things are composèd here
Like Nature, orderly and near:

. . .

6

Humility alone designs

Those short but admirable lines,
By which, ungirt and unconstrained,
Things greater are in less contained.
Let others vainly strive t' immure
The circle in the quadrature!
These holy mathematics can
In every figure equal man.

Just as the 'beasts are by their dens expressed' in stanza 2, the modest 'lines' of the family seat reveal the moral qualities of the Fairfaxes and provoke a complex network of allusions to the unsolved problem of squaring the circle (i.e. transforming a circle into a 'quadrature' or square of the same area), to the ideal proportions of the human form, and to the symbolism which associated the mortal body with the square and the immortal soul with the circle.

Already in these first few stanzas, the poem's preoccupation with ideas and images of enclosure and restraint has been established: the vaulted brain, the shell of the tortoise, the 'hollow palace' of the tomb (stanza 3), the 'bee-like cell' of Romulus (stanza 5), the boundaries set to human nature by the physical and symbolic properties of circle and square. The 'holy mathematics' of stanza 6 generates the playful conceit that when the 'Master *great*' squeezes himself into the narrow confines of his home, 'the swelling hall / Stirs, and square grows spherical' (stanza 7), and hints at a correspondence between the formal qualities of the house and the formal qualities of the poem in which it is being celebrated. The 'short but admirable lines' of *Upon Appleton House* – Marvell's favourite octosyllabics, which are one foot shorter than the iambic pentameter usually deemed appropriate for 'great' subjects – are carefully built into stanzas comprising four rhyming couplets. (Such a symmetrically satisfying arrangement of eight-syllable lines into eight-line units had been called 'the square or quadrangle equilater' in Puttenham's treatise, *The Arte of English Poesie* (1589).) And since Marvell probably had William Davenant's recently published epic, *Gondibert*, in mind as a literary counterpart to the ostentatious architecture of the age (Wallace, pp. 239–40), his earlier references to 'this sober frame' and the 'orderly and near' composition to be found 'here' may be taken to indicate a community of values between general's house and tutor's poem. Of both, it could be said that 'Things greater are in less contained.' Certainly, the method of constructing self-contained stanzas out of couplets which are themselves metrically and syntactically self-contained gives an epigrammatic tightness to a poetic enterprise of considerable length and scope.

Having paid the customary tribute to the social virtues that survive at Nun Appleton and restated the theme of Nature's superiority to Art (stanzas 8–10), Marvell offers to entertain 'each pleasant footstep' of our prospective tour through the 'fragrant gardens, shady woods, / Deep meadows, and transparent floods' with an account of the 'progress of this house's fate' – a narrative 'opportunely' prompted, like so much else in the poem, by something that catches his eye. The sight of 'that neighbour-ruin' – 'The quarries whence this dwelling rose' – brings to mind an event which laid the foundations of the family fortunes, and the connotations of the word 'house' are accordingly extended to take in the Fairfax dynasty as well as the Fairfax residence. In 1518, Sir William Fairfax of Steeton had married Isabel Thwaites, a wealthy orphan whose inheritance included Bishop's Hill in York and the estate at Denton mentioned in stanza 10. It was shortly after the dissolution of the monasteries in the reign of Henry VIII that the ownership of Nun Appleton was transferred to the Fairfaxes – a fact alluded to in stanza 35. There is no documentary evidence, however, to authenticate the story that Marvell tells in stanzas 12–34. As Lee Erickson has demonstrated, *Upon Appleton House* itself is the only authority for the account of Isabel's confinement by the abbess of the Cistercian nunnery and the subsequent legal order which sanctioned Sir William's forcible rescue of his bride (p. 160). It looks as if Marvell seized upon the historical marriage and the existence of the 'neighbour-ruin' as the basis for a heroic myth that would serve the dual purpose of glorifying the house of Fairfax and providing a foil for the present Lord's retirement from active life.

It is with the benefits of a religious seclusion that the representative of 'the subtle nuns' begins her seduction of 'the blooming virgin Thwaites':

13

'Within this holy leisure we
Live innocently, as you see.
These walls restrain the world without,
But hedge our liberty about.
These bars inclose that wider den
Of those wild creatures callèd men.
The cloister outward shuts its gates,
And, from us, locks on them the grates.'

But an innocence which depends on the evasion of trial and danger rather than on self-control is merely 'a fugitive and cloistered virtue' – a perversion of true morality which gives itself away by its crafty perversion of language: it is really the nuns, not the world and its 'wild creatures', whom the walls and bars are designed to 'inclose'. Moreover, this is not a genuine retreat from worldliness, since the 'holy leisure' of the cloister breeds its own temptations, which are proffered with an ingratiating skill reminiscent of the voice of Created Pleasure. The inexperienced Isabel is no Resolved Soul, however, and by the end of stanza 25, 'The nun's smooth tongue has sucked her in.' Sir William hesitates – 'He would respect / Religion, but not right neglect' (stanza 29) – but eventually he breaks through the nunnery's double defence of walls and superstitions and carries off his prize (stanzas 32–4). His action is justified not only by the 'lawful form' granted by the court (stanza 30), but also by historical necessity. Like Cromwell who 'Urged his active star', he has a destiny to fulfil:

31
Is not this he whose offspring fierce
Shall fight through all the universe;
And with successive valour try
France, Poland, either Germany;
Till one, as long since prophesied,
His horse through conquered Britain ride?
Yet, against fate, his spouse they kept,
And the great race would intercept.

As the progenitor of a line of Protestant heroes culminating in the Lord General of the Puritan armies, it is appropriate that he should triumph symbolically over the 'wooden saints' and 'holy-water brush' of Roman Catholicism in the mock-heroic battle of stanza 32; and it is equally appropriate that the nunnery and its lands should come into the possession of his family as a result of the Reformation. The words that bring this section of the poem to a close render with epigrammatic vigour the verdict of history:

Though many a nun there made her vow,
'Twas no religious house till now.

One of the famous descendants of the union of Sir William and Isabel was responsible for the sight which next engages the poet's attention:

36
Who, when retired here to peace,
His warlike studies could not cease;

But laid these gardens out in sport
In the just figure of a fort;
And with five bastions it did fence,
As aiming one for every sense.

Whichever Fairfax this was, his career was a mirror image of that of the Cromwell of 'An Horatian Ode', who 'could not cease / In the inglorious arts of peace' and emerged from his 'private gardens' to pursue 'adventurous war'. There is no question of judging between Cromwell's emergence and Fairfax's withdrawal, however, since both were heroic choices made by men who merited the 'immortal garland' which Milton had said was 'to be run for, not without dust and heat'. The distinction the poem invites us to consider is that between the morally enervating and life-denying enclosure of the nunnery and the well-earned retirement of a true Christian warrior who, like the Resolved Soul, maintains his vigilance against subversion by the five senses. Moral alertness need not preclude innocent enjoyment, of course, and Marvell plays along with the military conceit created by the gardener in his description of a day among the flower-beds (stanzas 37–40) – from dawn, when 'the morning ray / Hangs out the colours of the day', to dark, when the stars 'patrol' the night sky. Sensuous and witty pleasure reaches a climax in the 'fragrant volleys' with which Lord and Lady Fairfax are saluted as they inspect the 'parade' of flowers: 'Whose shrill report no ear can tell, / But echoes to the eye and smell'.

But such playful fantasy – harmless enough in itself – is put into perspective by the abrupt change of mood which accompanies the recollection of that other garden beyond the five bastions that 'fence' this private world – yet another of the enclosures of the poem:

41

Oh thou, that dear and happy isle
The garden of the world ere while,
Thou paradise of four seas,
Which heaven planted us to please,
But, to exclude the world, did guard
With watery if not flaming sword;
What luckless apple did we taste,
To make us mortal, and thee waste?

Identifying himself with the misery and guilt of his countrymen, the poet puts the metaphors that he had previously used 'in sport' at the disposal of a more sombre vision. War 'doth overgrow' the former 'nursery of all things green', and in place of 'garrisons' of flowers, 'We ordnance plant and powder sow' (stanzas 42–3). In this context, Fairfax's retreat to the secluded delights of Nun Appleton must once more come under scrutiny:

44

And yet there walks one on the sod
Who, had it pleasèd him and God,
Might once have made our gardens spring
Fresh as his own and flourishing.

There is certainly a note of regret here, in the thought of what might have been if the Lord General had chosen to assert rather than resign his power. But to read serious criticism of his behaviour into this passage, as some commentators do, is to ignore the force of the proviso in the second line. Marvell regarded history as the product of a complex and mysterious relationship between human initiative and divine will, and Fairfax was no more to be condemned for pursuing his personal destiny than Cromwell was for urging his active star or Sir William for taking measures to ensure that 'the great race' would not be intercepted by 'the subtle nuns'. The active and contemplative lives are not antagonistic absolutes, but alternative paths by which individual human beings may fulfil the purposes of God. What matters, in any particular set of circumstances, is the degree of moral responsibility that goes into the act of choosing between them; and the next stanza leaves no doubt as to Marvell's respect for the man who laid down supreme command of the parliamentary forces with the words, 'What my conscience yields unto as just and lawful, I shall follow; and what seems to me to be otherwise I will not do. My conscience is not satisfied, and therefore I must desire to be excused':

45

For he did, with his utmost skill,
Ambition weed, but conscience till –
Conscience, that heaven-nursèd plant,
Which most our earthly gardens want.
A prickling leaf it bears, and such
As that which shrinks at every touch;
But flowers eternal, and divine,
That in the crowns of saints do shine.

This tribute concludes the didactic and panegyric phase of the poem, and with the 'invisible artillery' of the eyesight turning 'the battery of its beams' from 'proud Cawood Castle' – once the seat of the Archbishops of York and so still an emblem of prelatical ambition – to play 'o'er the meads below', Marvell effects a skilful transition to the more subjective and lyrical episode that is to follow.

Up to this moment, our consciousness of the speaker as a presence has largely been derived from the frequent demonstrative phrases – 'this sober frame', 'that neighbour-ruin', 'these gardens', 'these bastions' – and the repeated adverb 'here', reinforced by imperatives, exclamations, and questions. These linguistic features have served to root the poet's discourse in a specific location and to establish both his involvement with his material and his relation with his auditors. Now, at last, Marvell projects this persona in the pronoun 'I', and although he remains merely an observer for the time being, the emphasis begins to shift from the things observed to the process of observation. The keynote of this section is sounded in the word 'unfathomable', which looks forward to the metaphor of the sea, and also suggests the mysteriousness of the visionary realm we are about to enter: 'And now to the abyss I pass / Of that unfathomable grass.' Both aspects of the word are picked up in the next stanza:

> To see men through this meadow dive,
> We wonder how they rise alive,
> As under water, none does know
> Whether he fall through it or go.

To contemplate this wonderland of changing perspectives, where normal hierarchies break down, is as disorientating as being 'under water': men are 'like grasshoppers', 'grasshoppers are giants', 'green spires' of grass become 'precipices tall' (stanza 47); meadows become oceans, mowers become 'mariners', flowers are plucked from the sea-bed (stanza 48).

Nature and art are confused as experience takes on the qualities of a theatrical illusion: 'No scene that turns with engines strange / Does oftener than these meadows change.' A masque of 'tawny mowers' is said to 'enter next' – like a group of performers at a court entertainment – only to be metamorphosed into a band of Old Testament Israelites, before whom 'the grassy deeps divide' as they make their way 'on foot through a green sea' (stanza 49). Within a few lines, they have become cruel soldiers who 'massacre the grass along', and in case that metaphor should seem excessively fanciful, one of them holds up his scythe with 'the edge all bloody'. The 'bloody Thestylis' greedily snatches up the fledgeling rail that has been accidentally butchered, and delivers a jolt to our sense of literary propriety by breaking the fictional frame of the poem with a jibe at the imagination that created her:

51
When on another quick she lights,
And cries, 'He called us Israelites;
But now, to make his saying true,
Rails rain for quails, for manna, dew.'

Undaunted by this interruption, the poet continues to read the scene before him metaphorically. The fate of the hapless bird, whose humble obscurity could not save it from the ravages of war, is philosophically lamented (stanza 52); the meadow strewn with mown grass is likened to a battle-field, 'quilted o'er with bodies slain', and the women turning the hay with pitch-forks are said to 'represent the pillaging' (stanza 53); the 'victors' of this harvest triumph dwindle, by way of a comic allusion to the fragrance of 'Alexander's sweat', into mere rustic revellers dancing 'in fairy circles' (stanza 54).

The climax of the mowing sequence is reached in the visual and historical kaleidoscope of stanza 55:

When after this 'tis piled in cocks,
Like a calm sea it shows the rocks,
We wondering in the river near
How boats among them safely steer.
Or, like the desert Memphis sand,
Short pyramids of hay do stand.
And such the Roman camps do rise
In hills for soldiers' obsequies.

Such is the deceptive nature of the senses, that we seem to see the boats on the river beyond the flat expanse of the meadows actually sailing between the piles of hay – an astonishing sight which appears to give literal force to the metaphors of 'calm sea' and 'rocks'. And in the long view of history, the great civilizations of the past – with their pyramids and burial mounds – belong to the same transient order as the grass that falls before the mower's scythe.

The theatrical engines turn again and the 'scene' presents a 'new and empty face of things', which begets a series of fantastic images, culminating in a picture of the villagers' cattle let out to graze on the common land from which the hay has been cleared away – an idea which prompts mischievous glances at the egalitarian policies of the Levellers and an incident from Davenant's *Gondibert*. Seen from the distance, these cattle inspire the most bizarre and brilliant of all Marvell's manipulations of perspective:

58
They seem within the polished grass

A landskip drawn in looking-glass,
And shrunk in the huge pasture show
As spots, so shaped, on faces do –
Such fleas, ere they approach the eye,
In multiplying glasses lie.
They feed so wide, so slowly move,
As constellations do above.

Reduced in size like a landscape-painting reflected in a mirror, they seem no bigger than spots on human faces or than fleas placed ready for inspection in multiplying glasses (the forerunner of the microscope) but not yet subjected to magnification. Their almost imperceptible progress as they graze their way in formation across the featureless plain – beautifully suggested in the slow movement of the poetic line, with its long open vowels and medial caesura – reminds the observer of the passage of the stars across the night sky. Such a stanza is more than a dazzling display of metaphysical wit. In its demonstration of the capriciousness of the faculties of sight and imagination, which can bring cattle and fleas and constellations together in a single act of perception, it becomes a paradigm of Marvell's expressive methods and of his central insight as a poet: that nothing is quite what it appears to be in a world which changes shape and size and significance as we alter our angle of vision upon it or filter it through the transforming medium of the human mind.

The 'pleasant acts' of this pageant of nature are concluded by the flooding of the river, which 'makes the meadow truly be / (What it but seemed before) a sea'. Once again, the distinction between the actual and the metaphorical is obliterated and the familiar scene dissolves into a series of paradoxes: 'The river in itself is drowned'; eels 'bellow in the ox'; boats sail over bridges; fishes scale the stables (stanzas 59–60). While the traditional symbolism of civil war as a flood has an obvious bearing on this evocation of a world turned upside down, it is an impoverishment of the meadow-sequence to reduce it to 'an allegorical masque' of recent English history, in which the slaughtered rail is to be interpreted as Charles I, the 'quick' rail seized by Thestylis as Scotland, and the inundation as conflict within the parliamentary ranks (Allen, pp. 131–8). More important than any specific contemporary allusion is the overwhelming impression of disorder created by the break-down of stable relationships between perceiver and perceived, language and reality, poet and poem.

It is from such disorder that refuge is sought among the trees:

61

But I, retiring from the flood,
Take sanctuary in the wood,
And, while it lasts, myself embark
In this yet green, yet growing ark.

This second occurrence of the pronoun 'I' inaugurates a new movement in which the speaker will become much more intimately involved with the natural surroundings. No longer permitted to stand apart as an ingenious reporter of the passing show, he is himself threatened by the rising flood-water, and his retreat into 'this yet green, yet growing ark' signals another attempt to 'restrain the world without'. The pun on the word 'embark' brings into sharp focus the dual impulse to preserve the self intact by riding out the flood of the age's turmoil and to lose the self by merging it with nature. Either course lacks that positive commitment to the larger purposes of God and history discernible in Noah's preservation of 'all creatures' from the Flood of the Old Testament. And a similar judgement is silently implied in the emblem of the 'double wood of ancient stocks' which converges at a single point, just like the long 'pedigrees' of the Fairfaxes and the Veres: 'Of whom though many fell in war, / Yet more to heaven shooting are' (stanza 62). Indistinguishable both symbolically and syntactically – does the relative pronoun refer back to the 'double wood' or the 'two pedigrees'? – forest trees and family trees fulfil, according to their kind, the alternative destinies of self-sacrifice and self-perfection. This timely reminder of the moral perspectives established earlier in the poem is the prelude to Marvell's version of the woodland experience found in the works of Milton, Lovelace, and Benlowes.

As we might expect, he eases us into it by way of visual and imaginative transformations. What 'the eye' perceives from a distance as a single mass ('wood not trees'; 'one great trunk') has a quite different appearance close to: 'within / It opens passable and thin.' A simile which likens the widely spaced trunks to 'the Corinthian porticoes' of classical architecture slides into a metaphor which conceives them as the 'columns' of a 'temple green', beneath which 'the wingèd choirs / Echo about their tunèd fires' (stanzas 63–4). We have entered a cathedral of the woods – one of nature's sacred places, like the 'close covert by some brook, / Where no profaner eye may look' in Milton's 'Il Penseroso'. Within its precincts, as in the 'well ordered stately grove' of Lovelace's 'Aramantha', are to be found emblems of a natural order that has been lost to the world outside. The nightingale sings 'the trials of her voice', while 'listening elders prick the ear' (stanza 65); the stock-doves, 'whose fair necks are graced / With nuptial rings', offer a 'sadder, yet more pleasing sound' (stanza 66); the 'careless' poet catches a precious glimpse of the 'hatching throstle's shining eye' through 'the hazels thick' and witnesses the spectacle of the heron teaching its young to fly (stanza 67). These are not random observations, but a coherent vision of life's generative cycle: the single nightingale, the married doves, the thrush sitting on its eggs, the parent heron encouraging its offspring to be independent of the nest.

In the next three stanzas, an ideal of good government is discovered in 'the hewel's wonders':

68

He walks still upright from the root,
Measuring the timber with his foot,
And all the way, to keep it clean,
Doth from the bark the woodmoths glean.
He, with his beak, examines well
Which fit to stand and which to fell.

The ambivalent language – 'upright', 'measuring', 'examines well', 'fit to stand' – presents the woodpecker simultaneously as a natural phenomenon, observed with loving accuracy, and as a moral force, whose activities are like those of a stern but incorruptible magistrate. After references to 'the axe' and the 'tainted side' of 'the hollow oak', it is difficult not to see a reaction to the beheading of Charles I in the couplet that concludes stanza 69: 'Who could have thought the tallest oak / Should fall by such a feeble stroke!' And although the quest for the precise identity of the 'traitor-worm' may be fruitless (the names of Strafford and Laud have been put forward), the next stanza has a political resonance which suggests that more is behind it than the generalized view of human sinfulness favoured by some interpreters:

70

Nor would it, had the tree not fed
A traitor-worm, within it bred,
(As first our flesh corrupt within
Tempts impotent and bashful sin).
And yet that worm triumphs not long,
But serves to feed the hewel's young,
While the oak seems to fall content,
Viewing the treason's punishment.

The harsh facts of the real world of politics are so transmuted in this woodland vision of a society kept clean by 'the holtfelster's care' that even the felling of 'the tallest oak' has a natural fitness and occasions no resentment.

In interpreting what he saw in the forest emblematically, Marvell had before him the example not only of other poets, but also of the natural philosophers of the seventeenth century, who acknowledged that the physical universe was a source of moral and spiritual wisdom as well as an object of scientific study. Bacon had set 'the book of God's works' side by side with 'the book of God's word' in his *Advancement of Learning* (1605), and Sir Thomas Browne had declared in *Religio Medici* (1643) that 'there are two Books from whence I collect my Divinity; besides that written one of God, another of His servant Nature, that universal and publick Manuscript, that lies expans'd unto the Eyes of all'. Robert Boyle, the famous experimental chemist, was to enjoin the readers of his *Occasional Reflections* (1665) to profit from the riches that lay unheeded around them:

> And indeed, the World is the great Book, not so much of Nature, as of the God of Nature, which we should find ev'n crowded with instructive Lessons, if we had but the Skill, and would take the Pains, to extract and pick them out: The Creatures are the true Aegyptian Hieroglyphicks, that under the rude form of Birds, and Beasts, &c. conceal the mysterious secrets of Knowledge, and of Piety.

It is to a place in such company that the poet lays claim when he describes himself as an 'easy philosopher', but the epithet should put us on our guard. This philosopher at ease – 'careless' was his word earlier – is also one who has come by his insights without the kind of efforts implied by Boyle's words 'Skill' and 'Pains'. Indeed, the whole passage has a playful air which suggests an element of self-mockery:

71

Thus I, easy philosopher,
Among the birds and trees confer.
And little now to make me wants
Or of the fowls, or of the plants:
Give me but wings as they, and I
Straight floating on the air shall fly:

. . .

72

Already I begin to call
In their most learn'd original:

And where I language want, my signs
The bird upon the bough divines.

As so often, Marvell treats his inherited material with a mixture of sympathy and scepticism. Lovelace's Aramantha had become 'conversant in lays / Of birds' when she fled to the 'yet living wood', and Milton had conjured up a 'strange mysterious dream' beneath the trees in 'Il Penseroso'. Man's yearning to recover a primal harmony with his environment – to be one with the fowls and plants – and to gain access to truths beyond the reach of reason found expression in such woodland ecstasies, and that yearning leaves its mark on *Upon Appleton House*. The fantasy of 'floating on the air' is wryly, but regretfully, subverted by the reservation, 'Give me but wings as they'; and to call the language of the birds 'their most learn'd original' is at once ironic (birdsong is far from scholarly) and a gesture towards the belief that the unfallen creation enjoys a purity of spiritual knowledge unattainable and inexpressible by sinful man.

The attempt to extract not just 'instructive Lessons', but also 'mysterious secrets' from the natural scene comes to a climax in stanza 73:

Out of these scattered sibyl's leaves
Strange prophecies my fancy weaves:
And in one history consumes,
Like Mexique paintings, all the plumes.
What Rome, Greece, Palestine, ere said
I in this light mosaic read.
Thrice happy he who, not mistook,
Hath read in Nature's mystic book.

But doubts must be entertained about any prophecies that are woven by 'fancy' and identified with the oracles inscribed on dead leaves and scattered by the enigmatic Sibyl of Cumae. And there is self-deflating irony in the extravagant assertion that all the wisdom of the ancient world can be read in the patterns created by sunshine dappling through foliage. Unlike the revelation contained in the Mosaic books of the Bible, this 'light mosaic' – as ambiguous as the phrase itself and 'light' in the same way that the philosopher was 'easy' – is too insubstantial to be of lasting significance. 'Thrice happy', indeed, would be the man who could decipher the hieroglyphics of 'Nature's mystic book' and be confident that he was 'not mistook'. But Marvell's faith in the mind's ability to be sure of anything is not strong enough for him to endorse his own half-comic claim to visionary gifts.

The poet now surrenders himself to sensuous enjoyment of nature:

'languishing with ease' upon 'pallets swoll'n of velvet moss', his 'panting brows' soothed by the breeze, he gratefully relaxes from the strain of mental activity under the influence of the 'cool zephyrs': 'Who, as my hair, my thoughts too shed, / And winnow from the chaff my head' (stanza 75). He feels as secure from 'the world' as the 'subtle nuns' were in their walled enclosure, and more secure than Damon, whose body and mind fell to the power of Juliana:

76

How safe, methinks, and strong, behind
These trees have I encamped my mind:
Where beauty, aiming at the heart,
Bends in some tree its useless dart.

Submitting himself totally to the 'silken bondage' of the woodbines and the 'gadding vines' – plants, as the speaker of 'The Garden' knew, are so much more rewarding than women – he fantasizes about escaping forever from the dangers of sexual and military warfare beyond the protective screen of the trees: 'And, oh, so close your circles lace, / That I may never leave this place' (stanza 77). As the flood recedes, to reveal a landscape cleansed and restored to pristine innocence, he quits his hilltop refuge and descends to the river, which is 'the only snake' in the paradise of 'these meads' and which becomes a perfect emblem of the identification of self with scene achieved in the act of reflection or contemplation: 'Where all things gaze themselves, and doubt / If they be in it or without' (stanzas 79–80). Garlanded 'with heavy sedge', like the river-god Camus in Milton's *Lycidas*, he devotes himself to fishing, that most leisurely of all occupations: 'Abandoning my lazy side, / Stretched as a bank unto the tide' (stanza 81).

Then, in a fine comic transition back to the panegyric mode, the tutor-poet is surprised out of his indolence by his pupil, and shamefacedly acknowledges his truancy from the responsibilities of adult life:

82

But now away my hooks, my quills,
And angles – idle utensils.
The young Maria walks tonight:
Hide, trifling youth, thy pleasures slight.
'Twere shame that such judicious eyes
Should with such toys a man surprise.

Even 'loose Nature' recollects herself at the approach of Mary Fairfax and a breathless hush falls over the evening scene. It is an enchanted moment, suspended 'betwixt the day and night', like that which attends the passage of the kingfisher, that 'sapphire-wingèd mist', when the shadows cast by the setting sun creep silently 'from underneath these banks' and extend like black shutters ('eben shuts') across the river (stanzas 84–6). A more conventional, less magical, tribute follows:

87

'Tis she that to these gardens gave
That wondrous beauty which they have;
She straightness on the woods bestows;
To her the meadow sweetness owes;
Nothing could make the river be
So crystal pure but only she;
She yet more pure, sweet, straight, and fair,
Than gardens, woods, meads, rivers are.

This may owe something to Waller's fanciful praise of Sacharissa in 'At Penshurst':

Her presence has such more than human grace,
That it can civilize the rudest place;
And beauty too, and order, can impart,
Where nature ne'er intended it, nor art.

But in Marvell's hands, it transcends the purpose of hyperbolical flattery and serves to concentrate in the person of Mary Fairfax all the qualities of the estate that has been celebrated at such length and with such ingenuity in the work that is now drawing to an end.

For 'The young Maria' is to carry the central significance of this supreme example of the country house poem. Unlike the nuns in their cloister and the poet in his ark of trees, she has not sought to 'restrain the world without', but has faced its temptations and overcome them. It is no accident that the images of stanza 90 recall the mock-heroic battle of the nunnery story: Mary has withstood the attacks and ambushes of young men, with their artillery of tears and sighs and praise. And she owes her readiness to meet this traditional test of virtue to the loving but firmly Puritan regime of the 'domestic heaven', where she has been 'nursed, / Under the discipline severe / Of Fairfax, and the starry Vere' (stanza 91). Such preparation was particularly needful for this young woman, since she has as heavy a burden of historical destiny to bear as her ancestor, Sir William, whose action had ensured the foundation of the 'great race' of the house of Fairfax. Because she is an only child, the future of the dynasty now depends on the kind of marriage she makes. Marvell discreetly contrives to compliment not only the daughter, but also the father, who had demonstrated his trust and devotion (and made her a more attractive match) by entailing part of the family estates upon her, rather than letting everything pass to the next male heir:

93
Hence she with graces more divine
Supplies beyond her sex the line;

. . .

While her glad parents most rejoice,
And make their destiny their choice.

'Meantime,' says the poet, Mary will continue her education among the fields and flowers of Nun Appleton: '(Till fate her worthily translates, / And find a Fairfax for our Thwaites)' (stanza 94).

Turning to address the 'woods, streams, gardens, meads', which surpass the most famed groves and gardens of antiquity and modern Spain as Mary surpasses 'all virgins', the poet contrasts the 'rude heap' of 'Gulfs, deserts, precipices, stone' that constitute the postlapsarian world with the landscape he has been evoking:

96
Your lesser world contains the same,
But in more decent order tame;
You, heaven's centre, Nature's lap,
And paradise's only map.

Nun Appleton may not be paradise, but in an England devastated by the taste of a 'luckless apple', it is the 'only map' Marvell and his employer's family have of that lost perfection. And with these thoughts, night closes in and the poem concludes with a set of virtuoso variations on its recurring motifs of inversion, enclosure, and correspondence:

97
But now the salmon-fishers moist
Their leathern boats begin to hoist,
And like Antipodes in shoes,
Have shod their heads in their canoes.
How tortoise-like, but not so slow,
These rational amphibii go!
Let's in: for the dark hemisphere
Does now like one of them appear.

The verdict of Marvell's most sustained meditation on the question that most preoccupied him as a lyric poet seems to be that a human being like Lord Fairfax, who has played an active part on the public stage and earned his retirement, or like Mary Fairfax, who is preparing herself for the time when she will take up her appointed rôle, has the right to enjoy the peaceful seclusion of such an earthly paradise as Nun Appleton. But its oblique judgement on himself – effected with humour and self-mockery, but nonetheless serious – is that in the end it is not enough to be an 'easy philosopher' or to languish 'with ease', abandoning oneself to an existence of pleasure and leisure. The attempt to 'exclude the world' and construct a cloister or an ark for the preservation of the self is placed in a proper moral perspective by the very structure of this remarkable poem, which sets the experiences of the poet-tutor uncompromisingly between the panegyrics to the disciplined and heroic Fairfaxes, who are content to submit themselves to the will of God and 'make their destiny their choice'.

8

Panegyrics and satires

The poet who determines to enlist for active service on 'the public stage' must abandon not only the 'calm leisure' of 'some secret nest', but also the personal tensions and playful ironies of the lyric mode. Under the pressure exerted by the aims and methods of political rhetoric, analysis tends to give way to persuasion and ambiguity to be resolved into party oppositions. Nevertheless, the once commonly held view that the fruits of Marvell's commitment to the causes of the Protectorate and the Country party are of little interest has been challenged in recent studies (notably those by John M. Wallace, Annabel Patterson, and Warren Chernaik), which have recognized in the Cromwell poems of the later 1650s and the verse and prose satires of the 1660s and 1670s the same realism and the same creative questioning of literary tradition that characterizes his pastoral and Petrarchan masterpieces. This final chapter will provide a brief survey of Marvell's adaptation of the modes of panegyric, satire, and prose polemic to meet the changing political realities of the England of Oliver Cromwell and Charles II.

'The First Anniversary of the Government under His Highness the Lord Protector' was advertised in the official journal, *Mercurius Politicus*, in January 1655 and published in the same month by the Government printer, Thomas Newcomb. It seems likely, therefore, that Marvell's public tribute to the man whose fitness 'for highest trust' he had privately conceded in 'An Horatian Ode' was issued with a propaganda purpose and with the approval of the authorities. In order to understand its nature as a literary and a political document, it is necessary to know something of Cromwell's career since his victory over Charles II at Worcester in September 1651. Bribery and nepotism were rife among the surviving members of the Long Parliament – The Rump – and Cromwell eventually lost patience with this increasingly unpopular body. On 20 April 1653, he called in his soldiers and brought its rule to an abrupt end. Fearful that a freely elected House of Commons would reinstate the monarchy, the army leadership gathered together an assembly of godly men, which met for the first time on 4 July 1653. Millenarian excitement was running high, and Cromwell himself shared the expectation that the apocalyptic prophecies of the Scriptures were about to be fulfilled. In his address to the Nominated Parliament, he looked forward to the imminent establishment of the Kingdom of God, in which Christ would reign with his saints for a thousand years:

> I say, you are called with a high call; and why should we be afraid to say or think, that this way may be the door to usher in things that God hath promised and prophesied of, and so set the hearts of his people to wait for and expect? . . . Indeed I do think something is at the door. We are at the threshold, and therefore it becomes us to lift up our heads and to encourage ourselves in the Lord. And we have some of us thought it our duty to endeavour this way, not vainly looking on that prophecy in Daniel, *And the Kingdom shall not be delivered to another people.*

The radicals, led by a small but influential group of Fifth Monarchists who identified themselves as the saints of the prophecies, pushed for extreme reforms which threatened the legal system and the rights of property, and on 12 December the moderate members voted to dissolve the assembly and surrender their authority to Cromwell. On 16 December 1653, he accepted the title of Lord Protector under arrangements set out in a document known as the Instrument of Government. These provided for a balance of power between the Protector, a Council of State, and an elected House of Commons. When the first Protectorate Parliament met on 3 September 1654, however, it immediately introduced measures to restructure the constitution in its own favour. Exasperated by the recalcitrance of the new assembly, Cromwell dismissed it on 22 January 1655 and assumed direct military control through ten major-generals appointed as district governors.

When Marvell was composing his poem, presumably in the weeks preceding the anniversary of the Protectorate in December 1654, there was still a hope that the rift between Parliament and Protector could be healed and the new constitution made to work. Certainly the whole thrust of his celebration of the past year's achievements is directed towards rallying support behind the system of mixed government enshrined in the Instrument. And although his admiration for Cromwell himself is wholehearted – betraying none of the troubled ambivalence of 'An Horatian Ode' – 'The First Anniversary' is no mere court-poem of the kind perfected by Edmund Waller to forge an idealised image of the Stuart monarchy. Marvell's task as panegyrist to the Protector was to find ways of extending the sanction of heroic and mythic status to the rule of the man who had overthrown the 'ancient rights' of kingship without simply repeating the commonplaces of royalist eulogy, as Waller was to do in his own anniversary offering, 'A Panegyric to My Lord Protector'.

Taking his cue from the occasion of an anniversary, he begins by setting Cromwell apart from the ordinary race of men in his mastery of time. While others sink beneath 'the weak circles of increasing years', he alone 'with greater vigour runs, / (Sun-like) the stages of succeeding suns' and 'shines the jewel of the yearly ring' (line 1–12). In a bold figure, Marvell transfers to the Protector the traditional symbolism of the sun, not in order to invest him with the mystique of royalty, but to distinguish him from 'heavy monarchs' who 'make a wide return, / Longer, and more malignant than Saturn' (lines 13–16). The conventional correspondence between king and sun, which was a fundamental feature of Stuart symbolism, is exposed as a falsification of reality. By both astronomical and astrological analogy, kings in their tardiness and evil influence are more like Saturn, which takes longer than any other planet known in the seventeenth century to complete its annual course. So whereas Cromwell 'in one year the work of ages acts', the 'earthy projects' of kings are passed on uncompleted from father to son (a mocking explanation of the value placed by royalists on the hereditary principle). Moreover, kings, heedless of 'sacred prophecies', do nothing to further the purposes of God and their reigns run to waste as they 'with vain sceptre strike the hourly bell' (lines 19–42). Not so the providential leader, who seeks to bring himself and his nation into harmony with the divine will:

> While indefatigable Cromwell hies,
> And cuts his way still nearer to the skies,
> Learning a music in the region clear,
> To tune this lower to that higher sphere. (lines 45–8)

This image leads into an extended simile which invites comparison with its source in Waller's panegyric 'Upon His Majesty's Repairing of Paul's'. Long over-due repairs to St Paul's Cathedral had been initiated by James I in 1620, interrupted, resumed by Charles I in 1633, and finally abandoned at the outbreak of the Civil War. Waller transforms this unimpressive record by invoking the story of Amphion, who raised the walls of Thebes by playing on a golden lyre:

> When the first monarch of this happy isle,
> Moved with the ruin of so brave a pile,
> This work of cost and piety begun,
> To be accomplished by his glorious son,
> Who all that came within the ample thought

Of his wise sire has to perfection brought;
He, like Amphion, makes those quarries leap
Into fair figures from a confused heap;
For in his art of regiment is found
A power like that of harmony in sound.

Marvell may well have intended to lay bare the truth behind this rhetoric in his earlier jibe that 'one thing never was by one king done' (line 22) and to offer a facetious challenge to royalist wit in his elaboration of Waller's Amphion couplet into a brilliant eighteen-line fantasy of stones dancing 'up in order from the quarries rude' and 'flocking marbles' uniting 'in a palace' (lines 49–66). But the more serious point of the simile is to enhance the achievement of 'our Amphion' in presiding over the establishment of a new constitution. Waller's poem had ended with the truism that 'The task is easier to destroy than build', and the Cromwell of Marvell's own 1650 ode had appeared to be a destructive force that could rend 'palaces and temples' and 'ruin the great work of time'. Since then, the primary problem facing the nation's leaders had been to devise 'another mould' for the state which would ensure stability without sacrificing what had been fought for in the 1640s. Applying the Amphion allusion to the Protector by way of a topical play on the word Instrument, Marvell emphasizes again how much has been accomplished in the course of the past year:

Such was that wondrous order and consent,
When Cromwell tuned the ruling Instrument,
While tedious statesmen many years did hack,
Framing a liberty that still went back. (lines 67–70)

Although the propagandist function of the poem demands that Marvell present the current situation in a favourable light, he manages to keep in touch with political realities by focussing sharply on the intransigent fact that makes it so much more difficult to institute a new system of government than to raise a city or repair a cathedral: 'All other matter yields, and may be ruled; / But who the minds of stubborn men can build?' (lines 77–8). In his account of the constitution of the Protectorate, he uses the architectural conceit he had played with in the Amphion simile to assert the positive aspects of the stresses and strains that threaten any human society with disintegration. Wisely deployed, as they are in the structure devised by the Instrument of Government, those very stresses and strains, held in equilibrium by the overseeing Protector, provide a guarantee of stable rule and individual rights:

> The Commonwealth does through their centres all
> Draw the circumference of the public wall;
> The crossest spirits here do take their part,
> Fastening the contignation which they thwart;
> And they, whose nature leads them to divide,
> Uphold this one, and that the other side;
> But the most equal still sustain the height,
> And they as pillars keep the work upright,
> While the resistance of opposed minds,
> The fabric (as with arches) stronger binds,
> Which on the basis of a senate free,
> Knit by the roof's protecting weight agree. (lines 87–98)

Marvell now returns to his conception of Cromwell as an agent of providence, consulting the 'sacred prophecies' ignored by worldly monarchs and tuning 'this lower to that higher sphere'. If only the kings of Europe would follow his example and 'humbly tread / The path where holy oracles do lead' (lines 107–8), then the great events foretold in the Book of Daniel and the Revelation of St John might be fulfilled: 'How might they under such a captain raise / The great designs kept for the latter days!' (lines 109–10). But these apocalyptic hopes, already disappointed at home by the failure of the Nominated Parliament, are being thwarted by the 'regal sloth' of foreign princes, who leave Cromwell to pursue 'the monster' of Antichrist 'in dark nights, and in cold days alone' (line 127). The Protestant dream which had inspired Cromwell in his speech of July 1653 is another of those answers to the loss of paradise and the 'slow-chapped power' of time, which compel Marvell's imaginative assent, only to be tempered in the expression by conditional tenses:

> Hence oft I think if in some happy hour
> High grace should meet in one with highest power,
> And then a seasonable people still
> Should bend to his, as he to heaven's will,
> What we might hope, what wonderful effect
> From such a wished conjuncture might reflect.
> Sure, the mysterious work, where none withstand,
> Would forthwith finish under such a hand:
> Foreshortened time its useless course would stay,
> And soon precipitate the latest day.
> But a thick cloud about that morning lies,
> And intercepts the beams of mortal eyes,
> That 'tis the most which we determine can,
> If these the times, then this must be the man. (lines 131–44)

But, 'alas', the chosen hero, who seems born for the great task of bringing in the millennium, is hindered by the apathy of mankind: 'The ill delaying what the elected hastes' (line 156). And indeed, this man of unparalleled courage and integrity, who has come unscathed 'through storms of thundering lead' and remained 'unstained' by the exercise of power, may be at risk from the sins of his own countrymen. His life has more than once been attempted in 'poniarding conspiracies, / Drawn from the sheath of lying prophecies' (lines 171–2) – a reference to plots by Levellers and Fifth Monarchists; and the recent accident in Hyde Park, when the coach he was driving overturned, is interpreted as a warning to a people whose 'brutish fury' makes them unworthy of such a leader. In a typical moment of literary self-awareness, Marvell seizes on Cromwell's narrow escape from death to absolve himself from the taint of sycophancy which clings to the art-form he is practising. Extravagant praise is more justified and less compromising in an elegy than in a panegyric: 'So with more modesty we may be true, / And speak, as of the dead, the praises due' (lines 187–8).

Death would, in fact, have been England's irreparable loss, but Cromwell's gain, since it would have sent him to his reward in 'the kingdom blest of peace and love' and released him from the burden of serving 'thankless men' (lines 215–20). This thought gives Marvell the chance to develop a point that Cromwell himself had been at pains to emphasize in a speech on 12 September, in which he had rebuked the House of Commons for seeking to interfere with the balance of power between Parliament and Protector:

I called not myself to this place. I say again, I called not myself to this place; of that, God is witness . . . I was by birth a gentleman, living neither in any considerable height, nor yet in obscurity. I have been called to several employments in the nation, – to serve in Parliaments, – and (because I would not be over tedious) I did endeavour to discharge the duty of an honest man in those services, to God, and his people's interest, and of the Commonwealth . . . after Worcester fight I came up to London to pay my service and duty to the Parliament that then sat . . . I say to you, I hoped to have had leave to have retired to a private life, I begged to be dismissed of my charge, I begged it again and again, and God be judge between me and all men if I lie in this matter.

These protestations seem to lie behind Marvell's defence of Cromwell against those who suspect him of self-interest or ambition:

For all delight of life thou then didst lose,
When to command, thou didst thy self depose;
Resigning up thy privacy so dear,
To turn the headstrong people's charioteer;

. . .

What since he did, an higher force him pushed
Still from behind, and yet before him rushed,
Though undiscerned among the tumult blind,
Who think those high decrees by man designed.
(lines 221–42)

The poet goes on to trace the steps by which Cromwell found himself compelled to suppress the Levellers and other 'ambitious shrubs' and finally, like 'Some lusty mate', to seize the helm from the 'artless steersman' in order to save the ship of state from 'whirling winds' and 'threatening rocks' (lines 257–78). Inherited ideas need to be revised in the light of what has happened since then. True liberty may best by secured by endorsing the providential leader's right to rule:

'Tis not a freedom, that where all command;
Nor tyranny, where one does them withstand:
But who of both the bounders knows to lay
Him as their father must the state obey. (lines 279–82)

Fifth Monarchists, Quakers, Ranters, Anabaptists, and Adamites are all glanced at in the ensuing diatribe against the 'frantic army' of sectarians and fanatics from whose anarchy the Protector's benevolent despotism is the one refuge (lines 289–324).

Again probably taking a hint from Waller's panegyric, which ends with 'our neighbour kings' looking on in amazement at Charles I's restoration of St Paul's, Marvell introduces a foreign monarch to voice the wonder inspired by the speed of England's progress under Cromwell:

'Is this', saith one, 'the nation that we read
Spent with both wars, under a captain dead,
Yet rig a navy while we dress us late,
And ere we dine, raze and rebuild their state?'
(lines 349–52)

Awed by the naval might built up by the 'one man' who 'although but named, alarms / More than all men, all navies, and all arms' (lines 375–6), this observer from overseas is even more perplexed by the paradoxical nature of Oliver Cromwell and the constitutional office he holds:

'He seems a king by long succession born,
And yet the same to be a king does scorn.
Abroad a king he seems, and something more,
At home a subject on the equal floor.' (lines 387–90)

The final couplet of this interpolated speech and the first couplet of the closing apostrophe to the Lord Protector draw attention to a tactical use of contrasting perspectives which is reminiscent of Marvell's lyric poetry:

> 'But let them write his praise that love him best,
> It grieves me sore to have thus much confessed.'
> Pardon, great Prince, if thus their fear or spite
> More than our love and duty do thee right. (lines 393–6)

What better way of deflecting the charge of flattery and special pleading that the art of panegyric attracts – and of shaming reluctant supporters at home – than to ascribe the highest praises of Cromwell to the grudging admiration of a hostile foreigner?

'The First Anniversary' is by far the most intellectually satisfying of Marvell's Commonwealth panegyrics. 'On the Victory Obtained by Blake over the Spaniards in the Bay of Santa Cruz, in the Island of Tenerife, 1657' sounds a familiar Marvellian note of regret that 'the sweet Canary Isles' have been contaminated by gold – 'that cause of war', which 'Kind Nature had from thence removed so far' – but the bulk of the poem is given over to conventional expressions of patriotism, glorifying Blake's 'conquering fleet' as the symbol of Cromwell's 'resistless genius' and his control of the 'boundless empire' of the sea. 'A Poem upon the Death of His Late Highness the Lord Protector' also contains much that is predictable – the storm that raged as he lay dying was a sign of 'what pangs that death did Nature cost' (line 112); 'Valour, religion, friendship, prudence died / At once with him' (lines 227–8); his 'honour, praise, and name' will live 'As long as future time succeeds the past' (lines 285–6). But more distinctive of Marvell's art is the view that his unspectacular death, from a physical decline exacerbated by grief at the painful last illness of his favourite daughter, was a fitting resolution of the tension between the private personality and the public image engendered by the duty imposed upon him as a providential leader:

> And he whom Nature all for peace had made,
> But angry heaven unto war had swayed,
> And so less useful where he most desired,
> For what he least affected was admired,
> Deserved yet an end whose every part,
> Should speak the wondrous softness of his heart.
> (lines 15–20)

Besides insisting on the human as well as the heroic dimension of the man, Marvell acknowledges with his customary realism that contradictory reactions were provoked by his career as soldier and statesman. It is therefore appropriate that he died on the anniversary of his victories over the royalists at Dunbar in 1650 and at Worcester in 1651:

> That so who ere would at his death have joyed,
> In their own griefs might find themselves employed;
> But those that sadly his departure grieved,
> Yet joyed, remembering what he once achieved. (lines 149–52)

And the harsh facts of Cromwell's unpopularity and isolation in his later years are faced in a characteristic simile which compares the vagaries of reputation to those of visual perception:

> The tree erewhile foreshortened to our view,
> When fall'n shows taller yet than as it grew:
> So shall his praise to after times increase,
> When truth shall be allowed, and faction cease,
> And his own shadows with him fall. (lines 269–73)

However devoted he may have become to Cromwell himself – and the passage beginning 'I saw him dead' (line 246) has the ring of genuine grief – the failure of the constitutional experiments of the 1650s marked the end of Marvell's hopes of seeing his ideals of order and freedom translated into permanent political reality. After this last tribute to the Lord Protector in 1658, he wrote no more panegyrics and fell back on satire as the only suitable poetic response to the new age that came in with Charles II.

He had tried his hand at the satiric mode as practised by Donne and Cleveland more than once already. 'Flecknoe' records his encounter with Richard Flecknoe in Rome during Lent in 1646, and makes witty capital out of the indigence, artistic pretensions, and Roman Catholicism of this poet–priest. The following is a representative example of its Clevelandesque conceits:

> So while he with his gouty fingers crawls
> Over the lute, his murm'ring belly calls,
> Whose hungry guts to the same straitness twined
> In echo to the trembling strings repined. (lines 41–4)

And the same brand of ingenious mockery is called upon to denigrate England's trading rivals, against whom 'Our sore new circumcisèd Commonwealth' was waging a naval war in the early 1650s. 'The Character of Holland', with its puns on 'pickled *Herring*, pickled *Heeren*' and its contempt for a country which is little more than 'the off-scouring of the British sand', is a light-hearted exercise in spite of its propaganda intention. Far more substantial and serious is 'The Last Instructions to a Painter', and though few would agree that it is 'arguably . . . Marvell's finest poetic achievement' (Farley-Hills, p. 76), a strong case has been made for regarding it as 'the first important Augustan political poem' (Fisher, p. 237) – one which anticipates the achievement of Dryden's *Absalom and Achitophel* in its attempt to present a sequence of public events in such a way that the sharp edge of contemporary issues is not blunted by the process of raising them to a plane of universal significance.

'Last Instructions' was written during the summer of 1667 and probably completed by early September. Like Marvell's other significant occasional poems, it cannot be fully appreciated outside the historical and literary contexts that gave rise to it. The poet had returned from a diplomatic mission to Russia and Scandinavia in January 1665 to find England once again at war with Holland. An English victory off Lowestoft on 3 June was celebrated by Waller in a panegyric entitled 'Instructions to a Painter, For the Drawing of the Posture and Progress of His Majesty's Forces at Sea', which cast an epic colouring over the event and transformed the Duke of York into a colossus bestriding the ocean and grasping 'the Indies in his armèd hand'. Waller's rhetorical fiction – 'First draw the sea, . . . Paint an east wind, . . .' – was soon turned to satiric effect in 'Second Advice to a Painter' and 'Third Advice to a Painter', both attributed to Marvell by some commentators. Fourth and fifth poems in the series also appeared in 1667, covering much the same ground as 'Last Instructions', and it may be, as Annabel Patterson suggests, 'that more than one poet was involved, and that the *Advices* were a group project' with which Marvell was closely associated (p. 167). Certainly they contribute, along with 'Last Instructions' (the only 'Painter' poem universally accepted as Marvell's), to a concerted attack on the administration of Edward Hyde, the Earl of Clarendon. Popular opinion had swung against the war, and peace negotiations were already under way by June 1667, when the Dutch admiral took advantage of England's naval unpreparedness to make a raid up the Thames and Medway to Chatham, burning a number of men-of-war and capturing the ship in which Charles II had made his triumphant return from exile. The Treaty of Breda was signed at the end of July and Clarendon was dismissed from office as Lord Chancellor on 30 August.

'The Last Instructions to a Painter' falls into five main sections, placed between an introductory passage on the art of painting and a concluding address to the king. Lines 29–104 offer suggestions for a series of individual portraits of leading members of the court; lines 105–522 describe the parliamentary session held between September 1666 and February 1667, during which a proposed excise on domestic goods was voted down by the Country party, and criticize the government's inadequate defence measures in the face of the continued threat from Holland; lines 523–760 present in humiliating detail the Dutch exploit of June 1667; lines 761–884 record how Peter Pett, the Commissioner of the Navy at Chatham, was made the scapegoat for the disaster and how peace was finally concluded amid dubious parliamentary manoeuvres by Clarendon and the Speaker, Sir Edward Turner; and lines 885–948 imagine Charles II reaching his decision to dispense with Clarendon as the result of a midnight visitation by, among other spectres, the shade of his father, who, 'turning his collar low, / The purple thread about his neck does show'.

Marvell signals his satiric intentions at the outset by inverting his model's appeal to the heroic conventions of historical painting. Waller had instructed his painter to elevate the subject-matter – 'Make all appear, where such a Prince is by, / Resolved to conquer, or resolved to die' (lines 17–18) – and had declared to Charles himself that 'no colours' could represent his 'great providence', 'nor pencil draw that care, / Which keeps you waking to secure our peace' (lines 317–19); Marvell advises *his* painter to consider whether 'our Lady State' is 'too slight', rather than too great, a subject for him: indeed, if he can descend to the rough work needed to 'daub a signpost' for an inn or scrawl obscene pictures on the ceiling of a bowling-alley, such a debasement of his art will 'suit our great debauch and little skill' and 'serve this race of drunkards, pimps, and fools' (lines 1–12). The court panegyrist had transformed the visit of the 'illustrious Duchess' and other ladies to the fleet at Harwich into a pageant of mythological splendour – 'The gazing sea-gods, since the Paphian Queen / Sprung from among them, no such sight had seen' (lines 81–4); the satirist calls for the portrayal of that same duchess, daughter to Clarendon and wife to Charles's brother, Duke of York, as she really was, 'to the life' (line 49):

> Paint her with oyster lip and breath of fame,
> Wide mouth that 'sparagus may well proclaim;
> With Chancellor's belly and so large a rump,
> There – not behind the coach – her pages jump.
>
> (lines 61–4)

The parliamentary debate about the excise is reduced to nothing more dignified than a contest of 'tric-trac' (backgammon) – 'Describe the

Court and Country, both set right / On opp'site points, the black against the white' (lines 107–8); and the members of the two Houses, who show little wisdom in playing 'the public game', are contemptuously listed according to their various species: 'early wittols', 'old courtiers', 'Expectants pale, with hopes of spoil allured', 'Court officers', 'procurers', 'the troop of Clarendon', the 'Mitre troop', the 'lawyers' mercenary band', the 'thrifty troop of privateers', the 'projectors', the 'Lord's sons'. But among these scramblers after wealth and position, there is a 'reserve' of undemonstrative but high-principled men – the nucleus of the Country party – who remain the best hope that commonsense and justice will prevail in the deliberations of Parliament:

A gross of English gentry, nobly born,
Of clear estates, and to no faction sworn,
Dear lovers of their king, and death to meet
For country's cause, that glorious think and sweet;
To speak not forward, but in action brave,
In giving generous, but in counsel grave. (lines 287–92)

After the coarse realism with which Marvell has been exposing political incompetence and corruption, the presentation of the Dutch fleet's progress up the Thames as a pastoral–mythological idyll is an effective way of highlighting the ease with which the raid was accomplished:

Ruyter the while, that had our ocean curbed,
Sailed now among our rivers undisturbed,
Surveyed their crystal streams and banks so green
And beauties ere this never naked seen.

. . .

His sporting navy all about him swim
And witness their complacence in their trim.

. . .

Aeolus their sails inspires with eastern wind,
Puffs them along, and breathes upon them kind.
With pearly shell the Tritons all the while
Sound the sea-march and guide to Sheppey Isle.
(lines 523–50)

On the British side, there is nothing but 'Confusion, folly, treach'ry, fear, neglect' (line 610), and the catalogue of disgrace is relieved only by the heroic death of a young Scots soldier who refused to desert his post on the Royal Oak. Marvell has recourse to the idealizing conceits of panegyric to transfigure an act that shames the nation by its lonely dedication to duty:

> Round the transparent fire about him glows,
> As the clear amber on the bee does close,
> And, as on angels' heads their glories shine,
> His burning locks adorn his face divine.
>
> . . .
>
> Down on the deck he laid himself and died,
> With his dear sword reposing by his side,
> And on the flaming plank, so rests his head
> As one that's warmed himself and gone to bed.
>
> (lines 681–90)

The reminiscence, in the final couplet, of the image used seventeen years before to convey Charles I's noble demeanour on the scaffold is evidence that such an instance of dignified and self-contained submission to the inevitable could still engage the deeper levels of Marvell's imagination; and the transcendent beauty of Captain Douglas's gesture here contrasts poignantly with the ugly and degenerate world depicted in the rest of the poem.

More in keeping with the realities of Restoration England is the last subject recommended to the painter: the king himself, his slumbers broken by the appearance of a naked woman at his bedside and his lust allayed by the shock of 'her touch so cold' when he 'with kind hand does the coy vision press' (lines 885–904). The idea of an allegorical embodiment of 'England or the Peace' (line 906) being mistaken by the lecherous monarch for another kind of night-visitor turns to witty account both the Advice-to-a-Painter convention in general (since such figures were common in the pictorial art of the age) and Waller's flattering conception of Charles II 'waking to secure our peace' in the original 'Instructions'.

In the concluding section, entitled 'To the King', Marvell asks Charles not to blame 'the Muse' for directing her satire against those at court who 'corrode' his light and 'undermine' both the realm and the monarchy itself by their ambition and greed. The party affiliation of the poet and the ultimate purpose of this long poem are clarified in the closing paragraph: the dangerous advisers who have sought to separate the king from his people – and loyal Englishmen know, of course, that 'the Country is the King' (line 974) – must be replaced by others who will put the interests of king and country before their own. Such men are to be found among that select band of patriots who were earlier distinguished from the rabble of parliamentary place-seekers:

> But they, whom born to virtue and to wealth,
> Nor guilt to flattery binds, nor want to stealth;
> Whose generous conscience and whose courage high
> Does with clear counsels their large souls supply;
> That serve the King with their estates and care,
> And, as in love, on Parliaments can stare,
> (Where few the number, choice is there less hard):
> Give us this court, and rule without a guard. (lines 983–90)

Back in 1650, Cromwell, the regicide, had been warned to keep his 'sword erect', since a 'forcèd power' would be impelled to maintain its authority by force. In 1667, Marvell argues that a legitimate king should be able to 'rule without a guard', provided he gathers about himself a court that respects both king and Parliament. The constitutional ideal is the same as that promoted in 'The First Anniversary': a distribution of power between Head of State, Council of State or 'court', and elected assembly. But whereas recent history had led him then to emphasize the guiding rôle of Cromwell as Protector, seven years of Charles II have now convinced him that justice and orderly government can best be guaranteed by a body of ministers chosen for their integrity, tolerance, and courage, who may be able to hold the balance between a feckless king and a wayward Parliament.

Whether or not the poet believed that there was any real chance of improvement once Clarendon had been removed, 'Last Instructions' maintains the politic fiction that evil counsel is a 'disease' (line 952) from which the king may recover. In later satires attributed to Marvell, the pretence that Charles was not himself the root of the nation's ills is dropped. 'The Statue in Stocks-Market', written some time between 1672 and 1674, concludes that the work being done to 'reform' the white marble figure of the king on horseback will never be completed: 'For 'tis such a king as no chisel can mend' (line 56). An earlier stanza had remarked on the appropriateness of its location:

> But a market, they say, does suit the king well,
> Who the Parliament buys and revenues does sell,
> And others to make the similitude hold
> Say his majesty himself is bought too and sold.
>
> (lines 21–4)

In 'A Dialogue between the Two Horses', dating from the end of 1675, Charles II's mount from Stocks Market is imagined in conversation with that of an equestrian statue of Charles I lately erected in Charing Cross. The upshot of their exchange of views is that things will never be 'mended' until 'the Reign of the Line of the Stuarts is ended' (line 158). A third poem, 'The Statue at Charing Cross', makes satiric play with the long-delayed unveiling of the bronze figure, originally cast in 1633, and now raised at his own expense by the Earl of Danby 'to comfort the hearts of the poor Cavalier' (line 17). Waller, writing on the same topic, had rejoiced that 'the First Charles does here in triumph ride', conveniently sited to 'See his son reign where he a martyr died'. The satirist thinks it would be kinder to turn the statue's face away from Whitehall: 'Though of Brass, yet with grief it would melt him away, / To behold every day such a Court, such a son' (lines 55–6). Particular contempt is reserved for Danby, currently the Lord Treasurer and leader of the Court party, who apparently considers his countrymen 'so Loyally tame' that they can be 'fooled with a sight' (lines 21–2) into forgetting government corruption and mismanagement. Although the authenticity of this group of works is in doubt, the tactic of undermining the propaganda value of royal statues is not unlike Marvell's practice of exposing the less than heroic truth behind the rhetorical excesses of Stuart panegyric. And the crude metre which is shared by all three sets of verses may not be the mark of an inferior or careless poet, but a literary equivalent to the rough daubing recommended to the painter in 'Last Instructions' – a medium deliberately chosen to reflect the degenerate subject-matter.

Although, from 1667 onwards, Marvell was active sporadically in what an enemy called his 'own proper trade of lampoons and ballads', the main outlet for his literary talent in the last six years of his life was the series of prose works which earned him his posthumous reputation as the defender of liberty. The first, and most celebrated, was his response to the virulent campaign being waged against the Dissenters by a rising member of the Anglican establishment, Samuel Parker. *A Discourse of Ecclesiastical Politie, wherein the authority of the Civil Magistrate over the Consciences of Subjects in matters of Religion is asserted; the Mischiefs and Inconveniences of Toleration are represented, and all Pretenses pleaded in behalf of Liberty of Conscience are fully answered* (1669) had been countered by John Owen, one of the leaders of Nonconformity, in a pamphlet which had drawn from Parker *A Defence and Continuation of the Ecclesiastical Politie*. In 1672, Parker had promoted the cause of intolerance and persecution a third time in a preface to a work by the late Bishop Bramhall. It was at this point that Marvell entered the fray with *The Rehearsal Transpros'd*, the title of which was derived from a comment on the plagiaristic practices of a figure representing the dramatist John Dryden in the Duke of Buckingham's burlesque, *The*

Rehearsal: 'Methinks, Mr. *Bayes*, that putting Verse into Prose should be called Transprosing.' The political situation confronting men of Marvell's persuasion was complicated by the Declaration of Indulgence issued by Charles II in March of the same year, which extended freedom of public worship to Roman Catholics and Dissenters alike. On the one hand, this relaxation of penal laws was welcomed and the satirist was able to exploit it as a weapon against Parker's advocacy of enforced conformity; on the other hand, the royal action was an example of that very tyranny of the civil magistrate over religious affairs which was at the heart of his dispute with the author of *A Discourse of Ecclesiastical Politie*, and it could be seen as one more step on the road to absolutism (and perhaps to Catholic domination of the government). As in 'Last Instructions', his purpose was to try to drive a wedge between the king and those of his advisers who, like Parker, were supporters of the high Anglican party.

To this end, Marvell sets out to discredit his opponent by subjecting his character, his arguments, and his style to a mocking analysis which will show him in his true colours: he 'transproses' him into 'Mr. Bayes', because he and the butt of Buckingham's play have so much in common, 'in their understandings, in their expressions, in their humour, in their contempt and quarrelling of all others' (p. 9); he proclaims him 'Buffoon-General to the Church of *England*' (p. 22); and he pours scorn on the fanaticism with which he pursues those 'Fanaticks' who do not submit to the authority of the state church – 'in my poor opinion I never saw a man through all his three Books in so high a Salivation' (p. 77). In particular he condemns the ill-mannered excesses of a controversialist whose 'only talent is railing' (p. 20). The spectacle of an ordained minister of the church 'raging bitterly against all the Presbyterians and other Sects' (p. 67) is not only amusing but also unbecoming, and Marvell is careful to justify his own comic treatment of 'Mr. Bayes' on the grounds of literary propriety: 'I shall, so far as possible, observe *decorum*, and, whatever I talk of, not commit such an Absurdity, as to be grave with a Buffoon' (p. 49). Indeed, the question of the proper stance to adopt in public controversy over matters of religion was one which was to exercise Marvell considerably. This first experiment will, he hopes, have demonstrated 'that it is not impossible to be merry and angry as long time as I have been writing, without profaning and violating those things which are and ought to be most sacred' (p. 145).

When he undertook a Second Part (1673) in answer to the violent personal abuse directed at him in Parker's *A Reproof to the Rehearsal Transpros'd*, he devoted a good deal of space to a discussion of the 'envious and dangerous employment' of those who 'take upon themselves to be Writers' (p. 159). Of all kinds of writing, *ad hominem* satire reflects least credit on the author:

It is one thing to do that which is justifiable, but another that which is commendable, and I suppose every prudent Writer aims at both: but how can the Author of an Invective, though never so truly founded, expect approbation (unless from such as love to see mischief at other men's expense) who, in a world all furnished with subjects of praise, instruction and learned inquiry, shall studiously choose and set himself apart to comment upon the blemishes and imperfections of some particular person? (p. 161)

Having elaborated these arguments at some length, Marvell effects a sudden reversal in order to exonerate himself and bring home to his readers the urgency of the enterprise he is engaged in:

And yet nevertheless, and all that has been said before being granted, it may so chance that to write, and that Satirically, and that a second time and a third; and this too even against a Clergyman, may be not only excusable but necessary . . . For it is not impossible that a man by evil arts may have crept into the Church, through the Belfry or at the Windows. 'Tis not improbable that having so got in he should foul the Pulpit, and afterwards the Press with opinions destructive to Humane Society and the Christian Religion. That he should illustrate so corrupt Doctrines with as ill a conversation, and adorn the lasciviousness of his life with an equal petulancy of style and language. In such a concurrence of misdemeanours what is to be done? (p. 163)

The key to his rhetorical strategy here, as so often in the poems, lies in the creation of an appropriate persona. In this instance, it is the familiar Marvellian figure – 'To speak not forward, but in action brave' – who has been impelled by a sense of moral and patriotic duty to emerge onto the public stage 'from that modest retiredness to which I had all my life time hitherto been addicted' (p. 169). He also takes pains to present himself, in sharp contrast to the bigotry and uncontrolled zeal of his antagonist, as a moderate adherent to the Church of England, basing his support for religious toleration on a disinterested concern for 'Humanity, Christianity, and Prudence' (p. 186). At other times, he is the fastidious man of true wit, who, while he finds 'very good sport' (p. 288) in the literary antics of 'Mr. Bayes' (like the two sophisticated observers, Johnson and Smith, in Buckingham's play), also disdains the task of anatomizing this 'noxious Creature' because of 'the offensiveness of the scent and fouling of my fingers' (p. 185). By his skilful management of this complex persona throughout the two parts of *The Rehearsal Transpros'd*, Marvell strives to keep the balance 'betwixt Jest and Earnest' (p. 187), and so win over both the wits and the moderate men who may as yet be uncommitted to the cause of toleration. Towards the end, however, in a characteristic ploy, he calls upon an impartial third party to pass judgement on the kind of acrimonious dispute into which he has allowed himself to be drawn. Introducing a long quotation from the work of Francis Bacon on the dangers and improprieties of religious controversy, he appeals to his opponent: 'Pray, Mr. *Bayes*, let us both listen, for I assure you, before he has done, he will tell us many a wiser thing than is to be met with either in *Ecclesiastical Politie* or *Rehearsal*' (p. 323).

When Marvell stepped into the arena again, it was in defence of *The Naked Truth. Or, the true state of the Primitive Church* by Herbert Croft, the Bishop of Hereford, which had been mocked by Francis Turner in *Animadversions Upon a Late Pamphlet*. Exerting his skill as satirist and polemicist in the cause of an author whom he commends as 'judicious, learned, conscientious, a sincere Protestant, and a true son, if not a father, of the Church of England' (p. 10), Marvell writes from the moderate Anglican position of tolerance and charity towards Nonconformists which Croft shared with other latitudinarian churchmen. The title of his response to Turner – *Mr. Smirke; Or, the Divine in Mode* (1676) – indicates that he is employing the same device that had served him well in *The Rehearsal Transpros'd*. Parker had been identified with Mr Bayes; Turner is given the name of a minor clerical character in Etherege's comedy, *The Man of Mode*, but also associated with its fashionable hero and the absurd fop who emulates him. After remarking that 'our ecclesiastical governors' seem determined to entertain the laity 'with new books of ridiculous and facetious argument', written by members of the clergy who are 'by their parts, their complexion and education unfitted for this jocular divinity' (pp. 6–7), he sets before us the latest 'close youth' to aspire to 'Ecclesiastical Preferment' by way of the office of 'the Church's jester':

> Yet to work he fell, not omitting first to sum himself up in the whole wardrobe of his function; as well because his wit consisting wholly in his dress, he would (and 'twas his concernment to) have it all about him: as to the end that being huff'd up in all his ecclesiastical fluster, he might appear more formidable . . . So that there was more to do in equipping of Mr. Smirke than there is about Dorimant, and the Divine in Mode might have vied with Sir Fopling Flutter. (pp. 11–12)

But although Marvell is still prepared to use the weapon of ridicule, he is increasingly impatient at having to cross swords with men who 'by their rash levity administer so much occasion upon the most revered subject, that one can scarce answer them in their own dialect without seeming, though never so averse, to border upon their profaneness' (p. 60). The very form of the 'Animadversion', which he had followed in *The Rehearsal Transpros'd* (itself subtitled *Animadversions upon a late Book*), committed the disputant to scoring points off his opponent in a tedious process of quotation and refutation. He tires of playing the same game as 'the great Animadverters of the times, the church-respondents in the pew' (p. 60). 'I must find some more expeditious way of dealing with him,' he admonishes himself at one point, 'and walk faster, for really I get cold' (p. 65); and he finally breaks off in disgust: 'I am weary of such stuff, both mine own and his. I will rather give him this following Essay of mine own to busy him' (p. 90). There follows *A Short Historical Essay Touching General Councils, Creeds, and Imposition in Religion*, in which he sets out his views on each man's right to liberty of conscience, 'without jesting, for the matter is too serious' (p. 125).

In the last of his important prose works, *An Account of the Growth of Popery, and Arbitrary Government in England* (1677), Marvell turned from ecclesiastical to political affairs and from satire and polemic to 'a naked narrative of some of the most considerable passages' (p. 263) in the parliamentary session that began in February 1677. Reflecting the widespread fears of a conspiracy in high places against traditional English liberties, he begins by describing the ideals enshrined in the mixed constitution and the Protestant religion. 'And yet,' he concludes, 'all this notwithstanding, there are those men among us, who have undertaken, and do make it their business, under so legal and perfect a government, to introduce a French slavery, and instead of so pure a religion, to establish the Roman idolatry' (p. 261). Such claims to perfection and purity in state and church are of course only part of a rhetorical strategy – at best another vision of paradise lost or never achieved – and the ensuing account of the political manoeuvrings between king and Parliament since the Dutch war of the 1660s, and more especially in the past eighteen months, leaves little room for optimism. Things have deteriorated even since the days of Clarendon: the members of the House of Commons that had been elected as long ago as 1661 have grown 'so familiar among themselves, that all reverence of their Assembly is lost' and 'they can see one another's votes through both throats and cravats before they hear them' (p. 331). The one glimmer of consolation, if not of hope, comes from the same quarter as in 'Last Instructions', though that 'gross of

English gentry' responsible for the defeat of the Excise proposals of 1666 seems to have been eroded by the passing years:

But notwithstanding these, there is an handful of salt, a sparkle of soul, that hath hitherto preserved this gross body from putrefaction, some gentlemen that are constant, invariable, indeed Englishmen; such as are above hopes, or fears, or dissimulation, that can neither flatter, nor betray their king or country: but being conscious of their own loyalty and integrity, proceed through good and bad report, to acquit themselves in their duty to God, their prince, and their nation; although so small a scantling in number, that men can scarce reckon of them more than a *quorum*. (p. 329)

Although many commentators have emphasized the gulf that separates the pastoral poet from the politician, two decades of public service did not radically alter a sensibility and mind that had always encompassed dissatisfaction with this world and the yearning for a better one within a larger and more realistic vision. The voices that complained to the 'unthankful meadows' for betraying a 'fellowship so true', cajoled a coy mistress into a desperate conspiracy to cheat time, and mourned over the devastation of England's 'paradise of four seas' by civil war were all called forth by the consequences of tasting the 'luckless apple' of the Fall. The power to move is undiminished, and perhaps the tones have been deepened and given greater authority by experience, in the voice that chided 'Mr. *Necessity Bayes*' in 1673:

You do hereby seem to imagine, that Providence should have contrived all things according to the utmost perfection, or that which you conceive would have been most to your purpose. Whereas in the shape of Man's body, and in the frame of the world, there are many things indeed liable to Objection, and which might have been better if we should give ear to proud and curious Spirits. But we must nevertheless be content with such bodies, and to inhabit such an Earth as it has pleased God to allot us. And so also in the Government of the World, it were desirable that men might live in perpetual Peace, in a state of good Nature, without Law or Magistrate, because by the universal equity and rectitude of manners they would be superfluous. And had God intended it so, it would so have succeeded, and he would have swayed and tempered the Minds and Affections of Mankind so that their Innocence should have expressed that of the Angels, and the Tranquillity of his Dominion here below should have resembed that in Heaven. But alas! that state of perfection was dissolved in the first Instance, and was shorter lived than Anarchy, scarce of one day's continuance. (*The Rehearsal Transpros'd*, Part Two, p. 231)

Select bibliography

I. Modern editions

Grosart, Rev. Alexander B., *The Complete Works in Verse and Prose of Andrew Marvell*, Fuller Worthies' Library, 4 vols. (Blackburn, 1875)

Margoliouth, H. M., *The Poems and Letters of Andrew Marvell*, 2 vols. (Oxford, 1927). 3rd edn revised by Pierre Legouis with the collaboration of E. E. Duncan-Jones, 1971

MacDonald, Hugh, *The Poems of Andrew Marvell*, The Muses' Library (London, 1952)

McQueen, William A. and Rockwell, Kiffin A., *The Latin Poetry of Andrew Marvell* (Chapel Hill, 1964)

Lord, George deF., *Andrew Marvell: Complete Poetry* (New York, 1968, reissued in Everyman's Library, London, 1984)

Smith, D. I. B., *The Rehearsal Transpros'd and The Rehearsal Transpros'd: The Second Part* (Oxford, 1971)

Donno, Elizabeth Story, *Andrew Marvell: The Complete Poems* (Harmondsworth, 1972)

II. Bibliographies and concordance

Collins, Dan S., *Andrew Marvell: A Reference Guide* (Boston, Mass., 1981)

Donovan, Dennis G., *Andrew Marvell, 1927–1967*, Elizabethan Bibliographies Supplements, 12 (London, 1969)

Guffey, George R., *A Concordance to the English Poems of Andrew Marvell* (Chapel Hill, 1974)

Szanto, Gillian, 'Recent Studies in Marvell', *English Literary Renaissance*, 5 (1975), 273–86

III. Biographical studies

Burdon, Pauline, 'Marvell After Cambridge', *The British Library Journal*, 4 (1978), 42–8

Erickson, Lee, 'Marvell's *Upon Appleton House* and the Fairfax Family', *English Literary Renaissance*, 9 (1979), 158–68

Hunt, John Dixon, *Andrew Marvell: His Life and Writings* (London, 1978)

Kelliher, Hilton, *Andrew Marvell: Poet and Politician, 1621–78*, Catalogue for an exhibition at the British Library (London, 1978)

'Some Notes on Andrew Marvell', *The British Library Journal*, 4 (1978), 122–44

Legouis, Pierre, *Andrew Marvell: Poet, Puritan, Patriot* (Oxford, 1965)

Tupper, Fred S., 'Mary Palmer, Alias Mrs Andrew Marvell', *Publications of the Modern Language Association*, 53 (1938), 367–92

IV. Collections of essays

Brett, R. L., ed., *Andrew Marvell: Essays on the Tercentenary of his Death* (Oxford, 1979)

Carey, John, ed., *Andrew Marvell: A Critical Anthology* (Harmondsworth, 1969)

Friedenreich, Kenneth, ed., *Tercentenary Essays in Honour of Andrew Marvell* (Hamden, Connecticut, 1977)

Lord, George deF., ed., *Andrew Marvell: A Collection of Critical Essays* (Englewood Cliffs, N.J., 1968)

Patrides, C. A., ed., *Approaches to Marvell: The York Tercentenary Lectures* (London, Henley and Boston, 1978)

Pollard, Arthur, ed., *Andrew Marvell's Poems: A Casebook* (London, 1980)

Wilding, Michael, ed., *Marvell: Modern Judgements* (London, 1969)

V. General critical studies

Allen, Don Cameron, *Image and Meaning: Metaphoric Traditions in Renaissance Poetry* (Baltimore, 1960)

Berek, Peter, 'The Voices of Marvell's Lyrics', *Modern Language Quarterly*, 32 (1971), 143–57

Berthoff, Ann E., *The Resolved Soul: A Study of Marvell's Major Poems* (Princeton, N.J., 1970)

Bradbrook, M. C. and Lloyd Thomas, M. G., *Andrew Marvell* (Cambridge, 1940)

Chernaik, Warren L., *The Poet's Time: Politics and Religion in the Work of Andrew Marvell* (Cambridge, 1983)

Colie, Rosalie L., *'My Ecchoing Song': Andrew Marvell's Poetry of Criticism* (Princeton, N.J., 1970)

Craze, Michael, *The Life and Lyrics of Andrew Marvell* (London and Basingstoke, 1979)

Creaser, John, 'Marvell's Effortless Superiority', *Essays in Criticism*, 20 (1970), 403–23

Cullen, Patrick, *Spenser, Marvell, and Renaissance Pastoral* (Cambridge, Mass., 1970)

Duncan-Jones, E. E., 'Marvell: A Great Master of Words', *Proceedings of the British Academy*, 61 (1975), 267–90

Eliot, T. S., 'Andrew Marvell', in *Selected Essays*, 3rd edn (London, 1951)

Empson, William, *Some Versions of Pastoral* (Harmondsworth, 1966)

Ferry, Anne, *All in War with Time: Love Poetry of Shakespeare, Donne, Jonson, Marvell* (Cambridge, Mass., 1975)

Friedman, Donald M., *Marvell's Pastoral Art* (London, 1970)

Greg, W. W., *Pastoral Poetry and Pastoral Drama* (London, 1906)

Grove, Robin, 'Poetry and Reader: Marvell's Triumphs of the Hay', *The Critical Review*, 23 (1981), 34–48

Guild, Nicholas, 'The Contexts of Marvell's Early "Royalist" Poems', *Studies in English Literature*, 20 (1980), 125–36

Hibbard, G. R., 'The Country House Poem of the Seventeenth Century', *Journal of the Warburg and Courtauld Institutes*, 19 (1956), 159–74

Hodge, R. I. V., *Foreshortened Time: Andrew Marvell and Seventeenth Century Revolutions* (Cambridge and Totowa, N.J., 1978)

Kalstone, David, 'Marvell and the Fictions of Pastoral', *English Literary Renaissance*, 4 (1974), 174–88

King, Bruce, *Marvell's Allegorical Poetry* (New York and Cambridge, 1977)

Leishman, J. B., *The Art of Marvell's Poetry* (London, 1966)

Lerner, Laurence, *The Uses of Nostalgia: Studies in Pastoral Poetry* (London, 1972)

Lord, George deF., 'From Contemplation to Action: Marvell's Poetical Career', *Philological Quarterly*, 46 (1967), 207–24

McClung, William A., *The Country House in English Renaissance Poetry* (Berkeley, Los Angeles, and London, 1977)

Nevo, Ruth, *The Dial of Virtue: A Study of Poems on Affairs of State in the Seventeenth Century* (Princeton, N.J., 1963)

—'Marvell's "Songs of Innocence and Experience" ', *Studies in English Literature*, 5 (1965), 1–21

Newton, J. M., 'What do we know about Andrew Marvell?', *The Cambridge Quarterly*, 6 (1972–3), 32–42

—'What do we know about Andrew Marvell? Further Notes', *The Cambridge Quarterly*, 6 (1972–3), 125–43

Osmond, Rosalie, 'Body and Soul Dialogues in the Seventeenth Century', *English Literary Renaissance*, 4 (1974), 364–403

Patterson, Annabel M., *Marvell and the Civic Crown* (Princeton, N.J., 1978)

Rivers, Isabel, *The Poetry of Conservatism 1600–1745: A Study of Poets and Public Affairs from Jonson to Pope* (Cambridge, 1973)

Røstvig, Maren-Sofie, *The Happy Man: Studies in the Metamorphoses of a Classical Ideal*, 2nd edn (Oslo, 1962)

Scoular, Kitty W., *Natural Magic: Studies in the Presentation of Nature in English Poetry from Spenser to Marvell* (Oxford, 1965)

Smith, Peter L., '*Lentus in Umbra*: A Symbolic Pattern in Vergil's Eclogues', *Phoenix*, 19 (1965), 298–305

Stewart, Stanley, *The Enclosed Garden: The Tradition and the Image in Seventeenth-Century Poetry* (Madison, Milwaukee, and London, 1966)

Summers, Joseph H., *The Heirs of Donne and Jonson* (London, 1970)

Tayler, Edward William, *Nature and Art in Renaissance Literature* (New York and London, 1964)

Toliver, Harold E., *Marvell's Ironic Vision* (New Haven and London, 1965)

Turner, James, *The Politics of Landscape: Rural Scenery and Society in English Poetry 1630–1660* (Oxford, 1979)

Wallace, John M., *Destiny His Choice: The Loyalism of Andrew Marvell* (Cambridge, 1968)

Wallerstein, Ruth, *Studies in Seventeenth-Century Poetic* (Madison and Milwaukee, 1950)

Warnke, Frank J., 'Play and Metamorphosis in Marvell's Poetry', *Studies in English Literature*, 5 (1965), 23–30

VI. Studies of individual works

'Bermudas'

Colie, Rosalie L., 'Marvell's "Bermudas" and the Puritan Paradise', *Renaissance News*, 10 (1957), 75–9

Cummings, R. M., 'The Difficulty of Marvell's "Bermudas" ', *Modern Philology*, 67 (1970), 331–40

Patterson, Annabel, '*Bermudas* and *The Coronet*: Marvell's Protestant Poetics', *English Literary History*, 44 (1977), 478–99

'The Definition of Love'

Bateson, F. W., 'Marvell's Impossible Love: A Comment', *Essays in Criticism*, 27 (1977), 109–11

Greenwood, E. B., 'Marvell's Impossible Love', *Essays in Criticism*, 27 (1977), 100–9

'The First Anniversary of the Government Under His Highness the Lord Protector'

Wilson, A. J. N., 'Andrew Marvell's "The First Anniversary of the Government under Oliver Cromwell": The Poem and its Frame of Reference', *Modern Language Review*, 69 (1974), 254–73

Zwicker, Steven N., 'Models of Governance in Marvell's "The First Anniversary" ', *Criticism*, 16 (1974), 1–12

'The Garden'

Berger, Harry, 'Marvell's "Garden": Still Another Interpretation', *Modern Language Quarterly*, 28 (1967), 285–304

Godshalk, William Leigh, 'Marvell's *Garden* and the Theologians', *Studies in Philology*, 66 (1969), 639–53

Kermode, Frank, 'The Argument of Marvell's "Garden" ', *Essays in Criticism*, 2 (1952), 225–41

Klonsky, Milton, 'A Guide through the Garden', *Sewanee Review*, 58 (1950), 16–35

'An Horatian Ode upon Cromwell's Return from Ireland'

Brooks, Cleanth, 'Criticism and Literary History: Marvell's "Horatian Ode" ', *Sewanee Review*, 55 (1947), 199–222

Bush, Douglas, 'Marvell's "Horatian Ode" ', *Sewanee Review*, 60 (1952), 362–76

Coolidge, John S., 'Marvell and Horace', *Modern Philology*, 63 (1965), 111–20

Duncan-Jones, E. E., 'The Erect Sword in Marvell's *Horatian Ode*', *Etudes Anglaises*, 15 (1962), 172–4

Reedy, Gerard, ' "An Horatian Ode" and "Tom May's Death" ', *Studies in English Literature*, 20 (1980), 137–51

Richards, Judith, 'Literary Criticism and the Historian: Towards Reconstructing Marvell's Meaning in "An Horatian Ode" ', *Literature and History*, 7 (1981), 25–47

Stead, C. K., 'The Actor and the Man of Action: Marvell's "Horatian Ode" ', *The Critical Survey*, 3 (1967), 145–50

Syfret, R. H., 'Marvell's "Horatian Ode" ', *Review of English Studies*, n.s. 12 (1961), 160–72

Wilson, A. J. N., '*An Horatian Ode upon Cromwell's Return from Ireland*: the Thread of the Poem and its Use of Classical Allusion', *Critical Quarterly*, 11 (1969), 325–41

'The Last Instructions to a Painter'

Farley-Hills, David, '*Last Instructions to a Painter*', in *The Benevolence of Laughter: Comic Poetry of the Commonwealth and Restoration* (London and Basingstoke, 1974)

Fisher, Alan S., 'The Augustan Marvell: *The Last Instructions to a Painter*', *English Literary History*, 38 (1971), 223–38

Gearin-Tosh, Michael, 'The Structure of Marvell's "Last

Instructions to a Painter'' ', *Essays in Criticism*, 22 (1972), 48–57

Miner, Earl, 'The ''Poetic Picture, Painted Poetry'' of *The Last Instructions to a Painter*', *Modern Philology*, 63 (1966), 288–94

'Mourning'

Delany, Paul, 'Marvell's ''Mourning'' ', *Modern Language Quarterly*, 33 (1972), 30–6

The 'Mower' Poems

Everett, Barbara, 'Marvell's ''The Mower's Song'' ', *Critical Quarterly*, 4 (1962), 219–24

King, Bruce, ' ''The Mower Against Gardens'' and the Levellers', *Huntington Library Quarterly*, 33 (1970), 237–42

'The Nymph Complaining for the Death of Her Fawn'

Guild, Nicholas, 'Marvell's ''The Nymph Complaining for the Death of her Fawn'' ', *Modern Language Quarterly*, 29 (1968), 385–94

Miner, Earl, 'The Death of Innocence in Marvell's *Nymph Complaining for the Death of Her Fawn*', *Modern Philology*, 65 (1967), 9–16

Thomason, T. Katharine, 'Marvell's Complaint Against His Nymph', *Studies in English Literature*, 18 (1978), 95–105

The Rehearsal Transpros'd

Anselment, Raymond A., 'Satiric Strategy in Marvell's *The Rehearsal Transpros'd*', *Modern Philology*, 68 (1970), 137–50

—' ''Betwixt Jest and Earnest'': Ironic Reversal in Andrew Marvell's *The Rehearsal Transpros'd*', *Modern Language Review*, 66 (1971), 282–93

Coolidge, John S., 'Martin Marprelate, Marvell, and *Decorum Personae* as a Satirical Theme', *Publications of the Modern Language Association*, 74 (1959), 526–32

'The Unfortunate Lover'

Duncan-Jones, E. E., 'A Reading of Marvell's *The Unfortunate Lover*', in *I. A. Richards: Essays in His Honour*, ed. Reuben Brower, Helen Vendler and John Hollander (New York, 1973)

Schwenger, Peter T., 'Marvell's ''Unfortunate Lover'' as Device', *Modern Language Quarterly*, 35 (1974), 364–75

'To His Coy Mistress'

Cunningham, J. V., 'Logic and Lyric', *Modern Philology*, 51 (1953), 33–41

Moldenhauer, Joseph J., 'The Voices of Seduction in "To His Coy Mistress": A Rhetorical Analysis', *Texas Studies in Literature and Language*, 10 (1968–9), 189–206

Upon Appleton House

Berger, Harry, 'Marvell's "Upon Appleton House": An Interpretation', *Southern Review*, 1, no. 4 (1965), 7–32

Gray, Allan, 'The Surface of Marvell's *Upon Appleton House*', *English Literary Renaissance*, 9 (1979), 169–82

Molesworth, Charles, 'Marvell's "Upon Appleton House": The Persona as Historian, Philosopher, and Priest', *Studies in English Literature*, 13 (1973), 149–62

Røstvig, Maren-Sofie, ' "Upon Appleton House" and the Universal History of Man', *English Studies*, 42 (1961), 337–51

Roth, Frederic H., 'Marvell's "Upon Appleton House": A Study in Perspective', *Texas Studies in Literature and Language*, 14 (1972), 269–81

Swan, Jim, ' "Betwixt Two Labyrinths": Andrew Marvell's Rational Amphibian', *Texas Studies in Literature and Language*, 17 (1975–6), 551–72